ABANDONING AN ALLY

ABANDONING AN ALLY

The Real Story Behind 70 Million Killed in China
and America's "Forgotten War"

JAMES FITZGERALD

ISBN: 0692482113
ISBN 13: 9780692482117

TABLE OF CONTENTS

NOTE to READERS;
Published history on China's fall to Communism boldly ignores
U.S State Dept. records of three crucial years. Other key docu-
ments have been spurned as well in favor of manufactured history.
The following pages will challenge and upset long- held concepts
of certain public figures of that era.

PROLOGUE

A s WORLD WAR Two ended, President Truman recognized "…
that Chiang's government fought side by side with us against
our common enemy…"[1] (Japanese Army records attest that China
was their most lethal enemy.) Washington records tell us that both
FDR and HST pledged vast aid to restore and rearm a devastated
China and within months, when Communist insurrection erupted,
China urgently requested that promised aid.

It was not to be. Two years later, U.S. Ambassador Stuart in
China described the situation "America still delays the long prom-
ised aid on which survival of democratic institutions depends."[2]
And "The Chinese people do not want to become communists,
yet they see the tide of communism running irresistibly forward."
Meanwhile in Washington, internal State Department memos

---

1 Truman, *Off The Record*, p.74
2 Foreign Relations of the U.S. *1948, vol. 7, p.155, Stuart to Sec. of State*

reinforced the "currently approved policy…to withhold export licenses for munitions shipments to China."[3]

President Truman and Congress, absorbed in near overwhelming problems at home and in Europe, were assured by trusted lieutenants that all was well in the East while one fifth of the world was consigned to a Communist overthrow. Once in power, the Reds launched a terror campaign that killed tens of millions. That cataclysmic fall of the largest country on earth, led to the 4th most violent war in U.S. history.* It was a cycle of treacherous, potentially inflammatory events, too hot for public consumption. The question today is; how long should history be denied in order to protect prominent legacies? As China challenges America for world supremacy, the background of U.S. – China relations is a subject area where American History should "get it right".

Washington records, incriminating personal papers, archived news reports and Communist records provide the backbone for this exposure of a monstrous tragedy in China and the price paid by young Americans.

It was Stalin's second attempt to enslave the largest nation on earth. China was first targeted by Soviet Premier Lenin in 1922 and by 1926 Stalin had Russian advisers imbedded in Sun Yat-sen's (Sun Yixian's) fledging Chinese government. When the Soviets incited their Red Chinese comrades to revolt, a young disciple of Sun moved decisively. Chiang Kai-shek (Jiang Jieshi) stifled the uprisings, deported the Russians and outlawed the Chinese Communist

---

3   Foreign Relations of the U.S. *1947, vol. 7, p.815,*

*The Korean War KIA rate (Killed in Action per Month) is exceeded only by that of the World Wars and the Civil War.

party. Free of turmoil, China made great economic progress through the early 1930s. That progress made China less vulnerable to Stalin's plots but threatened Japan's dominance in Asia. Japan attacked, expecting a quick victory but found their victim would not surrender. China tied down and bled the Japanese Army for three long years before America entered World War Two. Meanwhile, Stalin's Asian ambitions were interrupted when ally Hitler turned on his Soviet partner. Suddenly, Russia fought for survival and Moscow had no resources for the subversion of China.

However, International Communism was thriving. This was an era President Dwight Eisenhower defined as "harrowing decades that partly poisoned our national life."[4]

Disciples in the west eagerly took on the Red mission. But full support of China by America, the richest, most powerful country on earth, would render China invulnerable to Communist overthrow. America had to be turned against China and the only tactic available was the "Big Lie." Propaganda poured forth sanctifying the avowed terrorist who would soon enslave hundreds of millions and kill tens of millions. Despite his early advocating of terror, Mao Tse-tung (Mao Zedong) was acclaimed the "Enlightened leader of agrarian reformers," "The Great Teacher," "The most selfless man ever encountered." Conversely, his opponent, the head of China's government, who later rose from defeat and quietly founded a thriving democratic nation, was demonized as a cruel, corrupt despot. Nearly a 180 degree character reversal, but the enablers were skilled communicators, unhampered by ethics, and their anointed one, Mao, was a master propagandist.

---

4   Time Magazine, *Eisenhower on Communism, 10/13/52*

The key implementer of Moscow's overall strategy was a desk soldier with a talent for impressing politicians and collecting unearned accolades. A peculiar, aloof individual who exhibited something less than full commitment to the war effort and consequently lost authority as WW2 progressed. He was patron to an aging misfit colonel, who he rapidly promoted and foisted on struggling China. While courageous Americans fought and died conquering Hitler's Panzers in Europe and Tojo's Banzai warriors in the Pacific, America's military envoy to China turned from the war in China and transformed obscure Burma into a theater of the absurd. Despite incompetence that cancelled the U.S. war effort in Asia and invited an enemy offensive in China, the malevolent disciple succeeded in undermining the ally he was sent to aid, thereby advancing phase one of Moscow's plans for China.

At wars end, a new U.S President restored the discredited patron. Hailed by some as "The greatest living American", he was awarded authority over U.S. – China relations. The indifferent conference room warrior of WW2 found new levels of commitment and sacrificed all ethics in order to seal China's fate.

Dwight Eisenhower said we will never forget the "Harrowing decades that partly poisoned our national life." But until now, a half century later, the betrayers responsible for the death of tens of thousands of Americans and tens of millions of Chinese have been protected by a pervasive, drastic distortion of documented history.

The following pages try to avoid the insightful mindreading and unsupported adjective-laden prose and focus on what was said and what was done based on records. As the real story unfolds, maintaining objectivity will be a challenge.

For those who volunteered a few years and lost it all.
May future leaders aspire to such simple virtue.

1

A Season For
Revelations

A PRIL 1951, SPRING was in the air across the northern hemisphere. Iowa farmers planted with quiet optimism and in
Washington, buses disgorged lively students under canopies of
cherry blossoms. In Paris, patrons in sidewalk cafes tarried after
lunch, tilting their faces to the new spring sun and further east,
in Athens, families gathered, and dressed their young for Easter
processions. Much further east, on a small body of land jutting out
from the Asian land mass, trees were budding and wild flowers
sprouted along the roadway, but young minds were not pleasantly
occupied.

Charlie Company, 1st Marines moved forward between
lines of fleeing refugees. Charlie's mission: set up on Horseshoe

Ridge and stem the Red tide flowing south. The word came down expect a massive Chinese attack. Five months earlier, Mao Tse-tung (Mao Zedong), launched a surprise attack that pushed US/UN forces out of North Korea. Mao, not satisfied with saving his North Korean ally, wanted the South as well. At dusk, bugles sounded and waves of quilt-padded figures appeared advancing close behind the erupting earth of a rolling artillery barrage. A few too close to the fire stumbled and fell but the waves swept onward to meet their enemy. These were veterans. Some had fought the enemies of China for a quarter of a century, warlords, Japanese invaders and Mao's Reds before the fall. They were told they were they were defending their homeland.

Charlie watched dirty eruptions approach, felt the earth quake, heard the air rent by incoming and the firestorm engulfed them assaulting their senses, disintegrating and dismembering randomly. When it lifted, the enemy was through the barb wire and upon them. The fight increased in tempo and confusion until the remnants of Charlie, outnumbered and running out of ammunition, got the word to pull back 100 yards and regroup. The rear guard, were faced with crossing an open field while the enemy hosed it with machine gun fire. A few made it across when a cloud passed before the moon. Then the enemy got the range and put a bullet through Pfc Johnny Savoca's kidney. Corporal Barrish, trying to get his friend on a stretcher, was hit in the arm and chest. A few yards away, Pfc. Crow was wounded and then shifted to a seemingly safer spot where a sniper shot him through the heart.[1] Those who could move and fire a weapon formed into smaller units and counterattacked.

The survivors of Horseshoe moved on to assault or defend another hill. Charlie, like most combat units in Korea, was composed primarily of teenagers and 20 year olds seasoned with a few recalled vets of the "Canal", Tarawa or "Iwo". For many the next hill would be their last. Pfc. Crow and friends whose luck ran out on Horse Shoe Ridge were a fraction of the thousand Americans who died each month in the war that bled America for three long years. They were paying a debt, paying for history's deadliest betrayal. A subversion conducted by a few in Washington while America focused on solving Europe's problems.

While tens of thousands of Americans met death and dismemberment on the hills of Korea, an even greater horror was growing inside China, a terrorism that would consume tens of millions. The New York Times reported the new rulers of China, in power little more than a year, decreed the death penalty or life imprisonment for anyone who in any way opposed the government[2] and the CCP, the Chinese Communist People's Government went public in order to increase the effectiveness of their terror campaign. The government controlled Shanghai newspaper,[3] the Liberation Daily reported the execution of 208 counter- revolutionaries, who were made to kneel in a suburban lot one afternoon while a firing squad finished them off from the rear. To enhance the terror fac-

---

1 Berry, *Hey, Mac, Where Ya Been?* *P.215-217*
2 Ny Times, 3/10/51
3 Time Magazine, *Rubber Communist, 6/18/51*

tor, the newspaper printed the names of the victims and described the process.

Peking (Beijing) Mayor Peng Chen, chief organizer of the purges, hailed his Communist deputies:

Peng: How shall we cope with this herd of beastly despots, traitors and special agents?

Answer: Kill them!

Peng: Another thing. We have already disposed of a number of cases, but there are some still in jail. What shall we do with them?

Answer: Kill them all!

Peng: Another Thing. There are despots in the markets, among fishmongers, real estate brokers, water carriers, and night soil scavengers. How shall we cope with these feudal remnants?

Answer: Execute them by firing squad!

Time Magazine reported "… Chinese Reds by their own admission have bent all their efforts to turn father against son, mother against daughter. Wives are being handsomely rewarded for informing against their husbands, and children are organized into eavesdropping teams…" and "…. as in Russia, so also in Red China the state consists of soldiers, policemen, prisons and concentration camps."

American UPI correspondent Jack Belden, formerly an ardent admirer of Mao's Chinese Reds, reported "the increasing use of terror against any form of opposition, and extermination of large sections of the population."[4]

In his ruthless rise to power Mao's Red terrorism killed millions and once in control, he presided over the greatest human-induced

---

4 Chang and Holliday, *Mao. The Unknown Story, p.317*

death toll in world history. The key to his China takeover was the U.S. abandonment of the ally who'd saved countless thousands of American lives a few years earlier in World War Two, a treachery engineered within the U.S. government. President Dwight Eisenhower recalled "...many who moved among us ....their speech was pervasive and their vocabulary very clever. Remember? It went like this: after all we stand for political democracy and they stand for economic democracy ....." He pledged, "We must never forget that sophisticated lie..."[5]

The underlying tragedy of the monstrous horror that killed more than 60 million is that it could have been averted. There was nothing inevitable about the process that plunged China into murderous terror. History's oldest civilization had been progressing unevenly, but overcoming tremendous obstacles, until the betrayal.

---

5   Time Magazine, *Eisenhower On Communism, 10/13/52*

2

A New Beginning
in the East

B EFORE THE JAPANESE attack on Pearl Harbor on December 7, 1941, Americans remembered World War One and were engrossed in a continuing struggle to recover from the Great Depression. China was vaguely seen as a peaceful people under attack from cruel, aggressive neighbor, Japan. Few knew the Chinese traced their civilization back 5000 years and claimed with some justification that despite numerous wars, invasions and revolutions, their country had never launched a major invasion of a neighbor and its hundreds of millions lived within China's original boundaries.

Much of China's massive land area consisting of barren desert and mountains is unsuitable for agriculture. Other areas are marginally productive when weather allows. Throughout history, China's great population has been precariously balanced on relatively small fertile crop areas. Suitable land was farmed intensely and although crop production per acre was high, production per capita was marginal, floods, droughts and war brought famine. By the 20th century, despite its huge population, China's dominance in Asia was a thing of the distant past. After several aborted revolutions, the weak Emperor was overthrown and, in the resulting vacuum, the empire was fragmented into warlord-dominated provinces and European controlled port districts. Most Chinese clung to the lowest rung of society in their homeland. Life was cheap. A Westerner in one of the foreign port Concessions who beat and killed one of his Chinese servants might pay a fine of a dollar or less. A sign was posted on the gates of the park in Shanghai "Chinese and dogs not admitted."

Before the upheaval, under the Emperor's weak governance, the peasants in the countryside had evolved to a degree of anarchy that controlled the greediest landlords. When times were bad, landlords were expected to remit rents to alleviate suffering. The peasant wielding a scythe or sword was equal to his landlord who possessed no firearms. Failure to adjust rents could result in the landlord's demise.[1] At the same time, the weak government was careful not to over tax the peasants and cause revolt. When the Emperor fell, the new rulers, the warlords, swept away the delicate balance of power in the countryside. Using modern weaponry supplied by the Europeans and Japanese who controlled the ports, many warlords exacted extreme land rents and taxes from the peasantry. Meanwhile, dams, dikes and other infrastructure deteriorated from lack of maintenance. Millions died in floods and famine.

---

1   Fitzgerald, *Revolution in China*, p.42

In that tragic era a new political movement struggled to lead China. The philosophy of Sun Yat-sen stressed national unity, democracy, and livelihood. Sun proclaimed goals of uniting the country and eliminating foreign interests, giving the people a voice in government, and improving living conditions for the Chinese people. Two centuries of despots, warlords and foreign encroachments had generated a new political movement, but Sun Yat-sen died suddenly and the thriving movement needed a strong leader. Years passed before that vacuum was filled.

July 1928. "Thousands of people had come out to hail a victorious leader. Summer sun and the gay colors, flags and banners everywhere", a Danish correspondent described a young General's reception at one of several rail stops on a triumphant return from his campaign against the warlords of the North. "Four or five bands (all brass) were playing at the same time, each their own different melody, the shrill music helping to swell the chorus of cheers greeting the General as he stepped out of his compartment onto a small temporary platform nearby, from which he made a short speech. His voice was clear and carried well, his features were strong and intelligent, and he looked alert and full of energy. There was something convincing about Chiang Kai-shek when he spoke from a platform. But the task he had taken upon his shoulders of uniting the 400 million people in China in one ideal, which in itself would mean peace and independence to all Chinese subjects . . . such a task required a leader of quite superhuman qualities."

A few hours later, "he drove past the railway station outside Hsuchow, through the old city gates into the festively decorated city itself. Flaming inscriptions greeted him from every house wall, from temple doors and gates. Flags and banners and streamers everywhere. All the inhabitants of the town and several thousand soldiers were out to cheer the conquering hero on his entrance into their city. It was quite difficult for the man himself to get through the crowds."[2] Chiang had come a very long way from a poverty stricken childhood in the backwoods of China.

Born October 31, 1887, son of a rural salt merchant, according to available reports he was prankish as a child with a great tendency to get in and out of scrapes. During those years, China seethed from a recent defeat by the Japanese. The national humiliation produced a spirit of patriotism throughout China and young, impressionable Chiang was no exception.

Chiang, at age eight, lost his father and the family lost its income and position in the community. Many years later in a rare personal reflection Chiang recalled ". . . the indelible memory of my mother who endured so much in bringing up and educating a fatherless boy....It will be remembered that the Manchu regime was in its most corrupt state. The degenerated gentry and corrupt officials made it a habit to abuse and maltreat the people. My family, solitary and without what will influence, became at once the target of such insults and maltreatment ... indeed, the miserable condition of my family at that time is beyond description. It was entirely due to my mother and her kindness and perseverance that the family was saved from utter ruin." He continued and revealed a rare degree of humility "Now, while the trees by her grave have grown tall and thick, I cannot but realize how little I have accomplished and how I have failed to live up to the hopes she had placed

2   Tong, *Chiang Kai-shek, Vol. One, p. 156,157*

in me..."[3] At the time he voiced those sentiments, he was the leader and father figure of nearly one fifth of the world's population.

At age seventeen, Chiang shocked the locals by cutting off his pigtail, the symbol of loyalty to the Emperor. He decided on a military career and looked to Japan, the recognized center of military education in the Far East. His mother scraped enough together for passage to Tokyo where the military academy quickly rejected him. He returned home, applied and passed a competitive exam for entrance to the Paoting Military Academy. Although located in China, it was staffed by Japanese officers proud and arrogant after their recent victory over the Russians in the Russo- Japanese War. On at least one occasion, Chiang reportedly challenged instructors who spoke ill of China. He escaped with reprimand and at the end of the year was selected to go to Japan for further schooling.

Tokyo, at that time, harbored various Chinese rebel groups licking their wounds and plotting the next uprising. Sun Yat-sen's movement, organized as the Kuomintang (KMT) political party was the most prominent. Sun's first goal was forming a nation from the existing warring factions and freeing the country from exploitation by foreign interests. Young Chiang Kai-shek sought out Sun Yat-sen, then residing in Tokyo after an aborted revolution. When the young would-be revolutionary offered his services to the cause, Sun directed him to complete his military education.

Chiang graduated from Tokyo's Shinbo Goko Military program in 1909 and then served in the 15th Field Artillery Regiment of the Japanese Army. Revolt erupted again in China in October 1911.

---

3   Crozier, *The Man Who Lost China, P. 34*

Chiang and two others took unauthorized leave, donned civilian clothes to elude military police and boarded ship for Shanghai. On arrival, they slipped through the Manchu government police and reportedly packaged and mailed swords and uniforms back to their Japanese regiments. In total, approximately 120 rebels returned from Japan to join the ragtag military efforts of the new revolution.

Although revolutionary rhetoric was plentiful, weapons were few, and after some wrangling, leadership settled on the Shanghai Arsenal as the prime military objective. During the planning and organizing phase, Chiang Kai-shek rose to become informal Chief of Staff to local leader Chen Chi-mei. They planned a two-pronged attack. One group would open the revolt with an assault on Hangchow, the capital of Chekiang Province. The other, larger, group would attack the Shanghai Arsenal the following day to secure weapons. Both groups were outnumbered and poorly armed, and the Manchu government, well aware of the threat, reinforced their garrisons. Based on pure numbers and armament, the attacks appeared suicidal. The only rebel advantage was a revolutionary spirit that spawned a small group called the "Dare to Die Corps."

Chiang Kai-shek volunteered to lead 100 of the elites in the attack on Hangchow. Before the attack, he wrote his mother asking forgiveness for neglecting his filial duties, and telling how he wished his affairs and affects should be disposed, if he should die in battle telling her "I have sworn to give my life for the revolution."

His hundred, including two women rebels, using hand thrown bombs, stormed the fortress and drove out a much larger government force. Hangchow was the first city taken in the new revolt. A youthful Chiang Kai-shek had led the initial victory of the revolution and a writer singled out his exploits in a book entitled "The Record of the Independence of Chekiang."[4] The Emperor was deposed in the revolt, but Sun's party was not prepared for success. Intrigue produced chaos in Kuomintang ranks. One General was murdered, and the principles of Sun Yat-sen were soon shredded. Sun and his disciples retreated again to the expatriate community in Japan. While there, Chiang, somehow immune to penalties for his desertion from the Japanese Army, reportedly, contributed his views to periodicals. When Sun Yat-sen completed plans for his next revolution, Chiang again joined the fray and fought in Shanghai. The revolt failed. Chiang was captured, but managed to escape and flee with Dr. Sun to Japan.

In the following years, Sun's revolution sputtered against strong warlord forces. Chiang took on increasing responsibility and took his lessons in a world of intrigue and violence. He drew attention and escaped assassination on several occasions. In 1916, at age 29, he led a successful attack on the Kiangyin fortress on the Yangtse River. However, when opposing forces threatened; his troops deserted. Again, he managed to escape. At age thirty, he was impulsive, brave to an almost foolish extreme, yet, he seemed to have charmed life. He'd shown leadership under fire and evidenced a peculiar disregard for personal prestige, a characteristic he would soon display in dramatic fashion. It was said that his single-minded devotion to the Revolution was evident. Incorruptible himself, he was able to deal with others who were not. He carried loyalty to friends to an extreme and it seems, had a foul temper. Dr. Sun Yat-sen, after the assassination of his key lieutenant,

---

4 Tong. *Chiang Kai-shek, Vol. one, p. 14-17*

wrote Chiang addressing him with the customary respectful term "Elder Brother". "The sudden tragic death of Cha Ta-fu is a loss to me comparable to that of my right or left hand. When I look upon members of our party I find very few who are experts in war and also loyal. Only you, my Elder Brother, are with us, you whose courage and sincerity are equal to those of Cha Ta-fu, and your knowledge of war is even better than his. But you have a very fiery temper and your hatred of mediocrity is excessive. And so it often leads to quarreling and difficulty in cooperating. As you are shouldering the great internal responsibility of our party, you should sacrifice your ideals a little and try to compromise. This is merely for the sake of our party and has nothing to do with your personal principles. Would you, my Elder Brother, agree with this? Or wouldn't you?" On another occasion, after a display of anger Chiang wrote an apology "I have a bad temper and am usually lacking in good manners, I feel most ashamed of myself after careful reflection. I know myself that I have been ridiculous."[5] Although he continued to erupt when faced with particularly frustrating situations, he developed firm control when faced with important issues. Later, in his contact with one ally, he carried this self discipline to an extreme.

While turmoil continued in China, Lenin and his Russian Communists overthrew a fragile democratic government in Moscow. Fresh from their successful revolution, the Russian Reds shifted their attention to the ultimate Marx-Leninist goal of world domination and recognized the emerging upheaval in Asia. In 1922, Lenin wrote in the 10th anniversary issue of Pravda "China and India

---

5 Crozier, *The Man Who Lost China*, p.53

are seething. These two nations have a population of more than 700 millions. Add to them their Asian neighbors who are in like condition and they comprise over half the population of the earth." From that point on, the conversion of China to Communism became a key part of the Soviet plan for communist expansion and attempts at deep involvement in China politics followed. When the Soviet's initial efforts were rejected by the powerful warlord factions who were already well supplied by the Europeans and Japanese, they turned to Sun Yat-sen's Nationalist Kuomintang movement.

In 1919, Soviet Russia unilaterally renounced all exploitive treaties with China. Sun Yat-sen took note. Seeing a Russian connection improving his military strength vs. the warlords, he welcomed Soviet support, and they responded with weapons, ammunition and other much needed aid. The Russians also furnished an array of advisers who were soon involved in all civil and military functions in the KMT Party.

In 1923, Sun Yat-sen sent Chiang Kai-shek to Moscow where his young lieutenant met with Stalin, Trotsky and other top government and military officials. Viewed later, Chiang's reports displayed the political insight that allowed him to survive and rise in the turmoil of China politics. He first advised Sun to avoid all foreign connections and go it alone, using the Communists in Russia as an example. They'd advanced after their revolution despite a lack of foreign recognition. Although he recognized Red success in Russia, Chiang advised Sun Yat-sen the Russian Communists were not to be trusted. Sun, after his series of failed revolutions, needed Russian military aid and was willing to take the risk.

Soviet advisory aid first came in the form of Michael Borodin, an international Communist. Born in Russia, he'd moved to the U.S. with his parents, was educated there and for a time, ran a business school in Chicago. He'd joined the Communist International movement as an agitator in Mexico and later, was deported from Scotland. He'd also served as advisor to Turkey's ruling Pasha. Borodin came with high recommendations, personal charm and air of sincerity. When he declared for Sun Yat-sen's three principles, he was completely accepted in the KMT and appointed official advisor to the Party. By 1924, Borodin arranged a resolution allowing Communists to join the KMT. Conditions were added requiring an oath of obedience to the KMT party.

Although Sun Yat-sen's principles were widely accepted and aroused the patriotism of the masses, Sun knew the most powerful warlords, could only be brought into line with military force. Chiang, during his Moscow visit, had discussed staffing and general plans for a military academy. In 1924, Sun Yat-sen founded the Whampoa Military Academy and appointed Chiang Kai-shek to head it. Chiang, on his long rail trip across Siberia to Moscow, became acquainted with Soviet General Blucher, a.k.a. Galen. Sun named Galen Chief of Staff of an academy heavily staffed by Russians. The school's planned enrollment of 300 was expanded to 500 when 3000 applied. Chiang focused totally on the Academy and its students and despite the Russian staff, he was able to establish and control the development of cadets. He instilled the "dare to die" spirit he'd learned as a revolutionary, as the core ideal for the student body. To counteract traditional Chinese warfare practices emphasizing passive methods, he installed "mien-Tso-fa" wherein any commander from platoon leader to Commandant who retreated without orders, was summarily executed.[6] He later organized the Nationalist Army around leadership from the Whampoa Military Academy, a group loyal only to him. Whampoa discipline and commitment, along with the Nationalist fervor then sweeping China and Russian aid, combined to give Chiang a small effective army.

As the military situation improved, the political scene fragmented. Less than a year after the military Academy opened, Sun Yat-sen died leaving no directions for succession to the leadership of the Party or the Republic. The fledging nation grieved. For many Chinese, Sun personalized their hopes for a brighter future, and he'd become the spirit of a new China. In the void remaining, Sun's closest aids attempted to fill the gap by directing separate government functions with Chiang in charge of all military matters. The others soon fell out among themselves and plotting, intrigue and rebellion provided a climate for Communist expansion and anarchy.[7] During this period, Chiang remained in the field, leading military campaigns against various rebellions. His junior officers, former academy cadets, performed very well under fire. On one occasion, a KMT division of 7000 was defeated. Chiang reportedly arrived the following day and led a furious counterattack that dispersed the enemy and added to his reputation.

---

6   Liu, *A Military History of Modern China*, p.13
7   Tong. *Chiang Kai-shek, Vol. One*, p. 80,81

The political pot continued to boil and an assassination left one of the ruling group, Wang Ching-wei, as head of the Kuomintang Party. The Russians saw Chiang Kai-shek as the future leader of the Nationalist movement. However, they intended to convert him and the evolving Kuomintang Party leadership to Communism, or failing that, take over the government as they'd done in Russia only a few years earlier. Future Communist leaders Mao Tse-tung and Chou En-lai (Zhou Enlai) were already active in the KMT at lower levels.

On June 4, 1926, Chiang called a meeting of the Kuomintang leadership and urged decisive action on a northern expedition to conquer warlord-dominated provinces. The Reds, intent on Party domination, rather than military efforts to unify the country, objected. As Red opposition solidified, the Nationalist Army incurred disciplinary problems that were traced to Chinese Reds incited by their Soviet advisers. While Chiang resolved his army problems, a struggle for overall control of the KMT party erupted on March 20, 1926 with a general strike in Canton. Chiang Kai-shek moved in quickly. He disarmed the strikers and presented the KMT party and the Russian advisers with a "fait accompli." One Russian adviser, Stepanov reported "they (the Russians) were not using Chiang, but were being used by him."[8] Chiang quickly removed all Russians from administrative and executive positions and redefined their role as "advisers."

Chiang Kai-shek emerged from the attempted coup as the undisputed leader of the National Revolutionary Army and a power figure in the government-controlled provinces of China. Although

---

8   Liu, *A Military History of Moderrn China*, p. 24

much of the country remained controlled by warlords and foreign interests, the people across China were beginning to hear of a new and different political party. The KMT movement's appeal to the youth swelled the army's ranks and modest military successes allowed personification of the KMT movement to gradually fall on Chiang Kai-shek.

Despite this personal recognition, prospects for his Northern Expedition waned. Army growth required money. Unlike warlord troops, who lived off the people, Chiang paid his soldiers regularly and required they respect the rights of civilians. However, the enthusiasm of the poor produced little revenue and the Nationalist government faced a new cash problem. Soviet Russia reacted to their lessened role in China by restricting aid volume, and selling supplies at high cash prices. Meanwhile, western powers and Japan saw Nationalist fervor as a threat to their domination of Chinese ports. Rather than aid China's new government, they enforced an arms embargo.

Chiang's options were severely limited. The Nationalist government could yield to the Soviets and gain arms and supplies and sacrifice Sun's revolution to Communism, or yield to the threat posed by the alliances of hostile warlords, give up hard won progress and compromise Dr. Sun's goals. Chiang saw his deferred northern expedition as a third and more favorable alternative. Beyond existing Nationalist borders, lay North China with large arsenals and plentiful supplies. The problem was Northern warlord troops outnumbered Nationalist Government forces by more than two to one. Despite this imbalance, Chiang called a meeting of Kuomintang leadership, overcame resistance from Borodin and

Chinese Reds and gained government approval to lead the Army northward.

When Chiang marshaled his army and moved north, results of his rejection of traditional warlord practices became apparent. He'd organized his army on political principles. Embedded Kuomintang party officials insured that Dr. Sun's Three Principles were followed. His paid troops were strictly prohibited from using aggressive behavior toward the people they encountered. As the Army advanced, word preceded it. Government soldiers did not loot. For the rural peasants, this was nothing short of amazing. The Nationalist propaganda was true. The Army was "one with the common people." This not only eased the acceptance of an army entering enemy territory, but, as fraternization with the locals developed, it provided valuable information on the enemy's situation.[9] The acclaim of the people and positive remarks of foreign observers resulted in a great rise in the prestige of the young commander. A leader was emerging, something the country lacked since the death of Dr. Sun.

Through most of 1926 and into 1927, Chiang battled the warlords in the north and a series of Moscow directed insurrections at home. He came to see the Chinese Communists as willing to destroy all in order to take power. For the Reds, Chiang Kai-shek's emergence as a national leader positioned him as the principal enemy. Chiang pleaded for unity. "...China is half dead and it devolves on us to resuscitate her. It is necessary that all should co-operate and fight for liberty and justice so as to enable China to regain her

---

9   Tong, *Chiang Kai-shek, Vol. One, p. 101*

position in the world." Orders from Moscow directed otherwise. The Reds plotted within the KMT to undermine Chiang and other non-communist officials.[10] They incited and organized agitation, disruption, strikes and riots and they resorted to terrorism to solidify their hold in localities where they'd seized power. Chiang abandoned the olive branch, declaring "Whoever goes against the aims and methods indicated by Dr. Sun Yat-sen will not be a comrade but an enemy who must not remain among us."

From Moscow, on November 30, 1926, The Kremlin called on the Chinese Communist Party workers to do "their most to strengthen the political work among the troops...bringing to fulfillment the Chinese revolutionary ideology."[11] Stalin specified, "Work must be intensified in the rear and within the divisions of Chiang Kai-shek, in order to disintegrate them..." The lines were drawn.

Civil unrest increased. On March 10, 1927 Chiang again sought to warn the insurgents and calm the waters, but there was no turning back. Three days later, Red elements in the KMT issued orders to return all power, political, military, financial, and foreign affairs to the party where they felt they could seize power from the KMT committees. Chiang struck quickly, sending the Peking police on a raid of the Soviet Embassy where they seized incriminating documents, evidence that dispelled any remaining doubts on Red Chinese allegiance to Moscow. Chiang summoned all military leaders, set up a purge committee and issued orders to disarm all Communist strikers. On April 12, violence erupted in Shanghai.

---

10 Tong, *Chiang Kai-shek, Vol. One*, p.143
11 Liu, *A Military History of Modern China*, p. 40

A Communist led attack on the 26th Army Corps headquarters provoked counter fire from the troops. In the subsequent violence, arrests and executions, the Communists claimed they lost 300 killed and 5000 missing. The Nationalist claimed to have captured 3000 rifles, 20 machine guns, various pistols, 800,000 rounds of ammunition, seven cart loads of axes and 2000 long handled pikes. Five days later, Red leadership declared Chiang Kai-shek guilty of a great massacre of the people and oppression of the party and put a price on his head. Chiang, in control of the police and the army, detained all the Russian advisers, arrested 2000 Chinese Reds and gave all Communists at large 10 days to report, or face a firing squad. He then formed a government in Nanking (Nanjing), reaffirmed Sun Yat-sen's three principles and called for a total break with the Reds. Russian advisers Borodin and Galen left reluctantly. They'd worked closely with Chiang Kai-shek held him in high regard. In departing, Borodin doubted Chiang could succeed in his plans for China; "I am convinced that he is honest in his fight for the Nationalist cause, but he is not enough of a personality to carry his works alone, to take upon himself the gigantic task of liberating and reconstructing China."[12]

In order to succeed, Chiang Kai-shek had transformed himself from reckless combat leader to wily political operator. One who could play off opposing forces, unite disparate interests, and take one step back to gain two steps forward, yet always able to move swiftly and effectively when required. Would it be enough?

---

12 Crozier, *The Man Who Lost China*, p.110

3

TURMOIL AND PROGRESS

D URING 1927 AND 1928, Chiang Kai-shek's National army conducted a successful campaign that resulted in the subjection of much of North China to Nationalist rule. The resources of the North became available to the new China. Chiang had achieved military success in the north against great odds while defeating Communist insurgency at home. He was becoming the recognized leader of China.

His next step was unprecedented in world politics. Within the KMT, non-communist factions entertained long smoldering resentments, differences fueled by Chiang's meteoric rise to national prominence. Chiang Kai-shek abruptly announced his retirement. He left the party with directions to regain unity, outlaw the Communists and he laid down specific conditions for his retirement. First: that both factions resolve their differences and he offered to be a sacrificial lamb. If either faction decided he should be punished, he would regard whatever punishment is meted out as a mark of extraordinary honor. Second: he urged completion of the final phase of the Northern Campaign and third: he called for a "thorough cleansing" of areas where the Communists had turned to violence and terror.

The China Weekly Review said: "Where is there any man who has been willing to give up his hard-fought-for post and voluntary retire to private life, for no other reason than the preservation of the Party and the salvation of the country from further bloody internecine warfare?"

The view from the left presents his resignation as a cynical maneuver by an absolute ruler who could easily reclaim his position. This describes a capability but not a motive. All evidence indicates Chiang suffered from a lack of control throughout his career on the mainland. Modern China had no absolute ruler prior to Mao Tse-tung.

Chiang retreated to the mountains of his native province and announced he intended to spend five years studying politics, economics and military tactics and then turned to his personal affairs. His first marriage, arranged when he was14 years old was a disaster. His wife failed to persuade him to give up his commitment to the revolution and they divorced. He visited Japan and renewed acquaintance with former instructors and military commanders. Later, while visiting at the family home of Dr. Sun in Canton, Chiang Kai-shek met a beautiful young U.S. educated woman with a grasp of politics, a love of China and a rich father. Mayling Soong was initially not interested, but Chiang persisted. They married on December 1, 1927 and became inseparable. The new Mme. Chiang Kai-shek participated fully, from top-level meetings with foreigners where she served as Chiang's interpreter, to organizing refugee relief when war erupted. She gained the distinction of being the only First Lady of World War Two to be injured by enemy action. Her beauty and charm enhanced Chiang's national and international image, but, in dealing with Americans, her advice, at times, may have inhibited his talent for decisive action.

Chiang Kai-shek's absence from power was short lived. Without a strong national figure to symbolize a united China, warlord armies emerged. KMT leadership, incapable of firm decision or effective action, requested Chiang's return. He accepted and pledged to complete the northern campaign to unify the country. In the brief period without a strong Nationalist government, the unconquered northern warlords had gathered their strength and the weakened Nationalist government had not capitalized on the resources newly available in the north. Nationalist forces were still heavily outnumbered by better-equipped northern forces. Once again, Chiang relied on spirit and discipline to overcome the odds.

As the end of the decade approached, the Reds erupted in Canton once again. The Nationalists reacted quickly and violently, overcoming the insurgents and executing suspected Communists including a few Russians. The Chinese Communist Party, the CCP, was outlawed and Chiang moved toward complete suppression of Red influences in the government and the army. The Russians responded by cutting off all aid.

Chiang Kai-shek soon had to meet an entirely different set of challenges. Inside the country, the initial flush of patriotism among the powerful had passed and provincial governors, former warlords, were beginning to chafe under the authority of the central government. Rebellion was in the air and the Communist movement, although suppressed, was not extinguished. On July 31, 1931, three men concealed along the roadside fired on Chiang's car. They missed, were captured and later admitted a communist political faction in Canton had sent them on the assassination mission. When the Russians cut off aid, Chiang turned to Germany for military help and advisors. The dismantling of the German army, after their defeat in World War One, left Germany with a surplus of talented, top level military people. From 1927 on, Germans provided China with the advisors needed to prepare his army to defend China against a recognized threat from Japan.

Unfortunately, time for developing national strength was limited. Chiang's leadership and the growing strength of China were becoming evident to the world. Neighboring Japan watched and saw the new China as a threat to its dominance in Asia. In 1928, Japan took its first aggressive step by sending military forces into the province of Shantung to obstruct the Nationalist campaign in North China. They failed on that occasion but it signaled things to come.

In 1931, Japan invaded Manchuria (Man zhou). China, still in the process of a merging of factions and private armies, was easy prey. In 1933, Chiang sought to buy time by signing an agreement giving Japan virtual control in Manchuria. Public sentiment called for resistance against the invaders and political factions in northern China agitated for military action. Chiang refused to move until his army was prepared. He restrained angry troops and citizens reminding them "we must remember what we have suffered and set apart 10 years for developing our national strength and 10 years for training our people..."[1]

Along with accelerated military development, Chiang used his position as "Father of the New China" to launch a "New Life Movement" to prepare the civilian population for the upcoming struggle. He based it on guidelines of behavior gathered from Confucius and other Chinese sages. Four principles were li, yi, lien and ch'ih meaning property, justice, honesty and a sense of self-respect. Chiang announced the program at a mass meeting and then had 100 groups of students organized and trained to bring the new program to the public throughout the country. It was a call for integrity, courage and self-sacrifice. One offshoot was an anti-opium campaign aimed at eradicating widespread opium smoking and drug trafficking within six years. An ambitious goal, opium smokers and opium commercial interests could not be denied by proclamation. China was the world's largest producer. The crop employed at least one million families and produced great profits for powerful vested interests.[2] Chiang took a practical approach. The government took control of the trade and then gradually strangled it, reportedly reducing opium usage 80% by 1937.

From 1931 onward, increasing Japanese oppression in Manchuria aroused many Chinese against Chiang Kai-shek's low profile strategy. He was increasingly vulnerable to claims of appeasement. The loudest voice came from the Communist enclave. The remote, barren refuge of the Communists had nothing of value to attract the Japanese; consequently, the Reds had nothing to

---

1   Liu, *A Military History of Modern China*, p. 160
2   Tong, *Chiang Kai-shek, Vol. One*, p.29

lose by leading the cry for war. Meanwhile, part of Chiang Kai-shek's war preparation plans called for the final elimination of Mao and his faction. On December 7th, 1936, Chiang began his move on the Reds when he flew to Sian to enlist the forces of Chang Hsueh-liang, known as the "Young Marshall." Although the Young Marshall had been a critic of Chiang Kai-shek's seeming appeasement of the Japanese, he professed loyalty to China and his domain was close to the Red enclave and a logical point to launch anti-Red operations.

At 5 AM, on the morning after Chiang's arrival in Sian, he'd completed his early morning exercises when he heard gunfire and found a force of nearly 100 troops attacking his sentries. Chiang and two of his men scaled a 10-foot wall. He fell thirty feet into a moat and severely injured his back. Climbing out under fire, he stumbled away, down the mountainside only to fall into a cave. The second fall immobilized him completely. His pursuers discovered him lying partially clothed, shaking with rage. His captors carried him down the mountain to the offices of the Young Marshall who addressed him respectfully as "Generalissimo." Chiang retorted: "Since you call me Generalissimo, then you are my subordinate. If you recognize me as your superior officer, you must immediately escort me back to Loyang. Otherwise, you are a rebel. If I am in a rebel hands, then you can kill me immediately. Apart from that there is nothing more to be said." He refused to respond further for several days. Despite the young Marshal's posture of courtesy and respect, his assault had killed or wounded more than 40 of Chiang's entourage.[3]

---

3   Crozier, *The Man Who Lost China*, p. 183

News of Chiang's capture spread quickly and plunged the nation into gloom and anxiety. One report described "A pall of gloom had fallen over most of the nation." Another reported, "Children could not sleep, soldiers wept, and illiterates badgered those who could read the newspapers in order to learn the most recent dispatches from Sian."[4] The kidnappers soon found that despite the outcry against Chiang's "appeasement", all of the powerful leaders throughout the country called for Chiang's release. Meanwhile, in Sian, during the days of silence, the Young Marshall and his 2nd in command browsed through Chiang Kai-shek's papers and found his plans to resist the Japanese invaders. According to one flattering report, they hurried to repent: "If I had known but ten or twenty percent of what you have said in the diary, never would this rash act have happened. Now I sincerely realized that my own views were mistaken. Since I know the greatness of your leadership, I feel I would be disloyal to our countrymen if I did not do my utmost to protect you." Chiang broke his silence: "Send me back to Nanking." On December 25, 1936, Nanking received news of Chiang's release and the city erupted with joy, firecrackers and cheering crowds. Many people held parties to celebrate.[5] Any doubts on Chiang's position in hearts and minds of the people were dispelled. The Young Marshal's explanation for his actions didn't convince Chiang. He placed his former captor under long-term house arrest

A different view of the Chiang's release sees him saved by Stalin whose order to release Chiang is relayed to the Young Marshall by Chinese Red, Chou En-lai. Most proponents of that view also

4   Crozier, *The Man Who Lost China, p. 184*
5   Ibid, *P. 188-189*

insisted the Chinese Reds were simple agrarian reformers entirely separate from Stalin's influence. Difficult to accommodate these contradictory concepts of Stalin's influence on CCP affairs.

However, a new day was approaching in the Nationalist/ Communist relationship in China.

4

THE CONTENDER

YEARS EARLIER, WHILE Chiang Kai-shek solidified his leadership
of the Kuomintang Party and the country, the beleaguered
Communist Chinese faced a different situation and found a new
leader. Mao Tse-tung also came from rural China, but from com-
paratively well-off parents. It was said that Mao's father started
with a few acres of land and improved his situation by lending money to other peasants at usurious rates. Youthful Mao, on occasion,
rebelled against his father and showed indications of sympathy for
the downtrodden. At age 17, he entered primary school. The year
was 1910, a year of severe drought and resulting famine. It's reported, in that situation, Mao collected rents for his father during
his school holiday, and when he encountered tramps or paupers he
gave them some of the money he'd collected. The following year
Mao entered the middle school in Changsha. The city had a history of unrest and was about to erupt once again. As Chiang had

done, Mao cut off his queue and joined the revolutionary army. His duties included daily drill and mundane domestic chores, cooking and carrying buckets of water. By February 1912, he decided the life of the Revolutionary soldier was not for him. He considered and then dismissed learning a trade or applying for a government position. He was admitted to the Hunan First Middle School but left the school within six months and moved into cheap lodgings in the city. It's reported he spent his days in the library devouring socioeconomic classics, history, geography, and newspapers.

The following year Mao gained admittance to a training school for primary school teachers. Mao recalled, "I have never been to university, nor have I studied abroad. The groundwork of my knowledge and scholarship was laid at the first teacher's training school which was a good school." Mao spent over five years in the school, leaving in the summer of 1918. It was the year of Sun Yat-sen's second revolution. Fighting flared up in Hunan, and although Mao had been involved in student antigovernment activities; rather than reenlist in the revolutionary forces he reentered the Teachers Training School. He wrote thoughtful articles and arrived at conclusions such as "No crime is greater than the repression of man's nature."[1] Principles he soon discarded. Within a decade he would declare "To put it bluntly, it is necessary to create terror for a while in every rural area...."[2] Another of his early enlightenments was: "One should not stop one's pursuit of the truth until the aim is achieved and only then can one have ambition."[3] Pursuit of truth

---

1 Fitzgerald, *Revolution in China*, P.44

2 Mao Tse-tung, *Selected Works of Mao Tse-tung*, Vol. one, p. 29

3 Fitzgerald. *Revolution in China*, P.46

soon gave way to acceptance of Leninist dialectics wherein opposites and contradictions become identical when the party could benefit from such interpretations.[4] Soon, concern for man's nature and concern for truth would no longer exist for Mao Tse-tung.

On May 29, 1918, Mao resigned from the chairmanship of the student society and moved to Peking. There, he gravitated to various revolutionary and anarchist student societies and related later "My interest in politics increased and I myself became more radical." The following year he returned to his home, near Hunan, with a new bride and took a teaching job at the primary school. In Hunan, Mao gave public lectures on Marxism and the Revolution. He also edited and contributed to the Hsiang River Weekly Review criticizing Western political leaders and advocating a union of Communist republics. He verbally espoused democracy, attacked warlords and demanded release of imprisoned revolutionaries. As Mao's emergence as a radical populist gained attention, the government took notice and suppressed his weekly review.

Mao again retreated to Peking where he adopted a lifestyle of poverty and studied socialist and communist manifestos. The following April, he moved to Shanghai in what he called, "probably a critical period in my life." He took a job as a laundryman and experienced manual labor for the first time in his life. In July, he returned to Hunan, took a position as director in the teacher's training school, while he pursued political studies and activism. He was enthralled with Communism. He wrote, "Socialism is certainly the cure for the ills of the world and also suitable for the future

---

4   Mao Tse-tung, *Selected Works of Mao Tse-tung, Vol. one, p.337*

reconstruction of China. I think that the first thing we must do is to organize a party . . . the Communist Party, which will be the promoter, propagandist, vanguard, and commander of the revolution. Unless it is organized, the revolutionary and labor movements in China cannot have a nerve center." Mao's efforts in organizing the labor movement, inciting strikes and spreading propaganda led him to the position of Chairman of the Hunan Association of Trade Unions. In December 1922, he met with the governor of Hunan and presented a list of radical demands. When the governor issued an order for young Mao's arrest, he fled to Shanghai.

In 1923, when Russian Borodin eased Chinese Communists into Sun Yat-sen's Kuomintang party, Mao Tse-tung was elected as delegate to the National Congress of the new KMT government. However, his rise to prominence peaked when Communist prospects dimmed. He became ill and returned to Hunan to recuperate.

At that time, the Chinese Communist party, consistent with Marxist doctrine, focused on organizing workers and exploiting capitalist-labor conflict. While Mao languished in Hunan, his views gradually changed. During his convalescence and recuperation, he spent more time in contact with the peasants than he'd experienced during his protected childhood. He saw peasants who comprised 80% of China's population, providing a more logical base for the Chinese Communist Party than factory workers. On his return to party work, he gained recognition for his new views, but the party's prospects continued to decline. In 1928, after the first Red uprising and Chiang Kai-shek's move to suppress Communists, a dispirited Mao declared "Having fought in various places in the past year, we are keenly aware that the revolutionary upsurge in the country as a whole is subsiding. . . . Wherever the Red Army goes, it finds the masses cold and reserved . . . We have to fight the enemy forces hard whoever they are and scarcely any mutiny or uprising has taken place within the enemy forces . . . We have an acute sense of loneliness and are every moment longing for the end of such a lonely life."[5] During that period, Mao recorded how the Reds "requested" local support. He quoted a typical Red request to communities in their path: "The Red Army . . .makes every effort to protect the merchants-. . .(However), because of the current shortage of food supplies, we are writing you now to request that you kindly collect on our behalf 5000 dollars, 7000 pairs of sandals, 7000 pairs of socks and 300 bolts of white cloth. It is urgent that these be delivered before eight o'clock this evening.... If you ignore our requests, (it will be proof of your collaboration with reactionaries)...In that case we will be obliged to burn down all the reactionary shops in (the town)...Do not say we have not forewarned you!" Mao noted, "You can only expropriate once in a given locality, afterwards there would be nothing to take."[6]

In March 1928, Mao, by then a military commander, was criticized by the Hunan Special, Commissar for having not done enough burning and killing, and for having failed to carry out party policy. He apparently corrected his behavior and, as the Party turned to internal purges to purify the party, Mao was a leader rather than a subject.

---

5   Fitzgerald, *Revolution in China, p.127*
6   Short, Mao, A life, p. 231

"Reactionary subversion" was the term used to justify a reign of terror within the party. In 1930, party leadership ordered "the most merciless torture" to ferret out reactionaries. They warned that even those people who seemed very positive and loyal, very left-wing, must be doubted and questioned. Torture was progressive until the victim confessed. The first step was hanging by the hands and beating. Next came burning with open flames. One of the final steps that never failed consisted of nailing the victim's hands to a table and inserting bamboo splints under the fingernails. The methods were given names, "airplane ride," "sitting in a sedan chair," and torture continued until the victim blurted out names, any names that would halt the agony. As new names were investigated, the grim program expanded exponentially.[7] The program was not concerned with guilt or innocence. The continuous, pervasive terror decimated Party and Army ranks, but produced the uniformly obedient comrades later admired by western visitors to Mao's Yenan (Yan'an) headquarters. During the purge, Mao considered the suffering "irrelevant."

On the national scene, Chiang Kai-shek, from 1928 onward, faced several years of serious threats from the recently conquered warlord dominated provinces and Government troops were fully occupied suppressing dissident warlords. In order to control the growth of small, but aggressive Communist movements existing in several provinces, Chiang sent provincial troops against the Reds in a series of suppression campaigns. The campaigns had mixed results. In some encounters, Reds overcame provincial troops and persuaded them to join the Red cause. When Chiang Kai-shek

---

7   Short, Mao, A life, p. 274

finally succeeded in resolving his Northern unity problems, he sent government troops against the Communists. The Reds were no match. Starting in 1934, approximately 20,000 remnants of the several Communist Chinese movements sought escape by retreating westward toward mother Russia. They fled under relentless Government pressure. The first Red group, led by Mao Tse-tung, was driven out to remote thinly populated wastelands. Yenan, a barren cave village became Communist China's capital. Later Mao enshrined his escape to desolation and poverty as a glorious "Long March". When they finally stopped, the initial 20,000, despite forced recruiting along the way, had likely shrunk to less than the "whole army of 5000 men," Mao had claimed six years earlier. Chiang Kai-shek turned his attention towards the looming Japanese threat.

The much heralded Long March, rather than a planned military movement toward a specific destination, started out more as an aimless flight. Mao admitted later they set out on the Long March with several possible destinations in mind. Their remote final refuge was not part of an initial plan. They were simply fleeing from government suppression and seeking to unify all fragments at some point closer to the Soviet Union.

In their flight, they fought several rear guard actions. The Government, contending with larger Japanese problems, was satisfied to keep them moving toward isolation. It's generally agreed the trek of Mao's group covered 6000 miles in slightly over a year, averaging slightly over 16 miles per day. That is considerably below military standards for troop movements on foot; difficult terrain may have accounted for the shortfall.

Later, Red propaganda and western admirers, always seeking to present the Reds as a substantial entity, claimed as many as 100,000 set out. Pure logic and a few facts indicate it's a significant exaggeration. The overall movement consisted of the 1st, 2nd and 4th Red "armies". Before the Government encirclement and suppression campaigns, Mao recorded his first Army strength at 5000 men.[8] It's unlikely the Red army grew significantly while struggling under the government suppression campaigns that forced them to flee. It's also unlikely the 2nd or 4th armies exceeded the size of Mao's 1st Army since Mao was the Chairman of National Soviet Government. Simple arithmetic indicates the Reds set out with possibly 15,000 to 20,000 troops and Mao declared they had severe losses along the route. Chiang Kai-shek estimated 5000 survived the trek. One survivor described the Long March. "A great many soldiers and porters fell and died... there was no medicine for the sick... no one to give a peaceful burial to the dead...a condition to pitiful for the pen to describe... the morale of the officers and troops became utterly ashen hearted."

After years of fruitless struggle, defeat and terrifying purges, Mao needed a rallying cry. He propagandized the Long March as a glorious Communist achievement and raised it to the level of Moses exodus from Egypt. He proclaimed "We say that the Long March is the first of its kind ever recorded in history... It proclaims to the world that the Red Army is an army of heroes and that the imperialists and their jackals, Chiang Kai-shek and his like, are perfect

---

8   Mao Tse-tung, *Selected Works of MaoTse-tung, vol. One, p. 83*

nonentities… To sum up, the Long March ended with our victory and the enemy's defeat."[9]

Similar to other early Red achievements, later investigation cast a different light on the glorious victory. Decades a later former Red Army brat followed the Long March route, sought out survivors and was enlightened. She found that all top party and army leaders set out accompanied by their wives. 2nd Army records listed 10,068 starting out. Within six months they sustained 998 casualties and 208 defections to the enemy, but also 4004 desertions.[10] In order to replace massive desertions, males as young as fourteen were conscripted along the way and failure to meet recruiting goals led to death. Similar to Mao's previous "requests" from inhabitants along his route, all in their path who lived above subsistence level were defined as landlords and therefore subject to complete confiscation of all possessions. Any reluctance to cooperate resulted in "burning their houses, and digging up and destroying family tombs… Their families will be punished by death."[11] In the first stages of their flight, the Reds would occupy a city in their path and strip it of food, clothing and young males. Later in more barren areas where word of their looting had preceded them, they narrowly escaped with their lives.

Mao's glorious Long March put his band of survivors in a wasteland requiring continuous struggle to survive. From Moscow, Stalin contributed several modest cash payments allowing Mao to acquire very bare necessities. In December, 1936, Mao reflected on the Nationalist encirclement and suppression campaigns that

---

9   Mao Tse-tung, *Selected Works of MaoTse-tung, vol. One,* p.242

10   Shuyun, *The Long March,* P.69

11   Ibid, *p. 60*

continued to compress the Communist occupied area. He recounted his defeats. "In his fifth campaign... we milled around between the enemy's main forces and his blockhouses and were reduced to complete passivity... We showed not the slightest initiative or drive. In the end, we had to withdraw from our Kiangsi base area."

Mao lamented his situation "our enemy is big and powerful... The Red Army is small and weak... The Red Army is numerically small, its arms are poor and it has great difficulty in obtaining supplies such as food, bedding and clothing."[12] While the Reds initially confiscated food and other needed supplies from the local inhabitants, Mao Tse-tung soon realized a starving, and alienated population would produce even less food and begin a death cycle for his movement. He turned his army to agriculture, but the army and the people still existed on the edge of hunger, if not famine. In December 1936, Mao admitted they'd failed to smash the "encirclement and suppression" campaign of the Government forces and their areas had been "greatly reduced."[13]

The Reds soon found relief by going on the Government payroll. They joined Chiang Kai-shek's, United Front against the Japanese. For several years after joining, the Reds actively fought the Japanese invaders and received regular cash payments and other benefits from the National Government. Mao, ever tenacious, had survived government military attacks, and internal challenges, He completed the shift of Party focus from exploiting worker unrest in the cities to developing a base in the rural peasantry and rose

---

12   Mao Tse-tung, *Selected works of Mao Tse-tung, Vol. One, p. 197,198*
13   Ibid, p. 242

to become acclaimed as "The Great Teacher," the unquestioned leader of the party. That change in focus required exploitation of peasant-landlord conflict. While the Nationalist government had set a ceiling on land rents and had instituted a successful program to increase land ownership by tenant farmers, the program ground to a halt when the Japanese attacked. Mao exploited that situation.

Agriculture in China was unique in many respects. Land did not pass to the oldest male descendent, it was divided among all. A study by American, Dr. Lossing Buck, found three quarters of China's farm population owned some land, some of it only a fraction of an acre. He found that many tenant farmers were related to their landlords and the strong Confucian emphasis on family ties had an ameliorating effect on landlord rent gouging. Nevertheless, exploitation existed and then increased once the Japanese attacked and land rent control along with other government social and economic improvement programs were disrupted. Greedy landlords existed and Mao needed a theme of exploitation. The tenant-landlord situation was the only one available.

Initial phases of Mao's program, as it was implemented in the Red enclave, included kangaroo courts that divided the landlord's holdings and awarded them to the peasants. The landlord's fate could be dire. Mao's view was ". . . it is necessary to create terror for a while in every rural area..." and "...the only effective way of suppressing the reactionaries is to execute at least a few in each county."[14] In the microcosm that constituted the Red base area, a degree of discretion softened the impact on rural families. Later, as the movement grew, bureaucrats had little time for discretion.

---

14   Mao Tse-tung, *Selected works of Mao Tse-tung, Vol. One*, p. 29,38

The program, when applied on a large scale, used decision makers who knew nothing of the individuals and the family relationships involved. Policies were applied mindlessly and ruthlessly. When the Red cadres went out to the countryside and incited peasants to move against landlords, the ancient social fabric of rural China was shredded. The People's Revolution demanded enthusiastic participation by peasants against cousins and revered uncles, who were hauled before the People's Court to be abused and reviled. When more emphasis was needed, they were executed. Demands for efficiency required the People's Revolution to move aggressively to destroy the age-old Confucian emphasis on family ties and later to move against the nuclear family unit. Dedicated Communists could not be loyal to the new Socialist People's Revolution if they adhered to ancient decadent relationships.

While selective terror was the most efficient method of gaining control of the countryside, it had to be completely hidden from visitors. Mao, the Marxist ruthlessly advanced his program in the semi-barren countryside and Mao, the propagandist succeeded in concealing it from admiring visitors to his headquarters.

With no direct access to media, Mao relied on sympathetic western authors and correspondents to promote his movement as a substantial political and military entity in China. One seeming obstacle, the size of his capital, the control center of the Communist movement in a country of nearly a half billion people, was a cave and mud hut village of 25 to 30 thousand people. However, objectivity and logic did not interfere. Mao created what his visitors hailed as a model community in Yenan. The citizenry, ultra-disciplined survivors of the purges and the "Long March", were presented to a cult of admiring Western authors and correspondents. Influenced by the Great Depression, many visitors furnished unquestioning support for the spread of the new political religion. Some visitors to Yenan were former admirers of Stalin who'd been turned off by his purges, terror campaigns, his treaty with Hitler and his invasion of neighboring countries. In Mao Tse-tung, they found a new object for their political affections. Before long, pilgrimages to Yenan became an emblem of political enlightenment in liberal segments of western society.

Mao carefully developed a small masquerade community of disciplined citizenry and when membership in the United Front allowed free access to Yenan, townspeople welcomed visitors with rousing cheers. The guests heard stirring tales of bountiful harvests and of great Red victories over the Japanese. They were impressed with the uniform behavior and apparent commitment of the people and some thought they saw evidence of a small-scale, capitalism, even hints of an underlying democracy.

One military observer arrived during the early days of the United Front, when Mao's soldiers actively opposed the Japanese. U. S. Marine Captain Evans Carlson had both experience in China and the ear of President Roosevelt. Carlson, if nothing else, was a positive individual. Although he saw many fine qualities in Chiang Kai-shek, he reserved his highest praise for Mao and his Red forces. During a 1000 mile guided tour through Nationalist and Red guerrilla territories, he met with local Red leaders, and heard heroic tales of guerrilla operations against the Japanese. He saw none first hand. Based on his weeks living and traveling with a fragment of the Red Eighth Route Army, Carlson extolled its virtues and promoted

Mao's militia as a formidable force in China although he'd seen no substantial groups of troops. His enthusiastic mindset somehow saw Nationalist China, despite the enormous casualties, destruction and loss of productive capacity inflicted by the Japanese, as gaining strength while at war. Unfortunately, physically disabled President Roosevelt was not a traveling president. He relied on Carlson and others for on-site impressions.

By dispossessing landlords and temporarily giving land to the peasants, the Reds succeeded in gaining some repute as champions of the peasants. However, they soon found the disruption of the ancient family-based agricultural setup resulted in crop failures. Production, marginal at best in the semi-barren Red enclave, fell off dramatically creating a critical situation in the bare survival economy. Mao's solution was in the direction of his ultimate goal. Collectivization of agriculture was one of several areas where the great teacher seemed to have a blind spot. He firmly believed collective farms would produce more abundant crops when in reality, centuries of intensive effort in China had elevated output per hectare very near the upper limit. This problem had been recognized by China's leaders down through history, China simply had too many people and too little productive acreage. When the delicate balance was upset; people died. Decades would pass, and millions would die before the Reds grasped this simple fact. Mao's second ongoing error was his blind belief in Lenin's dogma on the method to achieve collectivization of agriculture." . . . the only way to bring about collectivization according to Lenin, is through cooperatives." Mao wrote "We have already organized many peasant cooperatives... of a rudimentary type... and must go through

several stages of development before they can become cooperatives of the Soviet type known as collective farms."[15] An update on
Soviet collective farms should have dampened Mao's enthusiasm. In
Russia and the Ukraine, by Stalin's count, 6 million Kulaks (small
landholders) died in the conversion to collectives. After the conversion, crop production fell, and a famine resulted in more death and
disaster. Thereafter Soviet agricultural production remained at a
permanently depressed level. The "Enlightened One" ignored recent disasters and blindly followed the Soviet model. He needed an
exploitable social grievance and he needed a method of controlling
the masses. Collectivization was his answer. He departed from that
goal and espoused private land ownership to gain peasant converts
only as temporary tactic, one to be fully propagandized and then
abandoned. Food shortages continued, but Mao relieved his perennial cash shortage by converting substantial acreage to growth of
opium poppies.

---

15   Mao Tse-tung, *Selected Works of Mao Tse-tung, Vol. One, p. 156*

5

A TEST OF NATIONAL CHARACTER

A FTER CHIANG'S RETURN from captivity in Sian, he realized the time for nation building had passed and elimination of the Red enclave would be more difficult than expected. Great strides had been made during the years of his Japanese "appeasement". He'd led the country through nearly a decade of economic development making unprecedented progress in agriculture, mining and industry. Railroad expansion nearly equaled progress of the previous 48 years. Thousands of kilometers of highways were built. Nationwide, construction of 33,000 km of telephone network was completed. Imports of luxury goods decreased while imports of machinery and other industrial and utility equipment increased as China expanded the manufacturing sector. American Ambassador Nelson Johnson reported "An observer ...cannot but be impressed by the energy with which the Chinese government is pushing its program of economic reconstruction on all fronts, agricultural, industrial and communications."[1] The British commercial counselor noted "the increasing, justified confidence which the Chinese themselves as well as the world at large have in the future of this country, a confidence based on the remarkable growth of stability achieved in recent years and the improved political, financial and economic conduct of affairs- government and private."[2]

Meanwhile, by 1937, the nation had enough of Chiang Kai-shek's apparent appeasement of the Japanese. It's generally agreed Red envoy Chou En-lai visited Chiang and convinced him Mao's CCP would cooperate in a fight against the Japanese invaders. This Red Chinese commitment coincided with Russian aims to keep the Japanese fully occupied in China, and relieve pressure on neighboring Russian Siberia. Consequently, faithful Communist Mao Tse-tung pledged obedience to Chinese Army orders and committed to fight the invader.

Chiang Kai-shek's United Front contained all political persuasions willing to confront the Japanese and all participants were paid by the National Government. The increase in total Chinese army units was modest. The Communist Chinese added four divisions totaling approximately 30,000 men.[3] Other private armies contributed a few more divisions to the 325 division Nationalist Army.

Although the world vaguely sympathized with China's situation, outside aid was not forthcoming. The United States at that

---

1   Fairbank, *The Cambridge History of China, Vol. 13, Part 2, p. 164*

2   Ibid, *p.164*

3   Ibid, *p. 613*

time followed a policy of appeasement toward Japan. The U.S. failed to enforce its then existing "Open Door Policy" and accepted Japan's exclusion of U.S. ships from Chinese ports. When the Japanese sank the American gunboat Panay, killing crew members, Washington meekly submitted a verbal protest. Meanwhile, the Western nations, who'd carved up China's port districts during the past century, saw Chiang's earlier efforts to unite China as a threat to their interests. The British enjoyed major concessions in China, including complete sovereignty over the port of Hong Kong, and were reluctant to face a strong united China in the future. The French in neighboring Indochina similarly turned away. China fought alone.

By 1937, Chiang Kai-shek and his German advisors had made substantial progress in arming China, but less than needed. Many doubted that China could withstand the expected attack from Japan.[4] For the Japanese, virtual control of Manchuria and encroachment in North China was not enough to satisfy their goal to be masters of Asia. Japan suddenly attacked south into the Chinese heartland. All progress in China towards Sun Yatsen's goals ceased and China fought for survival. Chiang Kai-shek would soon face decisions that would destroy masses of people and infrastructure in order to save the majority of his people and the nation.

In addition to the Japanese onslaught, China had residual internal problems. Chiang officially commanded 325 Army Divisions, plus the few added by the United Front and a number of irregular units soon involved in guerilla activities. While the Japanese attack

---

4   Chiang Kai-shek, *China's Destiny and Chinese Economic theory*, p. 128

tended to solidify most of the warlords under Chiang, several secretly sought separate peace with the Japanese. Some assumed the role of puppet rulers in Japanese occupied China and fought alongside the Japanese. In addition, the availability of Chiang's warlord armies varied. Some confined their operations to defense of their own territories, and were not available for strategic attacks or defense of lands beyond their borders. His core Army, led by Whampoa Academy graduates had gained tactical skills from the German advisers and possessed do or die courage, but they fought Japanese aircraft, tanks and artillery with rifles and machine guns and were decimated.

When the Japanese attacked, they expected to soon annihilate all Chinese opposition and they believed Chiang's government would collapse in a few months. They were astonished to find China absorbing severe losses, finding replacements and continuing the fight. Official Chinese records show 3,211,419 casualties from 1937 to 1945 and 14 million drafted. Of those enlisted, approximately one of every four men became a casualty[5] and lack of medical facilities meant a high proportion of casualties died on the battlefield. As the Chinese fought stubbornly, Japan had to commit more and more troops. In 1937, they'd launched the invasion with 21 divisions, by 1941 they needed 40 divisions to maintain a stalemate with Chiang's forces.[6] Japanese military writer Masanori Ito described the situation. "Although inferiority in weapons and lack of training had caused the Chinese forces to suffer heavy losses, this did not prevent the Chinese Army

---

5 Chiang Kai-shek, *China's Destiny and Chinese Economic theory, p. 136*
6 Ibid, *p. 205*

from maintaining a first line strength of 7 million, harassing the Japanese army to exhaustion. Therefore no devastating blow had ever been dealt on the main force of the Chinese Army. . . The Japanese army merely succeeded in occupying towns, points and railways... as far as the Japanese army was concerned, this was undeniably a defeat. . .some suggested Japanese army should contract the war areas, ... But... once the Japanese army drew back, they (the Chinese) would give chase."

When the U.S. joined the war on Japan, the Japanese army had already lost 1,150,000 killed in China. On the front lines, it was a battle of attrition. Chiang's armies fought and retreated to fight again. When suicidal defenses were needed to rearguard the relocation of factories, his best troops were sacrificed in order to stave off collapse. People and territory were sacrificed to buy time. He believed relief would come when America entered the war against Japan. He didn't foresee the form of future U.S.-China relations.

As the Japanese advanced in China, lightly armed defenders resisted successfully on occasion, but at great cost. Heroic stands resulted in defenders slaughtered to the last man and China's best divisions were wiped out. Rank had no privileges; even Mme. Chiang Kai-shek was strafed and injured. Civilians were killed indiscriminately. As major cities fell, news of atrocities reached the West. The "Rape of Nanking" headlined the story of a two week Japanese orgy of rape and slaughter that included the bayoneting of woman and children. They killed more than a quarter of a million civilians in one city. Military prisoners were used for decapitation contests, bayonetting practice and/or buried alive.[7] The world was shocked, sympathized and did nothing.

In October, 1937 the United Front forces succeeded in trapping a Japanese division numbering 20,000. The enemy attempted to advance south through Shansi province through a mountain pass and connected valley. After the Japanese dispersed the local warlord's troops, Chiang sent in government troops who, at great cost, blocked the advance and bottled the Japanese up in narrow confines. 15,000 Red troops of the United Front attacked and harassed the Japanese flanks and rear. The Japanese lost approximately one third of their forces in repeated assaults against the Nationalist blocking force and in defense against hit and run attacks by Red guerillas. It was a small ray of light in the dismal period of Chinese defeat and retreat. Mao seized the opportunity to propagandize the action. He claimed a brilliant Red victory, proof of great Communist efforts in the war against the Japanese invader. A better concept of Red contributions to the battle was indicated by their report of 300 dead and 900 wounded. Meanwhile, Chiang's Nationalist blocking force under continuous air, artillery and infantry attack for a full month took heavy losses.[8] In the scope of Nationalist China's war with Japan, this was a minor encounter. Mao's propaganda raised Red engagements to near mythic proportions.

Six months later, in April 1938, Chiang's Nationalist forces achieved a more substantial victory over the Japanese invaders. Taierchuang, a town obstructing the Japanese advance toward the

---

7   Chang, *The Rape of Nanking.*

8   Hanson, *Humane Endeavor*, p. *104, 108*

interior became the scene of a critical battle. When the Japanese attacked, Chinese reinforcements cutoff the enemy's rear echelon and supply lines and the town's defenders surged forth and slaughtered the enemy infantry. The country was ecstatic. The Japanese were not invincible after all. Unfortunately, the elation was short-lived. The Japanese corrected their tactics and resumed the offensive with full support of tank, artillery and air attacks and gained their objective.

The Japanese Air Force, in addition to supporting army operations, conducted daily air raids on principal cities. China, with no air force and no anti aircraft weapons, was defenseless. At one point, waves of bombers assaulted the relocated capital, Chungking (Chongqing), twenty two hours each day.

As China struggled alone, Soviet Russia stirred. Stalin, always concerned that Japanese aggression in China would spill over into neighboring Russian Siberia, decided to support his former enemy. The Soviet dictator, realizing the insignificance of Mao's CCP, ignored the Chinese Reds completely and contributed combat aircraft and pilots to Chiang's fight against Japanese air supremacy.

Unfortunately, Russian support was short lived. In 1939, a shock wave hit the western world and affected China immediately. Stalin suddenly concluded a friendship treaty with former archenemy, Hitler. With that treaty, Stalin believed threats from both Germany and Germany's Asian ally, Japan, were eliminated. Support of Nationalist China was no longer advantageous for the Soviet Union. Chiang lost his Soviet air squadrons and Mao Tse-tung redirected his Chinese Communists "The Sino Japanese war affords our party an excellent opportunity for expansion.

Our fixed policy should be 70% expansion, 20% dealing with the Kuomintang (The National Government) and 10% resisting Japan. There are three stages in carrying out this fixed policy: the first is a compromising stage, in which self-sacrifice should be made to show our outward obedience to the Central Government, and adherence to the Three Principles of the People (nationality, democracy, and livelihood, as outlined by Dr. Sun Yat-sen), but in reality this will serve as camouflage for the existence and development of our party. While waiting for an unusual turn of events, we should give the Japanese invader certain concessions."[9]

The "10% resisting Japan" soon turned into quiet cooperation. Despite these internal directions, Mao and his supporters in the West continued to broadcast and amplify claims of aggressive Red actions against the Japanese.

China's desperate fight was typified by the Japanese Army's advance on the major city of Hankow. With no air defenses, Japanese air raids, along with advancing ground forces, turned the city into a scene of chaos. "While columns of ragged and bloody wounded struggled in, the evacuation of civilians began. In the last weeks, 40,000 moved out crossing rivers in boats and junks or overland in wagons and handcarts to Changsha, capital of Hunan. Trainloads of half- starved, tattered war orphans gathered up from the battle zones by a woman's committee organized by Mme. Chiang Kai-sheik were fed and washed and marched in clean blue overalls to riverboats for evacuation. The dismantling of factories and equipment for the long haul to the interior, organized by the industrial cooperatives, was underway. The wounded looking for a hospital

9 Wedemeyer, *Wedemeyer Reports,* p. 253

that had already been dismantled sat or lay on the pavement, worn out, unable to go further. Among the last-ditchers of Hankow was Mme. Chiang Kai-shek…"[10]

When Japanese advances were delayed or occasionally stopped by stubborn defenders who died at their posts. Critics in the West faulted Chiang Kai-shek for sacrificing his best troops. But Chiang had a plan. A mass movement was underway, "huge slow motion upheaval, was relocating the working capacity of Free China to the west. A steady trudging toiling stream of people carried goods and equipment and themselves out of the area of the invader into the independent zone. Boats, trains, carts, pack animals and coolies, under repeated bombings, shared in the inland trek from Nanking (Nanjing) and other cities. Factory machinery, government records, university libraries, the contents of hospitals, arsenals and offices, were transported in boxes slung on shoulder poles or packed in sampans and pulled up stream by straining teams moving foot by foot over the rocks and road less banks. In the age-old method of moving vessels up the rapids, the great-muscled coolies, hundreds to a load, bent double against the ropes, slowly hauled the burdens to the free land beyond the Yangtze gorges. A whole textile mill was packed into 380 junks of which a third sank in the rapids, were raised, repacked and started on their way again. Some factories were more than a year en route before renewing operation. Faculty and students of the universities organized into marching sections with foraging squads, police units and pack animals, walked to new locations in the west and southwest. A single coolie would trot by with a length of pipe over his shoulder. A

---

10   Tuchman, *Sand Against the Wind,* p. *192, 193*

cart would creak along with a load of parts. A boiler would be pulled along on rollers. Some of the machines were pulled by manpower over wooden rollers for 500 miles. When they had gone far enough, they dug caves in the rock cliffs along the Yangtze, and duplicated at least part of the arsenal that, six months earlier, had been operating in Canton."[11]

Although the enormous migration relocated 300 factories, the invaders took their toll. When the Japanese attacked in 1937, Chiang had already increased China's arsenal capacity sufficient to furnish rifles and machine guns for the entire army. Two years into the war, the relocated arsenals produced less than half of the army's needs and China had no other source of weapons. The destruction and tortuous relocation of arsenals reduced a typical Chinese Army division, equipped in 1937 with 7000 rifles and 200 light machine guns, to 2500 rifles and 100 light machine guns.[12] Incredible as it seems, more than half of China's soldiers went into battle unarmed, waiting to pick up a rifle from a fallen comrade.

Chiang's determined defense was not without costly mistakes. In order to halt the advancing enemy, he ordered demolition of selected Yellow River dikes. The flooding got out of control and huge losses of life and crop land resulted.

During China's desperate struggle, Mao's Reds improved their situation. In December, 1936, before the war, a depressed Mao Tse-tung had seen "world of difference between the Government forces and the Red Army. The Kuomintang controls . .. all... its political power is nation-wide" and "the Red Army is numerically

---

11 Tuchman, *Sand Against the Wind,* p. 196

12 Liu, *A MilitaryHistory of Modern China; 1924-1949, p. 203*

small, its arms are poor, and it has great difficulty in obtaining supplies such as food, bedding and clothing."[13] A year later, in 1937, Mao's forces enjoyed an unprecedented flow of cash when his ragtag forces were added to Chiang's United Front and the National Army payroll. The government paid the Reds at the same rate as the Nationalist solders, $7 per month for a private on up to several hundred dollars for a commander. The Red private pocketed only one dollar of the seven and the Commander received six dollars per month rather than several hundred. The bulk of government payments to Red solders went to Mao's treasury. At that time, the Red's also received grants-in-aid from the Nationalist government. For the sudden bounty, the Reds initially fought the Japanese aggressively in small-scale operations and claimed great victories. One report of a Japanese attack on the Reds cited 2000 attackers.[14] Engagements of this size merited little notice in Government Army reports.

After Stalin resolved his fear of a Japanese attack on Siberia and Mao redirected his CCP towards "70% expansion", Mao Tse-tung avoided alienating the Japanese. His military efforts were confined to attacks on puppet troops and isolated nationalist oriented groups. The goal was gain weapons and recruits. In remote Nationalist territories, the Reds would typically accuse a small Nationalist force of collaborating with the Japanese, surround it and either conscript or liquidate them. Red recruiting programs provided no time for gentle persuasion. Brutality, including burial alive, was more efficient.

---

13 Mao Tse-tung, *Selected Works of Mao Tse-tung, Vol. Onr, p. 197, 198*
14 Wou, *Mobilizing the Masses, p. 242*

However, even such radical recruiting couldn't account for the extraordinary growth claimed by the Reds. According to Mao's propaganda, the Eighth Route Army grew from 45,000 in 1937 when they joined the United Front, to 400,000 in 1940. A glaring exaggeration refuted by a Mao's own words and by simple logic. 400,000 troops "fighting furiously," against the Japanese enemy, as the Reds claimed, would have meant casualties in proportion to those suffered by government troops. No evidence of significant casualties was ever cited by Yenan visitors.

Mao's live and let live posture with the Japanese fit well with Japanese inability to defend the vast open areas overrun in their earlier campaigns. The quasi truce accepted Japanese control of major cities, utilities communications and railroads and allowed Mao's Reds to infiltrate and occupy the open areas and small towns. This arrangement benefited the Japanese in that as the Reds moved in, the Japanese were no longer targeted by Nationalist Chinese sabotage. For Mao the informal cease-fire was effective enough to allow his troops to cultivate crops in plain sight of Japanese blockhouses. Later in the war, as Nationalist China fought the great Japanese "Ichigo" offensive, Mao was able to report what he considered great success in Red development of Japanese occupied China. "The troops in the vicinity of the enemy's blockade lines or blockade ditches do not confine their production to agriculture but, as in the stable areas, have also developed handicrafts and transport. The fourth district contingent has set up a felt-cap Workshop, an oil press and a flour-mill, and in seven months has netted a profit of 500,000 yuan in local currency. Not only has it settled its own difficulties, but it is satisfying the needs of the people in the guerrilla zone. The soldiers now provide all their own woolen sweaters and socks."[15] Mao, ever the propagandist, continued to pretend such areas were guerilla zones where his Reds were battling ferociously against the Japanese. Also significant; Mao could find nothing larger than a felt shop and flour mill as examples of Red economic activities.

Possibly the greatest advantage the Reds gained from joining the United Front was the relaxation of barriers to visitors. The dry climate that kept the Reds on the verge of famine became an advantage compared to Chungking's oppressive humidity. Even the lack of intensive farming with its odors from human waste fertilizer and most important, freedom from Japanese air raids, all of it made a Yenan visit, in season, a welcome respite from Chungking.

Mao's principal disadvantage was the village itself. Caves and thatched roof mud huts made it distinctly unimpressive. A façade was constructed but visitors still had to energize an active imagination to see it as the capital of an important political movement exerting an influence on 20 % of world's population. Nothing about Yenan supported Mao's claims of substantial Red presence and influence in China.

One of the early propaganda efforts broadcast by visiting enthusiasts was Mao's claim to have conducted a "100 regiment offensive" against the Japanese. Literary and media admirers extolled it as a major military action. One version stated the Reds attacked with 300,000 troops in 105 regiments but then quantified Japanese reprisal strength at a modest 7000 infantry, 600 cavalry, 120 armored cars, 2 tanks and 8 airplanes.[16] Others vividly described the Japanese retaliation as the "new" tactic of *Senko-seisaku* ("three all")

---

15   Mao Tse-tung, *Selected Works of Mao Tse-tung, Vol. 3, p. 198*

16   Wou, *Mobilizing the Masses, p. 227*

principle . . . kill all, burn all, destroy all . . . which, ostensibly, left provinces blackened and populations massacred. The magnitude of Mao's and visitor's exaggerations can be gauged from Japanese records indicating that their retaliation for the great Red offensive killed 4500 and deported 17,000 to Manchuria.[17] When those figures are contrasted to the 250,000 Nationalist Chinese civilians killed by the Japanese in one city, Nanking (Nanjing), or the nearly quarter of a million killed in retaliation for Chinese rescue of a few Doolittle fliers, a true picture of Red war efforts and sacrifices can be seen.

With membership in the United Front, the Government relaxed the economic and military blockade of the Red Base Area. With this new freedom, Mao boldly proceeded with his 70% expansion goal in Free China territory, but then overstepped. In 1941, Mao moved his New Fourth Army, to take over new territories contrary to Government orders. Chiang's government forces attacked and the Reds were badly mauled by the Nationalist 40th Division. Mao reacted boldly by demanding legal status for the Communist Party throughout China, recognition of their quasi-governmental structures in "liberated" areas, enlargement of the Eighth Route Army from 3 to 12 divisions and authorization to keep the New Fourth Army south of the Yellow River. Chiang rejected the proposal and the charade of Red inclusion in a united effort against the Japanese, ended. Mao's troops were cut from the Nationalist Army payroll. The cash inflow the Reds enjoyed for four years ceased and barter with neighboring Nationalists areas was also cut off when Chiang Kai-shek reinstalled the blockade and sealed off the Reds.

---

17 Tuchman, *Sand Against the Wind*, p.216

Mao described his situation at that point. "For a while we were reduced almost to the state of having no clothes to wear, no oil to cook with, no paper, no vegetables, no footwear for the soldiers and, in winter, no bedding for the civilian personnel.[18] Mao's remedy was an increase in opium production. Despite Mao's despair, somehow a Western writer in Yenan at that time, described the Reds in the village of Yenan as "ruddier and healthier" than elsewhere in China and still another saw "a full belly, a warm back." These reports of conditions in the model city were presented as representative of conditions existing throughout the Red territory. Mao, the master propagandist, had an enthusiastic broadcast team. Unfortunately, Chiang Kai-shek lacked counter propaganda capability. False, unproven claims gained acceptance. Damage to the Government's cause was increasing. The Red propaganda campaign, unimpeded by reality, was gaining a momentum that would prove irreversible.

Through 1940 and 1941, the war wore on and China bled and fought alone. Chiang, desperate for air cover, after the Russians pulled out, arranged with the Italian Government to develop a Chinese Air Force. The Italians produced a formidable array of planes and pilots on paper. When Chiang called in a retired U.S. Air Force officer to evaluate his new Air force, Claire Chennault found it a farce. Chiang then turned to Chennault to salvage and lead the remnants of his Italian creation. They fought, but were no match for the Japanese.

Chennault next formed a group of American volunteers equipped with the only aircraft available; nearly obsolete American

---

18   Fitzgerald, *Revolution in China*, p.247

P-40 fighter planes. He developed tactics that enabled the "Flying Tigers", in their outmoded P-40s, to out fight the Japanese and provide a small ray of light in the dark days.

In April 1941, Soviet Russia further improved their relations with Japan by signing a non-aggression pact. The Soviets traded recognition of Japan's rule in Chinese Manchuria for Japanese recognition of Soviet rule in the Mongolian People's Republic. The resulting relaxation of tension along the Soviet-Manchurian border freed Russian troops to fight the Germans. It also allowed Japan to withdraw 100,000 men of the crack Kwantung Army from Manchuria. The Japanese needed these troops to execute their plans for attacks on the U.S. in the South Pacific and the British in Southeast Asia. Since the U. S. was supplying the Soviets desperately needed war materials, the Soviet-Japanese treaty releasing 100,000 Japanese to kill Americans in the Pacific should have been a subject worthy of discussion. There is no evidence of such an issue being raised with the Soviets.

Throughout the early defeats and retreats, Chiang Kai-shek believed if he could hold out by "trading space for time," America would provide the artillery and air power needed to attack and defeat the Japanese. There was no question of Chiang's support among the people. One visitor to a school in West China reported of Chiang, "...at whose name all students spring to their feet."[19] As China's situation worsened, Chiang retained the support of the people and his concept of Japanese military capabilities was proving accurate. The Japanese army was capable of conquering large areas, but they lacked the numbers to control the conquered areas.

---

19 Lautenschlager, *Far West in China*, p. 37

Although Mao's Reds moved into some of these areas, most of it was Nationalist governed. A government survey in 1939, before Red encroachments, reported 796 counties in conquered China theoretically controlled by Japan. Of this group, 63% were actually administered by the magistrates appointed by Chiang Kaishek. Another 31% of the counties were partially in the hands of loyal magistrates. The Japanese and their puppets controlled less than 20% of the territory behind Japanese lines. The invaders found themselves in an unprofitable quagmire tying down troops needed to achieve national goals elsewhere. But they still possessed potent military strength that could be focused on any point they chose.

In June 1941, a Time Magazine reporter made his way to the Chinese front lines and wrote one of the very few reports to come out of China on the situation at the front. It was six months before America entered WW2. Much of the Whampoa Academy officer corps had already fallen.

"China's army is the army nobody knows... the war front is days away from Chungking except by plane, and China has no planes to spare for junkets. China's army lies, and has lain for nearly two and a half years, on a tortured 2000 mile chain of fronts from the Yellow River to the upper end of the Burma Road. . . .

The only concepts which are as staggering as these vastnesses are China's materials lacks. Her huge army has become expert despite a most appalling want of arms and ammunition. . . . Its spirit is unmatched in Chinese history. It has a bitter determination.

There is no younger officer class in the world than that of the Generalissimo's crack divisions. Generalissimo Chiang is 53, Chen

Cheng (Sixth Area commander) is 41, Chen's Field Chief of Staff is 34. It would be hard to find a divisional or regimental commander in those divisions over 40. Regimental colonels are sometimes in their 20s.

One art these young officers have developed to its highest point is the skillful use of great superiority in numbers to compensate for shortages of equipment. The keen-weaponed spearheads of Japanese attacks are allowed to drive into the Chinese mass. Then the mass of Chinese gradually not only envelops the spearhead, but harasses its support and its supply lines.

China's best troops belie all the old saws about Chinese cowardice and indifference. They are husky, shaven-pated sons of the soil who, when they must, storm concrete casemates with nothing but hand grenades, who like better than anything else to close with the Japanese hand to hand.

Chinese troops have an added kind of courage: that of endurance. When food is short they can live for months on a pound of rice per day . . . a diet that will not much more than keep a man alive. They live through bitter winters in sleazy padded cotton uniforms. Most have no shoes, but they can march 40 miles a day when pressed. Furthermore, they endure endless defeat and disappointment without losing their sullen determination. Their determination is to drive the Japanese off the soil that they and their fathers have tilled for millenniums.

As for the U.S., a large-scale Chinese success would ease the future tremendously. The Chinese officers of the line think they could achieve that success, if only they had some artillery, and some scouting planes to go with it. They think they have learned a few things about how to fight a 20th-century war. But they are still forced to fight an 18th-century war without even having the 18th century weapon, artillery."[20]

As 1941 advanced, America maintained its neutrality but President Franklin D Roosevelt formally protested Japan's war on China and promised Chiang Kai-shek weapons, ammunition and aircraft to keep the million plus Japanese occupation troops from being deployed elsewhere. Foreign Minister T.V. Soong noted the Japanese responded to the Anglo-American protests by bombing Chungking, for twenty two hours each day. Without the aid promised by FDR, the city was defenseless. Soong cited "This awful demonstration of the difference between reality and promises …" Unfulfilled promises of aircraft to China were excused because aircraft were unavailable. Yet it was announced aircraft were being delivered to the Soviet Union. Soong pointed out that while promised aircraft were not being delivered to China, he saw an "American policy of appeasing Japan with materials of war … the very material and gasoline that are presently bombing Chungking … in order to keep Japan from attacking certain American supply routes to the south.

After the Japanese captured all major Chinese ports, they forced the British to shut down the Burma Road; China's last remaining supply connection to the outside world.

Only months later, the Japanese attacked Pearl Harbor and America declared war on Japan, Germany and Italy. The British reopened the Burma Road to supply China. But the rapid Japanese conquest of much of Burma cut off all incoming supplies to the

---

20 Time Magazine, *The Army Nobody Knows, 6/16/41*

hard-pressed Chinese forces. Thus China's situation, far from being improved over the years when she fought alone, was rendered more desperate. Soon, promised U.S. aid and emissaries would have unexpected consequences.

6

AMERICA ENTERS
WORLD WAR TWO

O N DECEMBER 7, 1941, Japan attacked Pearl Harbor and sank
or disabled most of the U.S. Pacific Fleet and, in the following months, inflicted a succession of defeats on American land
forces. Bataan, Corregidor, the entire Philippine Island chain,
Wake Island, Guam and other U.S. possessions fell. Britain lost
Singapore and Malaya and much of Burma. Previous U.S. intelligence reports from China, prepared by a Colonel Joseph Stilwell,
pictured Japan's army as third rate; it suddenly seemed they were
invincible. Americans read in the morning newspaper of a Japanese
submarine that surfaced and shelled the California shore. It was
the first foreign attack on the U.S. mainland since the war of 1812.
On the east coast, German U-boats sank American tankers and
freighters within sight of Atlantic City beachgoers. The U-Boat

assault throughout the North Atlantic Ocean threatened to put the American merchant fleet on the bottom and strangle Britain. The Axis powers, primarily Germany and Japan, seemed to easily overcome all opposition. American public morale plummeted with each new defeat.

In those dark days, China was a fluttering beacon. For four long years Chiang Kai-shek's ill-equipped army stubbornly fought, retreated and fought again incurring horrendous losses while facing the bulk of the Japanese Army. Japanese records show the Imperial Army totaled 51 divisions in early 1941. Forty of the 51 were engaged in China and Manchuria.[1] Stalin's 1941 non-aggression pact with the Japan released seven Japanese Army divisions from Manchuria. But 2/3 of Japan's Army remained tied down in China.

Through most of the war, the Chinese National Government, in addition to holding off Japan, also had to contain the small but potentially troublesome Chinese Communist forces. Some 20 divisions of the 325 division Government Army were drawn off from the critical mission of defending against the Japanese enemy, in order to contain the Reds.[2]

For the Allies, in that part of the world, (primarily U.S. and British forces), a critical point was reached. The Japanese attacked Australia by air but they needed additional ground forces for a successful invasion. Chiang's Chinese were pushed increasingly into the backwater areas of China and their supply routes were cut but to the great frustration of the Japanese, Chiang would not

1   Liu, *A military History of China, 1924-1949*, p. 205
2   Wedemeyer, *Wedemeyer Reports*, p. 280,281

quit, thus, Japanese troops could not be withdrawn. Meanwhile, the U.S., unprepared for all out war, instituted a complete mobilization of all resources. Armed forces had to be created from skeleton organizations. A war economy, capable of arming and supplying, not only the American Army, Navy and Air Force, but also Great Britain, the Soviet Union and China, was needed. This, from a U.S. industrial base still struggling from the depression of the 1930s. It was obvious to all; the mass of Japanese troops in China must be kept occupied in that land and not released to attack Australia or Hawaii. Continued Chinese resistance was vital to America. FDR made extravagant promises and assurances of aid to China while the Japanese offered China increasingly favorable terms for a negotiated peace. Chiang Kai-shek rejected Japanese offers and promised China would fight until Japan was defeated.

By 1942, Chiang had endured and overcome challenges that would fill ten normal life times. He had plunged into battles, evaded assassinations, escaped from enemy imprisonment, and formed a huge nation from disparate and conflicting groups. He had shown unshakeable tenacity and a deep belief in the Chinese people. He wrote "By the experience of 5000 years of rule....our people have acquired the virtue of understanding modesty, knowing humiliation, enduring disgrace and shouldering hardships. Because of understanding modesty, we are capable of accepting our lot. Because of knowing humiliation, we are capable of perseverance. Because we are capable of accepting a lot, we do not oppress or insult other races. Because we are capable of perseverance, we do not accept oppression or insults from other races. Because we are capable of enduring disgrace, the strength of our race is accumulated inwardly, and is not exposed outwardly. Because we're capable of shouldering hardship, the determination of our people is enduring and is not spasmodic." Hero, patriot, statesman, the only world leader to out maneuver the wily ruthless Joseph Stalin, Chiang Kai-shek was ill equipped to deal with China's new ally. In upcoming years, U.S. efforts in Europe and the Pacific would present America's warriors at their best. In far-off Asia, one American, supported by a powerful patron in Washington, would play a far different role.

Immediately after the Japanese attack on Pearl Harbor, Chiang Kai-shek contacted Roosevelt and Churchill to form a united defense against the Japanese. Chiang was the obvious choice for Supreme authority in the China-Burma Theater. A top level American Army leader would be assigned to serve as his Chief of Staff. The selection of the China Chief of Staff would be made by U.S. Army Chief of Staff General George Catlett Marshall. Marshall's impact on history, on America's present situation in world affairs is something that could not be predicted.

While Napoleon valued generals who were lucky in battle, George Catlett Marshall seemed lucky in career matters. Despite a complete lack of combat command experience and no meaning-ful experience commanding troops in peacetime maneuvers, he was selected over many more experienced senior officers for the Army Chief of Staff position. It is possible that more than luck was involved; Marshal's personal papers indicate that although his aloof, reserved demeanor largely precluded friendly messages to fellow officers, he maintained contact with General "Black Jack" Pershing, commander of U.S. forces in WW1 France. Pershing, although retired, retained a position of immense prestige in U.S Army and government circles. He'd been impressed by Marshall's handling of logistics for the U.S. role in the war-ending offensive in France. The Pershing connection may have been the key to Marshall's surprise elevation over many others seemingly more qualified.

Marshall's aloof posture combined with computer-like intellectual powers to produce an impressive figure in conference room meetings. His ability to quickly absorb, organize and emit information inspired awe. He regularly displayed his unique skill by collecting a lengthy list of questions from his audience and then answering each in detail, in the order collected. This "all in" procedure precluded any late questions inspired or modified by Marshall's early answers and to some extent lessened the overall effectiveness of the meeting, but all attendees left suitably impressed.

Nations at war need heroes particularly when early battles result in defeat. General Marshall began receiving accolades as the top military mind in America before the U.S. Army met the enemy. However, when war erupted, Marshall's rising star took a hit.

In early December, 1941, when Japanese diplomatic messages were decoded in Washington, it became apparent the Japanese would launch an attack to cripple the U.S. in the

Pacific, within hours. As the clock ticked down, the President's key people huddled, Marshal, a notorious 9 to 5 man, was absent. Whether he was at home or attending a meeting the evening before the attack is still open to question. On the morning of the devastating attack, he was horse back riding. After the attack, an official inquiry was impaneled to determine how the Japanese Navy could, after much advance warning by U.S. code breakers, make a devastating surprise attack on the key U.S. base in the Pacific and essentially sink the U.S. Pacific Fleet. The Panel found the Army responsible for the lack of alertness and response, General Marshall failed to keep his deputies and Army headquarters at Pearl Harbor informed on the probable outbreak of war at any time. The panel further reported Marshall had an admitted lack of knowledge of the condition of readiness of the Hawaiian command. It seemed the new Chief of Staff was suddenly in deep trouble. However, good fortune smiled again on George Marshall when President Roosevelt sealed all reports with a promise of an intensive investigation at wars end.[3] (At wars end, when the Pearl Harbor Hearings commenced, Marshall largely pleaded loss of memory. When pinned down by Congressman Keefe on his responsibility and failure to keep Pearl Harbor fully aware of the Japanese threat, Marshall diverted the responsibility aspect by admitting he had an opportunity to "Intervene and did not do it." He pleaded "I am not a book keeping machine..." and indicated the decoded Japanese threat was treated much like the other paperwork that crossed his desk each day.)

---

3   Cray, *General of the Army*, p.480.481

General Marshall was credited with the creation of an American Army from a bare, budget-scourged skeleton. It was an army created from the best raw material on the planet. An army that, with proper training and adequate weapons, could sweep all opposition aside, Marshall was responsible for all aspects of training, weapons, logistics, combat replacements, etc.

General Marshall was also America's voice in the early joint U.S.-British strategic decisions for the war in Europe and there he committed his second blunder. In the days immediately after Pearl Harbor, Washington focused on keeping Russia, as well as China and Britain, in the war. The fall of Russia would release masses of enemy troops and resources for attacks on Americans and British. The Soviet army was considered to be in immediate danger and in order to draw pressure off the beleaguered Russians, FDR gave Stalin's forces top priority. Military strategy was focused on developing British–American forces for an early invasion of Western Europe, an attack that would draw down German pressure on the Russian front. General Marshall accelerated U.S. Army training schedules to answer the crisis but his strategic judgement came into question when he became totally committed to a rash, early landing in France. "Sledgehammer" was a hastily planned Allied cross channel invasion and preliminary analysis exposed Sledgehammer as a recipe for disaster. Churchill charged it would "turn the Channel into a river of Allied blood." When Marshall's opposite number, Sir Alan Brooke asked "do we go west, south or east after landing, he (Marshall) had not begun to think of it." The Commander of

U.S. Army forces in the British Isles, General Mark Clark related "I pointed out that all we could count on using would be the 34th division then in North Ireland ... The 34th however, had little amphibious training, it lacked antiaircraft support and it had no tanks...."[4] Meanwhile, the Germans had 1.3 million troops in France and the low countries. Despite all the negatives, General Marshall was unable to back down from his all-out support of Sledgehammer and it cost him. Both FDR and Churchill were in close touch with all aspects of the war situation in Western Europe. The insanity of Sledgehammer was demonstrated months later, when a sizable cross-channel raid by British Forces suffered horrendous casualties. Two years later, after a massive buildup of U.S. and British forces, the success of Eisenhower's cross channel D Day invasion was no sure thing. From Sledgehammer onward, General Marshall seemed to back away from decision-making. He called for subordinates who would evaluate situations and bring him decisions.

President Truman, a staunch Marshall admirer, later described a typical Marshall/staff meeting; "He would listen for a long time without comment, but when he could stand it no longer, he would say, "Gentlemen, don't fight the problem, decide it." He'd spent hours listening and, as Chief of Staff, he possessed a unique overview of any situation his staff addressed. But he would contribute nothing to resolve the subject of the meeting. It seemed he was completely satisfied with any solution the meeting would generate. Surrendering decision making to qualified, well intentioned individuals i.e. Eisenhower

---

4   Clark, *Calculated Risk, p.v 34*

and MacArthur worked well in WW2. Unfortunately, General Marshall didn't limit his delegation of decision making to such individuals.

Government records and personal papers indicate General Marshall also possessed a peculiar inability to reverse a decision once made. Possibly due to his long career as a desk soldier, he had no exposure to crises that demanded the flexibility to reverse major decisions when conditions changed. He'd never experienced situations where surprise and shock were the norm. Marshall's commitments, not tempered by the cruel realities of combat or even the surprises faced in field problems, tended to be set in concrete.

His planning generated an American army eight million strong and in the course of his efforts, until he had key subordinates in place, he made decisions, but, it seemed he deferred making certain needed decisions. Problems and questions arose. Infantry training periods were shortened and green troops, those who survived their baptism of fire, were learning basic weapons handling while under enemy fire. Thus raw, inexperienced officers were leading ill-trained troops. Eisenhower, commanding the U.S. Army's first confrontation with German troops at the Kasserine Pass in North Africa, suffered a costly defeat. The story floated to cover the American debacle claimed U.S. troops were not "blooded" and therefore no match for veteran German troops. Eisenhower knew better. His troops had not received adequate training in the States. He swallowed his pride and requested experienced British officers to aid in retraining his Americans and he replaced a key commander, a Marshall favorite. The next confrontation with the Germans resulted in an American victory.

General Marshall's logistic skills also seemed open to question. After taking North Africa and Sicily, Eisenhower mounted an attack on the Italian mainland at Salerno. The landing nearly failed. In a rare assertion of his anger, an irate Marshall took issue with Eisenhower until Ike pointed out his superior's interference. Marshall, the logistician, had made drastic cuts in Eisenhower's invasion forces, moving infantry divisions and aircraft squadrons to England for the D-Day invasion of France nearly a year in the future.[5] An invasion Marshall was slated to lead.

After the D-day landings in France in June, 1944, and the bloody fighting through the hedgerows of Normandy that followed, American forces broke out and Patton's tanks raced across France. It suddenly appeared Germany could be conquered by Christmas. Then it all came to complete halt. Patton simply ran out of fuel. The official explanation was: a lack of port facilities in France had caused a bottleneck in the supply chain. It was claimed, capture of the extensive port facilities at Antwerp, Belgium would solve the supply problem. However, cranes and complex material handling equipment were not needed in order to pump petroleum at dock side. Major French ports such as Cherbourg and Le Havre and dozens of secondary ports capable of unloading petroleum were already in Allied hands. In addition to adequate French port facilities, a small diameter pipeline laid across the English Channel gushed fuel in

---

5   Perry, *Partners in Command*, p.229,230

coastal France. The only supply situation that had changed since D-Day, was the stretching of land supply lines as American tanks advanced further into Europe. Similar to the undersized pipeline, Eisenhower was given an undersized truck fleet. It was later revealed that, Russian Marshal Zhukov's armies, advancing on Germany from the East, deployed more Detroit trucks than Eisenhower's forces in the West. Antwerp Belgium port facilities were not needed to unload petroleum. Antwerp offered shorter trucking mileage to combat areas. Tanks required "x" gallons to travel "y" miles. Not a complex problem. Another glaring logistics error would soon appear where Marshall was directly involved in Burma.

Later, Marshall's replacement system was criticized for sacrificing combat unit morale and the lives of green replacements in the drive across France. The British rotated entire units out of combat to absorb replacements for dead and wounded. American units were not rotated out. Americans fought until they were used up, dead, dismembered or mentally disabled. New hastily trained replacements were fed in to fill the holes. Few had more than one trip to the rifle range before shipping out. Thrust into combat situations, many died before they learned basic survival measures.

Here again the situation changed but Marshall's early decision remained in place. In 1944, the early justification for shortened training schedules, taking pressure off the Russians, no longer existed. In the winter of 1942/43, German General Von Paulus surrendered his 6th Army to the Russians at Stalingrad. With that defeat, the German threat of conquering Russia ended. Russia was out of danger and the crises that may have justified pushing ill-trained Americans off to battle no longer existed. However, U.S. Army training schedules remained accelerated.

Weapons development was another area where Marshall's decisions or lack of decisions cost American lives. As the war advanced, the American public came to believe U.S. Armed Forces had the best weapons in the fight. Early in the war, Navy submarines had suffered from dud torpedoes, but the defect was soon corrected, and American submarines put Japan's cargo fleet on the bottom of the ocean. Navy Hellcats and Corsairs, flying from ultra modern aircraft carriers, ruled Pacific skies. The Air Force, connected to the Army on paper only, developed the P-51 Fighter and B-29 Bomber, far superior to any operational aircraft employed by enemies or allies in World War II. The small, 5 division, Marine Corps developed Amphibious Tractors, schooled the Army on Amphibious Landing tactics, pioneered the use of flame throwers and developed the concept of close air support.

Conversely, weapons development for U.S. Army ground forces was nearly nonexistent. With the exception of the Garand M-1 rifle developed well before General Marshall came on the scene, the American infantryman fought with outdated weapons. Americans machine gunners fired 500 rounds per minute. Germans responded with 1350 rounds per minute. Troops firing machine guns, mortars and other heavy weapons relied on the Colt .45 pistol for personal protection, The Colt 45 was designed for Philippine guerrilla warfare shortly after the turn of the century. One new weapon, the "bazooka," a close range anti-tank weapon, fired missiles that bounced off medium and heavy tanks. Perhaps the most glaring armament shortcoming was the selection of the Sherman tank as the mainstay of American armored divisions. The Sherman was no match for German armor. Tank crews considered it a death trap, calling it the "Ronson," the name of a then popular cigarette lighter. The U.S. Army in Europe had the advantage of air cover when weather allowed, other than that, they relied on initiative and courage to overcome serious weapons and training deficiencies.

Marshall's delegation of decision-making meant that Eisenhower and MacArthur made all operational decisions in Europe and the Pacific. Marshall's involvement was minimal. It would seem the U.S. Army Chief of Staff could have focused more on weapons development and training and replacement systems. That would, of course, have required modification and, in some cases, reversal of previous decisions. It was not to be.

General Marshall's aloof personality also didn't wear well in high stakes give and take with the President. Marshall rigidly guarded some aspect of inner self. In his personal papers he described one meeting with President Roosevelt "he finally came around to me, and I remember he called me George. I don't think he ever did it again. That rather irritated me, because I didn't know him on that basis. . . . I wasn't very enthusiastic over such a misrepresentation of our intimacy."[6]

---

6 Pogue, *George C Marshall, Statesman*, p. 651

One possible reason, for Marshall's icy demeanor was a tendency to avoid direct confrontations. When confronted with opposition that didn't shrink before his formal, remote posture, he avoided taking a stand, or making statements that might cause conflict. He preferred "in not antagonizing people but managing them."[7] Avoidance of direct confrontation required reliance on indirect methods of influencing people. Manipulating people without disclosing one's position requires a certain degree of subterfuge, even deception, tactics that foster dissension in a business or military organization. Marshall would use his people managing skills to great effect in the years to come but he would also become the managed one.

The thousands of telegrams, papers, memoranda and radio communications Marshall wrote or dictated during WW2, contain few blunt directives. Although his austere posture might suggest him to be the prototype authoritarian, his views were presented as wishes, suggestions or even more indirectly as expressions of concern.[8] When he did issue direct written orders, he seemed unable to follow-up and enforce them.

The General's use of assistants "who will solve their own problems and tell me later what they have done,"[9] was displayed during a top-level war council assembled to decide the goal of Allied operations after the Sicily campaign. Although Marshall was senior American officer present, "In three different arguments Churchill sought to influence Eisenhower, upon whom

---

7   May, *The Truman Administration and China, p. 31*

8   Perry, *Partners in Command, p.19*

9   Ibid, *p.13*

the combined Chiefs of staff had rested responsibility for the key decisions on a post- Sicily strategy. Ike made the decision and the following day Marshall held a press conference and impressed correspondents with "an incredible performance" ..."The most brilliant interview I ever attended in my life," gushed one reporter.

While Marshall's delegation of decision making gave Eisenhower freedom to decide and act, absence of support came with it. During Marshall's 1944 visit to Eisenhower's HQ in France, Ike's cantankerous British subordinate, Bernard Montgomery, demanded a private meeting with Eisenhower's superior. Marshall complied and listened to a barrage of criticism of Eisenhower. Later, Marshall said he was furious "I came pretty near to blowing off out of turn." But he thought it better to "not meddle"[10] The situation required confrontation. Marshall did not confront. He listened and did nothing to resolve the problem and nothing to support his commander on the field of battle. Within a very few years, General Marshall would find reason to indulge in fateful meddling in the affairs of an ally.

There were also indications Marshall had a tendency to freeze onto premature decisions in personnel matters. He seemed to adopt and refuse to budge from a position of either blind support or total rejection of a particular individual.

Singling out the above from the huge array of problems Marshall faced would be unfair if it was not indicative of a serious command deficiency. Marshall had selected and promoted

---

10 Cray, *General of the Army, p.484*

well on two occasions when he had close association with the candidates. Not so with the swaggering Lloyd Fredendahl. Marshall simply liked his look. "I like that man, you can see determination all over his face." Marshall declared him "one of the best."

In 1943, the first Anglo-American offensive of the war was launched. The plan had the U.S. Army storming ashore on selected North African beaches and moving inland to attack Rommel's Afrika Korps from the west while British forces under General Montgomery attacked from Egypt in the east. Eisenhower, newly appointed by Marshall to command the North African invasion, Operation Torch, duly placed Lloyd Fredendahl in command of Central Task Force Torch. The first American confrontation with German troops resulted in a U.S. defeat at Kasserine Pass, Eisenhower found Fredendahl had holed up in a command post far behind the lines while his troops, lacking direction, retreated and surrendered. Eisenhower sent Fredendahl home. With revamped leadership and retrained troops, Americans outfought the Germans at Gafsa and El Guettar. Inexplicably, after Fredendahl was relocated to the United States, rather than being penalized, Marshall rewarded Fredendahl with a promotion to Lieutenant General.

As the war progressed, Marshall's shortcomings became apparent to both President Roosevelt and Prime Minister Churchill. As 1944 approached it came time to appoint a Supreme Commander of American and British Forces in Europe, Marshall, the assumed designee, was bypassed. His subordinate, Dwight Eisenhower, was awarded the prime military assignment of WW2. FDR lamely softened the blow by telling Marshall he couldn't sleep well if he, Marshall, was away from Washington.

Criticism of Marshall's performance in relation to the war in Europe could be offset somewhat considering the chaotic situation that existed when America entered World War II. However, Marshall's performance relative to China during World War II has escaped serious examination until now.

General Marshall, the strict "by the book" soldier immediately departed from Army protocols in his efforts for China. On the battlefield, a Marine PFC or an Army Private was expected, when ordered, to rise from his foxhole and expose himself to death or dismemberment. Officers in combat were quickly sacked for not following orders aggressively. However, in the early, desperate days of WW2, Marshall, granted a highly qualified subordinate the option to refuse one of the key assignments of the war and instead, appointed an aging misfit that he'd previously rescued from forced retirement.

The China Chief of Staff position, reporting to China's Head of State, required a high-ranking officer. Lieutenant General Drum was considered the best candidate. Then, in that hour of desperate need, when America saw only defeat in the Atlantic and the Pacific, Marshall, rather than simply assigning Drum, asked him if he'd like the assignment. Drum's first reaction was to opt out, but he quickly reconsidered and advised Marshall the following day. He was too late. Marshall had reached down into the ranks of newly promoted Generals. Although Chief of Staff

Marshall had declared his initial goal was to replace the Army's deadwood with men of action and initiative. One of the first two names he'd designated for promotion to Brigadier General was Colonel Joseph Warren Stilwell. With Drum out of the picture for a few hours, Marshall quickly gave Stilwell a position that would warrant his promotion to surprising heights. Stilwell's speedy advancement from Colonel to full General was unprecedented, particularly for an officer whose record displayed repeated problems with superiors, no significant record of achievement and recent negative fitness reports. Stilwell's performance in China would be absurdly negative for America and China but greatly benefit other interests.

Marshall cited Stilwell's fluency in Chinese and previous experience in China as reasons for awarding him the top post in China and later Marshall defended Stilwell's retention in China by declaring no other ranking officers were fluent in Chinese. But at the end of Marshall's earlier China tour, he'd reported his language classes had produced 30 officers fluent enough to negotiate in Chinese. Stilwell, for the most part, used an interpreter in dealing with Chiang Kai-shek and General Wedemeyer, who replaced Stilwell in China, was not fluent in Chinese and had no experience in country.

General "Vinegar Joe" Stilwell presented a public image of a forthright, outspoken warrior. From his initial appearance on the national scene, he was portrayed as fighting Joe Stilwell, a no-nonsense, man of action who sought out the hottest frontline combat and was beloved by the GI in the foxhole. Stilwell gave reporters extraordinary access and displayed a talent for caustic comments that showed well in print. However, Stilwell's public image had no basis in fact. He had no combat experience and similar to his patron Marshall, very little command experience in peacetime operations. While few American generals had combat command experience in 1941, none other than Stilwell devoted strenuous efforts to creating such an image. Early on, he resorted to dressing in an ancient campaign hat and shouldering an obsolete rifle to create the image of the battle worn, hard-bitten trooper. A sight that appeared ludicrous to troops serving under him but one that showed well in news photos.

Stilwell had evolved from a rebellious youth to an outspoken, acid tongued, non-conformist, mid level officer. He displayed a talent for languages and an ability to develop personal relationships with superiors. When assigned to Fort Benning, GA, his direct superior, then Colonel George Catlett Marshall rated Stilwell as "a genius for instruction." "Farsighted,... highly intelligent, . . . a leader, . . ." Marshall, enthusiasm, veering out of control, even described Stilwell as "tactful." Fellow officers, more familiar with Stilwell's vulgarities, thought less of his tact. His common usage included ethnic slurs and pejoratives, terms such as: limeys, frogs, huns, square heads, wops, chinks, gooks. One of Stilwell's colleagues saw him as "pretty close to a misanthrope."[11] A British view of Stilwell was later reported

---

11 Tuchman, *Sand Agauinst the Wind, p.127*

by legendary British General Sir Adrian de Wiart. "Stilwell is most friendly, but I can't feel sure of him...." de Wiart defined Stilwell "On the surface he is all honey, underneath a particularly vile form of vinegar" Churchill's chief military advisor, Sir Alan Brooke, defined Stilwell as "nothing but a hopeless crank with no vision."

Despite Stilwell's abusive expressions, on occasion, he seemed to wilt in high-pressure situations that called for forceful imposition of his will. Both the remote, aloof Marshall and the abrasive, abusive Stilwell evidenced one similarity when facing critical situations. It was a peculiar inability to give an order and see that it was carried out. On key issues, on many occasions, both Generals simply ignored disobedience of their direct orders. Vinegar Joe Stilwell would display this deficiency in a critical situation soon after he arrived in China.

General Marshall's legendary, icy demeanor was absent from his relationship with Stilwell. Most who knew both believed only Stilwell called Marshall by his first name "or was on terms of even the beginnings of familiarity."[12] The friendship is difficult to understand. Both served in the American Expeditionary Force, (AEF) in France in 1918, in staff positions well behind the front lines, but at different locations and at different levels of rank and responsibility. After the war, Marshall's and Stilwell's assignments to Tientsin, China overlapped by eight months. Stilwell's name doesn't appear in Marshall's papers, and he doesn't appear in Marshall's photos of social outings of that period. After Tientsin, Marshall

---

12 Wedemeyer, *Wedemeyer Reports,* p.122

was assigned to the Infantry School at Fort Benning Georgia. However it came about, it seems Marshall had been impressed by Stilwell. He held the post as head of the Tactical Section of the school open until Stilwell completed his China tour. Later, at Fort Benning, Marshall admitted the Base Commander asked him on three occasions to relieve Stilwell. Stilwell remained secure while Marshall remained in charge of the training program.[13]

After Benning, Stilwell was assigned to China. American military observers were inserted to evaluate and report on methods and capabilities of the combatants. Colonel Joseph Warren Stilwell headed the U.S. Army team in China.

Considered fluent in Chinese with experience in the country and a background in military intelligence, he seemed ideal for assignment to gain intelligence on Japanese military operations. However, once there, his activities included diversions beyond observation of military action. After the Japanese captured Nanking and rolled onward, a group of writers and reporters seeking protection holed up in the then neutral British concession in Hankow. Stilwell, through a friend at the American consulate, joined the group. It was 1938, the time of the United Front, when Mao's Communists joined the Chinese Government's fight against the Japanese. The Reds were represented in Hankow by the charming number two Communist, Chou En-lai, ever ready to convincingly present Communist Party line views. Stilwell and Chou reportedly socialized and discussed Chiang Kai-shek's

13 Lang, *General Stilwell in China*, p.67

many faults. Stilwell also met frequently with author Agnes Smedley, a fervent American Communist. The impressionable Smedley found Vinegar Joe "tough, gruff, battle scarred," although Stilwell had neither scars nor battles. One of the more worldly-wise authors present at these meetings believed Stilwell was captivated by Chou and Smedley and saw him starting to succumb to Communist influences.[14] Stilwell, also traveled widely and reported information not related to evaluation of Japanese military capabilities. Among varied subjects in his reports, after a fifteen minute meeting with Chiang Kai-shek and Mme. Chiang he reported penetrating insights on Chiang Kai-shek's motives (not good) and his shortcomings (many).

Later in 1938, Stilwell decided to spend the summer with his family in Hankow. He justified it as being ready to observe an impending Japanese offensive. Col. McCabe his direct superior in Washington had enough. He reprimanded Stilwell for "a serious error in judgment . . . when major military developments are in progress." and "coverage, quality and quantity of information received was not (repeat not) satisfactory." He was told the information conveyed could not justify the sums of G-2 confidential funds spent, and he should explain the "exact nature and value" of the information obtained by these expenditures. This latest entry on Stilwell's spotty record made him consider retirement. His age and history of being passed over for promotion put him in a position where he could be forced out of the army.

More serious than his digressions from duty, Stilwell's dismissive views of Japanese military capabilities would soon

---

14   Utley, *The China Story*, p.105

impact U.S. military operations. He maintained he could run the Japanese out of China in six months with only two U.S. Army divisions and properly equipped Chinese forces. As the Army's senior observer of Japanese military operations, his reports helped shape the U.S. Army's false confidence and setup a rude awakening when the Japanese attacked.

In 1939, Stilwell was ordered back to the United States to what he expected would be oblivion. "They're trying to put me out to pasture." He took a three-month holiday through Siam, Indochina, Malaya and Java. On August 3, 1939, he was still en route to his new assignment in the States when he learned he'd been promoted to Brigadier General by newly appointed Army Chief of Staff, George Marshall. After his sojourn through Southeast Asia, Stilwell took a one-month military leave and then took over command of a Brigade at Fort Sam Houston in Texas. In July 1940, he was assigned to command the 7th Division based at Fort Ord, California, seven miles from his home in Carmel and a few months later, Marshall moved Stilwell up to Major General. Fortune, in the form George Marshall, was smiling on Joseph Warren Stilwell.

When Marshall appointed Stilwell to represent America's military presence in China, he promised Chiang Kai-shek that Claire Chennault would be appointed Air Commander for the China Theater. Chennault, leader of the "Flying Tigers," American defenders of China's airspace, was at that time, the only American Commander with experience fighting the Japanese. However, before going to China and evaluating Chennault's performance, Stilwell insisted that an inexperienced Colonel Clayton Bissel be placed over the veteran commander. Bissel would make serious mistakes before Chennault was freed of his supervision. Marshall's promise, to appoint Chennault, was only the first of many U.S. promises to China to be broken without explanation or apology. Stilwell would repeat his preference for a comfortable intermediate between himself and an experienced combat commander later in Burma.

In addition to meteoric promotions, Marshall gave Stilwell authority not enjoyed by major Theater Commanders Eisenhower and MacArthur. Vinegar Joe controlled all aid to China. That authority conflicted with his primary assignment as Chief of staff for the Chinese Army. Control of aid to China gave Stilwell complete freedom to oppose his designated superior, Chiang Kai-shek. Any strategic or tactical issue could be subject to a Stilwell threat to hold up direly needed ammunition shipments. The threat of withholding weapons was a non-issue. China defenders received no weapons during Stilwell's tour of duty.

Before leaving Washington, before meeting Chiang Kai-shek, the Generalissimo of the Chinese Army and head of the Republic of China, Stilwell christened Chiang "the peanut." It would be a mild example of Vinegar Joe's future backbiting and slander.

When Stilwell arrived in Chungking, China and Japan were locked in a deadly standoff. Both had suffered casualties in the millions. China was nearly spent, but the Japanese had ambitions in the Pacific and Southeast Asia and realized further expansion in China was beyond their capability. Chiang Kai-shek looked forward to help from America with no warning of Joseph Stilwell's impact on his country.

Stalemate 1939- 1944

7

DEBACLE

G ENERAL STILWELL ARRIVED in China on March 3, 1942. Going
in, he evidenced feelings of resentment and possibly a sense
of inadequacy. "They remember me as a small-fry colonel that
they kicked around." He may have felt he was in over his head at
the start. Although he'd seen China's massive problems at ground
level, he knew nothing of the ancient cultural mechanisms that
allowed the KMT government and its ill equipped army to sput-
ter onward against the modern Japanese Army. On arrival, rather
than focusing on the huge, foreboding war in China as assigned,
Stilwell turned away to a small, seemingly more manageable theater of operations.

After meeting Chiang Kai-shek and staff, he noted them to
be "courteous, friendly and plan less." Although planning was
Stilwell's primary assignment, plan less they would remain. He
immediately turned from the million and a half Japanese troops

JAMES FITZGERALD

attacking China to a small campaign in neighboring Burma. The goal was: rescue the "Burma Road" supply line through that country. The initial British reaction to Stilwell's proposed campaign was negative. After reconsidering their strategic position, the British relented.

Initially, all went well for Stilwell. He convinced Chiang to give him command of two Chinese armies for his campaign to reopen the Burma Road. He was elated, after forty years of staff, attaché and classroom assignments, he would finally lead troops in battle. For Chiang Kai-shek, it was his first accommodation of a bad American proposal. Against his better judgment, the veteran leader yielded to plans created by a foreigner who had no experience in combat, no knowledge of Burma and scant time in command of troops in peacetime. Stilwell would face Japanese troops who were undefeated at that point. A foreigner commanding Chinese armies was unprecedented during Chiang's reign and Stilwell expressed amazement at the acceptance he received in this post.[1] For a limited time he referred to Chiang as the "Generalissimo" rather than "the peanut."

In his first command situation, Stilwell planned well enough based on his limited knowledge of the situation. He carefully positioned his forces on line, locating his armored reserve force close by for support of his frontline troops. Before major contact developed with the enemy, Stilwell complained that subordinate Chinese generals were not following his orders. Chiang flew in and laid down the law. The American general was in charge. Stilwell noted "I had full power to promote, relieve and punish any officer

---

1   Stilwell, *The Stilwell Papers*, p. 62

— 92 —

in the Chinese Expeditionary Force. (Jesus.) This is a new note in Chinese history." The press took photos and Stilwell's authority was a matter of public record.[2] It could not be withdrawn in private.

When the Japanese advanced on Stilwell's lines, the difference between planning and the confusion of battle emerged. A British-Burma unit far to the west called for help, and Stilwell abandoned his carefully laid plans and sent his armored reserve off to the rescue. The Japanese then attacked in force and pushed back the east end of Stilwell's line. With no reserves to reinforce or counterattack, the Japanese easily penetrated Stilwell's lines. As the battle degenerated, Vinegar Joe lost control. He went back to Mandalay "to try to stir up action." But he stirred nothing. Yet, he was the Commander in the field, publicly designated by Chiang Kai-shek.

Several recorded incidents indicate the real problem was Stilwell's inability to command in a crisis. In the midst of his crumbling defenses, he located one of his Chinese Generals. Chinese General Lo asked Stilwell to return to see him that evening. "Vinegar Joe" Stilwell, the Commander of operations, facing the need to make fateful decisions at any moment, left his subordinate undisturbed.[3]

As the military situation deteriorated further, Stilwell needed transportation to move troops to meet the enemy threat, but found reason to not commandeer a train "none of his staff was tactically authorized." Without the train, he was in drastic need

---

2 Tuchman, , *Sand Against the Wind, p.280*

3 Tuchman, *Stilwell and the American Experience, p.375*

of motor transport to transfer troops to strengthen weak points and failing that, to conduct an orderly retreat. He noted with disapproval there were 850 trucks and 65,000 gallons of gasoline nearby but "they were too busy hauling goods to China to haul my soldiers."[42] In contrast, while Stilwell did nothing, one of his subordinate Chinese generals commandeered a locomotive with 17 cars for movement of his troops. In a critical, life and death battlefield situation, Stilwell had the authority, and the responsibility to take over any resources he needed. He did nothing.

A closer look shows Stilwell also unable to confront and command one of his American subordinates. On March 24, 1942, he contacted his subordinate 10th Air Force Commander for desperately needed air support. The commander refused any operations before May 1, five weeks in the future. One week later; the same subordinate launched his aircraft to support a British operation. Stilwell was infuriated,[5] but did nothing. Similar to his publicly granted authority over Chinese forces, Stilwell had full power to direct, relieve and punish American subordinates. He used none of these powers. There exists no record of forceful attempts, by Stilwell, to command in the crisis. Consequently, no weak points were reinforced and no tactical moves were made. Based on Stilwell's personal papers and even the reports of a sympathetic author, it's apparent, Stilwell was unable to assert himself as the Commander. As his mission failed and his soldiers died, Stilwell's notes show

---

4 Tuchman, *Stilwell and the American Experience, p.369*

5 Ibid, *p.365*

a curious detachment and concern for self-image "The way the boys look at me in the jams, dead pan, to see how I take it. Now what are you going to do? . . . Will it break you down I wonder? I feel like an animal in a zoo." His mind seemed far removed from the crisis around him. But his worst performance was yet to come.

On May 1, with the situation, deteriorating, Stilwell ignored Chiang Kai-shek's orders to reassemble his forces at Myitkyina, Burma. He then refused air transport sent in to fly him out to headquarters in Chunking.[6] Instead, chastened by his inability to command, he simply walked away and took a one month leave while the enemy advanced through Burma toward China. He apparently had no stomach for further combat command responsibilities. Stilwell led 100,000 of Chiang's best troops into Burma. He walked out with a mixed group of 114 staff people and nurses. Ever conscious of image, he brought along a photographer and a friendly newspaper reporter who dramatized the flight as heroic struggle. Stilwell arrived in India unthreatened and unharmed while his troops continued to fight and die. Before walking out to India, he ignored his direct superior, Chiang Kai-shek in Chungking, and radioed halfway around the world to Washington his "last message for a while." He then destroyed the radio. His message was a self-serving lie. He reported "Hordes" of fleeing Chinese troops, "Control has entirely passed to small units."[7] Days later, he noted in his diary he was "just ahead of the Chinese Horde" and wrote of a

---

6   Chennault, *Way of a fighter*, p.160

7   Tuchman, *Sand Against the Wind*, p. 430 (see photo)

"deluge" of Chinese troops. But Stilwell not only left the battle before his troops, he took a safer route, further from the enemy than the routes taken later by Chinese Army units that retreated to India. During his flight to India, he saw none of his Chinese troops and he reached India well before any of his troops heading in that direction. Chiang Kai-shek, unable to get any response from his fleeing commander, cabled the commander of Stilwell's fifth Army. General Tu Yu-ming rallied three divisions and fought his way out to China. Other Chinese divisions of Stilwell's former command also conducted a fighting retreat. One general was killed in action. Stilwell's immediate subordinate, General Lo, remained at Stilwell's former HQ to exert some control over the situation. The next day, Stilwell apparently feeling vulnerable, lied to Marshall saying General Lo and the Chinese quartermaster had left Stilwell and his staff to their own devices. In Washington, Stilwell's patron came to the rescue. Incredibly, Marshall obtained Roosevelt's and Secretary of War Stimson's signatures on a commendation for Stilwell's performance. The only instance in U.S. history, possibly in world history, where a commanding general received a commendation for fleeing the battlefield, while his troops fought on.

Stilwell arrived in India unaware and apparently unconcerned about the fate of the army he led into Burma. He immediately gathered admiring news correspondents and made suitable ringing statements of going back in and beating the Japanese. His command failures disappeared under creative, portrayals of his leadership during a perilous trek to India. He was hailed in the media as slashing through dense jungle and mountainous terrain, confronted by wild beasts. But his personal photographer inadvertently presented another story. Photos show the group hiking along a clear trail and rather than donning his "trooper" costume, rifle and backpack, Vinegar Joe appears strolling along unencumbered. The party was served by mules, bearers and airdrops along the way. Stilwell's notes record attacks only from insects.

While the Japanese offensive advanced through Burma and threatened China, General Stilwell, Chief of Staff of the Chinese Army, resided in India for a full month. In the crisis, Chiang Kai-sheik's troops and Chennault's air force stemmed the tide. Meanwhile Stilwell, in India, worked his peculiar talent for self-promotion with Marshall and with the press. He took time to send many messages to Marshall in Washington, but after disobeying Chiang's instructions to assemble at Myitkyina, he severed communications with his immediate superior in Chungking. After several weeks in India, Stilwell claimed Chiang Kai-sheik, had undermined him. But Chiang had ordered Stilwell to retreat to Myikyina. The splintering of forces in all directions was evidence of a complete lack of control rather than secret orders. When Stilwell rediscovered his voice of authority in India, he installed a training program for a small portion of his former command. There is no record of any Stilwell queries on the armies he'd abandoned.

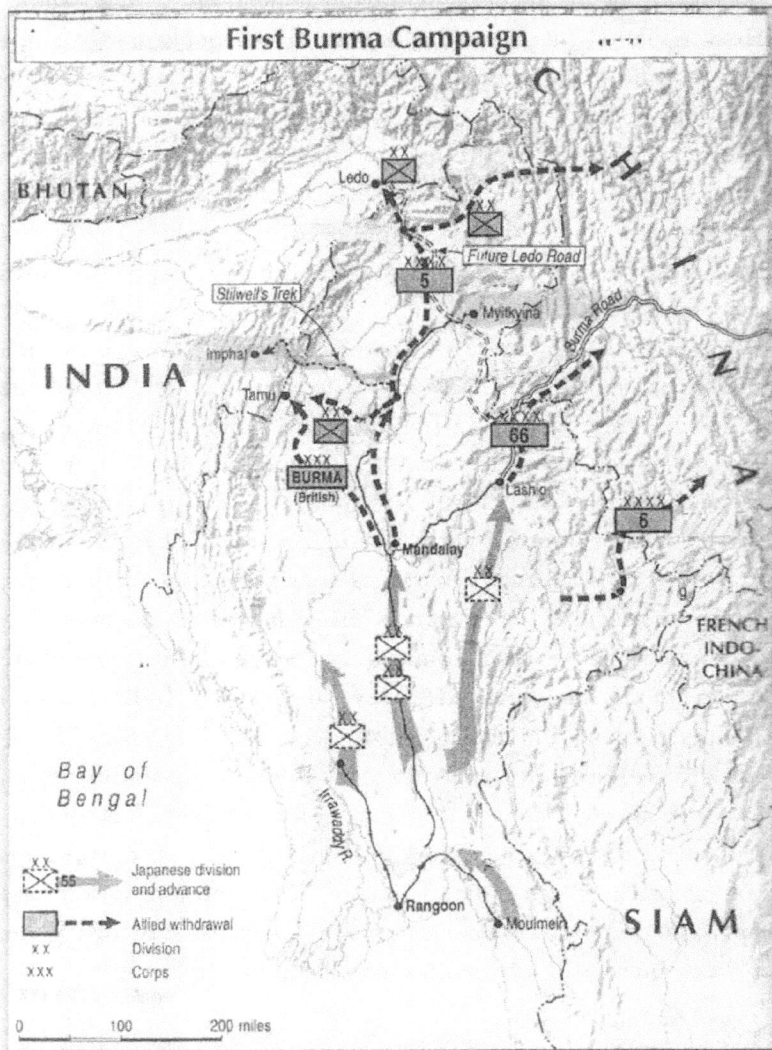

First Burma Campaign

Vinegar Joe's performance could be masked in a Washington focused on Europe but not in China. General Chennault's assessment of Stilwell's standing with Chiang Kai-shek was the Generalissimo had lost respect for Stilwell's ability as a field commander. Chiang Kai-shek, ever tactful with Americans, felt Stilwell's performance was so reprehensible that it would speak for itself, Marshall would take appropriate action and by not taking issue, he, Chiang, "would uphold the honor of a friendly nation". He did convey his assessment of Stilwell's overall performance to his Foreign Minister in Washington "I received your cable all the 15th asking my opinion about Stilwell to which I have already replied. So far, the China Theater has no organization or preparation for it. What is worse, not a single plan has been advanced for the minimum possible maintenance of the China Theater. As to a general plan for the establishment and maintenance of the air forces, tonnage of monthly air transport, and the timing of Army and Air Force operations and counterattack had not been treated as matters of importance. It seems that victory or defeat and the life or death of the China Theater had nothing to do with Stilwell. This man does not place much value on organization, concrete planning, and overall implementation. Possibly this is due to the fact that he is not familiar with the duty of the Chief of Staff. Failure of the Burma campaign is wholly attributable to strategic error, but Stilwell places all the blame on our ranking officers. He falsely reported that Lo Cho-ying had escaped to Paoshan.... He did not ask for my instructions before hand nor did he make any direct report to me. His undertakings were devoid of human feeling and reason. To uphold the honor of a friendly nation, I don't want to say much about Stilwell. At this moment, it is not necessary to hasten in responding to Marshall's inquiry. In the future, he probably will understand our reticence."[8]

Chiang's confidence in Marshall's judgement and reaction was badly misplaced, a costly mistake he would repeat in the future.

Apologists created a scenario of Stilwell being ignored and abandoned by his Chinese generals, but he had authority to execute any subordinate who disobeyed his orders. As General Chennault saw it ". . . but for . . . the ranking American officer in Asia and Chief of Staff of the Chinese Republic, it was a startling exhibition of his ignorance or disregard for these larger responsibilities."

When Stilwell disobeyed direct orders, abandoned his command, walked out to safety, and received a commendation, it seemed his penetration of Marshall's icy exterior gave him unlimited license. From that point on, he operated without restraints. On his return to Chungking and for the remainder of his tour, he savaged Chiang Kai-shek with a vengeance. He successfully buried a performance that, with out Marshall's protection, would have resulted in his recall and dismissal. In addition to the back-biting and undermining of Chiang Kai-shek, Stilwell, apparently without Marshall's knowledge, completely redefined his mission. Rather than prepare plans as Chief of Staff of the Chinese Army in China. He assumed a posture of commander-in—waiting for a second Burma campaign. As he told the reporters when he

---

8   Liang, *General Stilwell in China, p.44*

surfaced in India "we got a hell of a beating and we got to go back in and get it back."

Marshall gave lip service to Stilwell's planning duties, but apparently acquiesced to the focus on Burma.

Months after Stilwell's flight to India, the stories of his Chinese divisions were pieced together. The commander of his 38th division led his troops out through great hardship but in good order by a route closer to the Japanese lines than Stilwell's well publicized hike. The 200th division of Stilwell's Chinese fifth Army fought its way out along with the remnants of the sixth Army, to Yunnan, China. The 22nd and 96 divisions of the fifth Army struggled northward in varying directions and redoubled their traces . . . caught by monsoons in the high jungle to the northwest, those that survived were kept alive with food drops by U.S. and British Air Forces. Survivors of the 22nd reached India in July and August, months after Stilwell, while those of the 96th after an epic of endurance eventually made their way over the mountains to China. A year later "Chinese patrols crossing the trails used by the retreating troops and found "Skeletons lying in groups around every water hole and at the foot of every ascent. Tattered remnants of clothing, civilian and military...."[9] A stark contrast to their commanding general's "heroic trek" and early arrival in India.

---

9 Tuchman, *Stilwell and the American Experience in China*, p.384

8

EMPTY PROMISES

T HE OBVIOUS SOLUTION to the Japanese blockade of China's ports
was overland transport. Although the Japanese blocked the
land route through Burma, a logical supply route to China lay
through the Soviet Union. Unfortunately, the first supply run
through the USSR resulted in the Russians seizing the supplies intended for China. Rather than resolve the issue with the Soviets,
then the major recipient of U.S. Lend Lease aid, Washington simply abandoned the concept of supplying China through Russia.
Thus China was without land or sea supply lines.

Stilwell, having lost the Burma Road, proposed a venture that
would allow him to "go back in and take it back." He would construct a new supply road to China. The route he proposed would
wind through the remote edges of the highest mountains on
earth. Although it circumvented most of Japanese occupied south
Burma, some segments encroached on Japanese occupied territory.

Supposedly, the mountainous terrain would make it less accessible to Japanese attack, although the Japanese had displayed no inability to operate in mountainous terrain.

The proposed route, essentially a 1000 mile mountain road over extremely precipitous terrain, raised strong objections from all knowledgeable sources. In addition to requiring territory defended by the undefeated Japanese 18th Division, engineers charged with constructing the roadway and others familiar with the terrain vigorously opposed the route as unstable. They predicted annual rainfall totals of 150 inches with an intensity as high as 14 inches in 24 hours would cause washouts and avalanches that would not only shut down traffic, but would require the creation of repair stations and heavy equipment placements along the route. They estimated a major portion of road tonnage capacity would be needed to repair and maintain the roadway. Marshall ignored all negatives and continued his full support of the project.

The planned road, initially known as the Ledo road and later christened the Stilwell Road, was promoted as "The lifeline to China." Strangely, this "Lifeline" ignored China's immediate, desperate situation. The project, even if successful, would provide no relief for two years and road construction would require 50,000 American construction personnel and 30,000 locals. Stilwell, with Marshall's support, swept all objections aside. The new supply route became the justification for Stilwell's and therefore Marshall's total concentration on Burma at the expense of China.

China needed an interim supply system until the planned supply road was completed in the distant future. The answer was a modest air supply effort. Transport planes would carry supplies from India over the lower reaches of the Himalayan Mountains, the "Hump", to Kunming, China. Once operations began, tonnage was limited by the number of aircraft and the number of flights per day, but in the planning stages, Marshall's goals displayed the incongruity that would later typify U.S.-China relations. Logistician Marshall set ridiculously low tonnage goals which, in turn, undercut pressure to expand the fleet, and increase supplies to China.

The airlift started with a fleet of 100 aircraft, and was treated as an orphan. It provided a trickle of supplies to an ally whose weapons and ammunition were already depleted by five years of total war. Chiang requested 10,000 tons per month to support his army of 325 divisions. Based on General Marshall's U.S. Army budget, 325 U.S. divisions would require 6,825,000 tons per month. Stilwell and Marshall rejected Chiang's request for less than 1% of Marshall's U.S. budget as excessive. While Chiang's foot soldiers required much less than a more heavily armed and mechanized U.S. division, the Chinese divisions had suffered from continually diminished supplies for the past five years. After five years of exhausting warfare they needed much more than mere replenishment. The vast disparity in General Marshall's thinking is shown in that he used a rule of thumb that a rifleman in combat needed 150 rounds of ammunition per day. During Stilwell's tour, the average Chinese foot soldier carried 22 rounds of ammunition.[1] By Marshall's standards, this was enough to oppose the enemy with rifle fire for a few hours or, fire a machinegun for a few seconds. In the harsh, ruthless, world of Asian warfare Chiang's soldiers

---

1 Stilwell, *The Stilwell Papers*, p.208,209

frequently ran out of ammunition and were easily slaughtered by well-equipped Japanese.

Marshall's goal for the airlift to China was 4000 tons/month. By reducing Chiang's 10,000 ton goal to 4000, Marshall effectively reduced pressure to increase airlift capacity. Less than half of Marshall's 4000 ton goal reached China during the critical year when America had to keep China in the war.

The above tonnage included supplies for Chennault's U.S. 14th Air Force, (formerly known as the Flying Tigers) and significant tonnage for non-combatant U.S. and British staff people. Add to this Stilwell's diversion of Hump tonnage to prepare for his Burma campaign and the result was a U.S. ally relatively disarmed for nearly three years.

The integrity of Chiang's forces was clearly eroding. China's economy was wracked by inflation, and promised U.S. financial aid, aid not impeded by Japanese blockade, was held up in Washington. In the countryside, the former close relationship between the Nationalist foot soldier and the peasant farmer was strained. At times, unpaid, hungry troops resorted to scavenging whatever was available in order to survive. This aroused resentment in rural areas, which in turn reduced their dedication to the war effort, and impacted Chiang's image in the eyes of roving American correspondents who were unimpeded by communist style travel restrictions. China's deteriorating situation also provided fuel for Stilwell's State Department aides, always eager to disparage Chiang Kai-shek in their reports to Washington. For China, serious decline began while the country was purportedly under the umbrella of U.S. aid.

As America geared up war production, more transport planes could have been added and tonnage increased. But, even here, Stilwell operated from inexplicable motives. Without prior discussions with his superior, Chiang Kai-shek, Stilwell, refused additional transport planes to increase Hump tonnage. When Chiang became aware and questioned him, Stilwell claimed airfield capacity limited Hump operations to 100 planes. A lame excuse, two years earlier 14th Air Force commander General Chennault marveled at the quick mobilization of 120,000 coolies who built a 4800 Ft. runway for heavy bombers in 60 days. Stilwell then blamed the War Department and immediately sent an urgent damage control message to Marshall.

In midsummer 1942, additional transport planes were added to a flight of B-17 bombers that reached India en route to China. However, a crisis emerged in North Africa: Rommel's German Panzer Corps attacked and pushed back British forces. Rommel's objective was the Suez Canal, connecting the Mediterranean and Red Seas, lifeline of the British Empire. The alarm went up, and Marshall asked Stilwell to survey the situation of the B-17 heavy bombers then stationed in India on their way to China. Could they be transferred to Egypt to help stop Rommel? On June 23, 1942, without notifying Chiang, Washington ordered both the B-17's and the flight of transport planes intended for Hump duty, to Egypt. This diversion broke another specific Roosevelt promise to Chiang Kai-shek. When Chiang challenged the transfer, Stilwell claimed he had objected to the move. There's no record of Marshall overruling any of Stilwell's bizarre decisions during Vinegar Joe's China tour. It seems more likely Stilwell approved the transfer of the planes to

Egypt. Other than the simple malice displayed in Stilwell's private papers, his motives were obscure.

In January, 1943, a full year after America declared war, Air Force Commander, General Hap Arnold, visited the theater and promised to increase the transport fleet to 140 planes and promised to achieve the 4000 ton per month goal not achieved during the previous year. In June, 1943, a full year and one half after America entered WW2, tonnage airlifted to China inched up to 3000. Arnold also freed Chennault from reporting to Stilwell's appointee, Bissel.

When additional transport planes were available for Hump duty, a new restriction emerged. Stilwell appointee Bissell, responsible for constructing Hump airfields in India miscalculated and botched it. The fields were "a sea of mud" and had "no access roads". The fix took months. When finally ready, Marshall declared cargo planes were not available due to the demands of the Normandy invasion he expected to lead. Normandy was scheduled for one year in the future. Transfer of aircraft from Hump bases to England for the Normandy invasion would have required, at most, several days.

In the early days of the war, after the Japanese attack on Pearl Harbor, the depressing series of American defeats prompted a daring bombing raid on the Japanese homeland by American B-25 medium bombers. Damage would be minimal, but the goal was boosting morale on the home front. The mission required a bold new technique. Although medium bombers could not land on the relatively short flight decks of Navy aircraft carriers, after intensive pilot training, B-25 medium bombers could take off in that limited length and then land elsewhere. The Doolittle raid, named after its leader, required a Carrier Task Force to close within hundreds of miles of the Japanese homeland. A risky feat in itself, considering the superiority of Japanese naval strength at that time versus the depleted American Pacific fleet. According to plan, after attacking Tokyo and several other high profile Japanese targets the planes would fly on, land in Chinese Nationalist territories and join Chennault's 14th Air Force.

All went well until the U.S. fleet sighted small craft on their approach to Japanese home waters. Fearing the boats would trigger a deadly response from the Japanese Navy, Admiral Halsey launched the B-25s early and turned back. This meant the planes lacked adequate fuel to reach the designated Nationalist Chinese landing fields. It also meant they would reach China at night. Both problems could have been at least partially overcome if Chennault's spotters and forward airfield crews had time to select, set up and guide the planes to alternate landing sites, as they'd done many times for Flying Tiger aircraft in emergency situations. Unfortunately, Stilwell's appointee Bissell opted for secrecy. Bissel didn't advise anyone in China of the situation until a few hours before the planes arrived. The planes crash landed and were lost for future operations against the Japanese. Fortunately, most of the crews survived. But then, a great tragedy ensued. Most of the Americans who bailed out or crashed in Japanese occupied China, were spirited to safety by local Chinese. The aid of downed American fliers brought down the wrath of a Japanese Army outraged by the raid on their home islands. Fifty three Japanese battalions swept through Chekiang Province. By order of the Japanese high command, they slaughtered men, women and children to teach the Chinese peasants a lesson. Since the Tokyo raid was only symbolic, the U.S. morale boost was a costly one for ally China. The Japanese retribution reportedly killed nearly a quarter million Chinese.[2] In the history of China's war with the Japan, this was not a major Japanese offensive, yet the total fatalities approached the total of Americans killed in World War II. It was the type of war the Chinese had been fighting for years. Chiang Kai-shek was not consulted in advance of the Doolittle raid.

Chiang Kai-shek was coming to realize China had no voice in the planning and decisions affecting his nation's future. He recalled a comment by Ghandi, father of India's independence movement, "The West will never voluntarily treat us Orientals as equals. Why they do not even admit your country to their Combined Chief of Staff Conferences. If we are thus treated during war, what would be our position at the peace conference?"

As aid promises remained unfulfilled, Stilwell and Marshall found it advantageous to position China's pleas for help as demands from an ungrateful ward. A half-year after Pearl Harbor on May 17, 1942, Chinese Foreign Minister T.V. Soong was finally invited to a top level meeting with FDR, Churchill and Staff. He was forced to defer dealing with China's desperate, immediate needs and address the overall problem "—I believe you all know it, (China's desperate situation). China under such critical circumstances demands nothing from you Allies, but requests you to fulfill your promises." . . . "This is what I wish to tell you on behalf of the Generalissimo."

---

2 Chennault, *Way of a Fighter*, p.169

His eight-month wait for an audience and his plea were wasted effort.

Meanwhile, developments were underway in China that would ultimately constitute a greater threat than the Japanese Army.

9

THE ENABLERS

URING GENERAL STILWELL'S first year in China, other than his
Burma debacle, his impact occurred in non-military areas
where his ingrained hostility to Chiang Kai-shek and the Chinese
government blossomed and produced bitter fruit.

"Peanut" was Chief of Staff Stilwell's early name for his designated superior, the head of the Chinese Government, Chiang Kai-
shek. Official Army records passed this off later as a radio code
name but do not explain why such a demeaning term would be applied to a Head of State. In China, Stilwell abstained from applying
"Peanut" temporarily in favor of "Generalissimo" or "G-Mo" during
his elation over being the first foreigner to lead Chinese troops into
battle, but then reverted to using it after his abandonment of those
troops. From that point he descended to more disparaging terms:
"prejudiced, conceited despot, little dummy, grasping, ungrateful
little rattlesnake, the world's greatest ignoramus, slippery little

bastard" were some of his milder favorites. Only General Marshall and the Chinese Communists escaped Stilwell's backbiting venom. On several occasions, Stilwell referred to President Roosevelt, whose legs were crippled by paralysis, as "Rubber legs."[1]

Other than promoting a second Burma campaign, Stilwell dedicated himself to undermining Chiang Kai-shek. Any disgruntled Chinese aide or staff officer could unburden himself to Stilwell and be pumped for rumors of corruption, hoarding, and favoritism. All negative information was encouraged. When none was forthcoming, it was invented. Vinegar Joe then applied his considerable PR skills to disparage China's government in Washington. One member of his staff seemed to be solely occupied with developing an anti government propaganda program.

Before leaving Washington, Stilwell requested and was granted a specific State Department aide, separate from the U.S. Ambassador's staff in Chungking. John Davies had been raised in China, was fluent in the language and knew high ranking Communists. The Stilwell-Davies relationship began years earlier when Stilwell was posted as attaché' to the U.S. Embassy in China.

The level of urgency for Davies services in Stilwell's China headquarters is indicated by his arrival on station. Stilwell, on greeting him, said "there's nothing I can tell you about how to run your job. You're a free agent. . . ." Unfortunately for China, Davies soon moved on to serious activities. Although the Government had severed all relations with Chinese Communists, Chiang graciously allowed second ranking Red, Chou En-lai access to Government medical services. Chou was recuperating in

---

1 Tuchman, *Stilwell and the American Experience in China*, p.509

a Chungking hospital when Davies arrived on scene. Davies visited Chou regularly and faithfully transmitted the communist's claims and slanders verbatim to Washington. The incongruity of a U.S. State Department official recording and supporting an insurrectionist leader's charges against the government of a U.S. ally was one of many ignored in Washington during that period. Chou related to Davies stories of National secret police atrocities, Government hoarding of U.S. lend lease arms (there were none to hoard) and Government reluctance to fight the Japanese while dedicating all out efforts to annihilate the Mao's CCP. All claims were unsupported. All claims were transmitted directly to Washington, bypassing and escaping editing by experienced China hands in U.S. Embassy in Chungking. Chou's situation, residing in a Chungking Hospital, enjoying the medical care of his supposedly murderous enemy, aroused no skepticism in Davies or in his Washington colleagues.

On June 29, Davies reported "Chou said Chiang was to negotiate with Japan. He (Chou) hoped to put Communist forces under Stilwell's command to liberate Burma." Chairman Mao's internal directions to the party faithful expose the concept of Stilwell using Red troops as ridiculous. (Red Army troops had years earlier been converted to militia, part time farmers who planted, cultivated and harvested crops in order to survive, not liable to drop their scythes and hoes and walk to Burma to help Vinegar Joe Stilwell.) Chou also said the government had tried to conserve military strength by refusing to fight the Japanese. On July 5, Davies reported Chou claimed 441,000 Nationalist troops blockaded their small enclave. Available non-Red figures indicate the Government posted approximately 200,000 troops in that area to defend against the Japanese, as well as seal off the Reds.[2] Then, on July 10, Davies reported "Chou estimated Communist military strength at 500,000 to 600,000 men with 1 million rifles cached in various border areas of North China, Shantung and north of the Yangtze . . ." Chou didn't explain how a half million Red warriors could be blockaded for years by a smaller contingent of Chiang's purportedly inferior conscripts. Davies made no attempts to verify or qualify Red claims before passing them on to Washington.

On July 31, Chou En-lai, fully recovered, departed for Red headquarters in Yenan. Davies lacked Chou En-lai quotes for Washington, but he continued his line of anti- government propaganda. "Unless the U.S. imposed oppressive measures, the Chinese government would hoard lend lease supplies". He avoided quantifying the meager supplies reaching Chiang's armies. Davies also inserted a plug for Stilwell stating, "The Burma campaign should have an American commander." Although a Burma campaign had not been considered by Washington, it appears Stilwell and Davies were confident it would be adopted.

On August 6, 1942, Davies amplified his "hoarding" charges against the Chinese government. In his report to Washington, he openly referred to a letter by Red insurrectionist Chou En-lai suggesting the U.S. tighten control over Lend Lease aid to prevent Chinese authorities from hoarding, for other uses. But, there was no Lend Lease material to hoard, China was blockaded and Stilwell had complete control of the trickle of material flown

---

2   Tong, *Chiang Kai-shek. Vol.One p.237,238*

in over the Hump. Eighteen months later a new Ambassador to China publicly refuted the hoarding charge, but by that time, unchallenged for a year and a half, the charge had gained traction in Washington. Chou also proposed the U.S. should send representatives to Communist held areas on the "pretext" (?) of gathering intelligence about Japanese operations. Later Davies would use this intelligence gathering ploy and present it not as a pretext, but as the true objective for expanding his activities in China. From 1942 on, Stilwell and Davies regularly trumpeted the claim that the Nationalists would not fight and Chiang Kai-shek was waiting for America to defeat the Japanese. The relative contributions of China and America were apparent to any who were interested enough to investigate. Both the Japanese and the Chinese estimates agree the Chinese Army casualty count at the end of 1942 exceeded 2 million[3] and civilian deaths exceeded 10 million. The Chinese army lacked significant medical facilities for the wounded. Seriously wounded Chinese died and the Japanese killed all who surrendered. In comparison, America suffered approximately 100,000 ground troops killed in the war with Japan and no American ground troops were killed or wounded on Chinese soil. By late 1942, when the Stilwell-Davies misinformation campaign trumpeted China would not fight, China had lost millions, had inflicted over 1 million casualties on the Japanese and continued to tie down two thirds of the Japanese Army. A post war search of Japanese Army records showed conclusively that China inflicted more enemy casualties than the U.S. but the endlessly repeated slander accusing China

---

3   Liu, *A military history of Modern China*, p.145

of not fighting, gradually became accepted as fact. To fill out the fiction, Davies stated with increasing frequency that the Chinese Communists were fighting aggressively. None of the visitors to Red territory had ever seen a sizeable formation of the Red Army, much less seen it involved in hostilities with the Japanese. Yet, stirring tales of Red exploits abounded. Later, writings by Moscow's liaison to Mao's headquarters exposed a Red Chinese-Japanese truce during this period.

Davies also served as receptionist and host in order to conduct visitors to the proper contacts in Chungking. When radio news announcer Eric Sevareid was requested by a close friend of FDR to investigate the turmoil in Chungking, Sevareid found on boarding his India- China flight that one of his fellow passengers was John Davies. The flight turned out to be an adventure during which Davies and Sevareid became close friends. After 30 days of squalid life in Chungking, Sevareid decided he had enough of China. Davies had done his job effectively. Sevareid reported not only on Chungking but he also developed insights on the Communists in far-off Yenan. The Reds were helping the peasants and fighting the Japanese. They granted the people their civil rights and developed a solid base of goodwill. Conversely, Chungking resident Severeid somehow discovered Chiang's army had looted the rice harvest and millions were dying of starvation in provinces he had also not visited. While Davies did his "job", Stilwell, despite specific instructions from General Marshall to prepare strategic plans for China's military operations, prepared none. He did find time to note almost daily complaints about the weather and the shabby condition of the city (The Japanese rained bombs on the city every afternoon.) He also found time to compose poems of sympathy for his situation and time for poisonous diatribes on the head of government he was assigned to aid. He wrote ". . . when things go wrong the private can blame the general, but the general can blame only himself." Had Vinegar Joe actually done time under fire he would have realized when things go wrong, the private dies or is dismembered and the general is at worst reassigned.

Stilwell also seemed to have trouble consistently defining the supply situation. On June 25th 1942, he wrote "We fail in all our commitments and blithely tell him (Chiang) to just carry on old top."[4] Then six days later, he wrote "China has one friend, the U.S., a very generous one . . . the little jackass. We are doing our damnedest to help him..."[5] On November 26, he had another change of heart. He wrote "For our war. We are graciously allotted Lend-lease stuff we already have . . . Peanut and I are on a raft with one sandwich between us, and the rescue ship is heading away from the scene." Six months later, with no significant increase in tonnage over the hump, Stilwell wrote of Chiang, "this insect, this stink in the nostrils . . . we are breaking our backs to help him supplying everything ...."[6]

The above are Stilwell's milder epithets. The editor of The Stilwell Papers noted that Vinegar Joe's the most extreme verbal abuse exceeded acceptable limits and was deleted from the published text.

Stilwell also found time to compose and record his perceived victories over Chiang. At one point, he interrupted a meeting of

---

4   Stilwell, *The Stilwell Papers, p.119*
5   Ibid, *p.121,148*
6   Ibid, *p.171,210*

the U.S. Ambassador and Chiang Kai-shek. Against the advice of
the Ambassador, he handed Chiang an offensive letter. He rejoiced
later and composed a poem.

I've waited long for a vengeance
At last, I've had my chance.
I've looked at the Peanut in the eye
And kicked him in the pants.

The old harpoon was ready
With aim and timing true
I sank it to the handle,
And stung him through and through.

The little bastard shivered,
And lost the power of speech.
His face turned green and quivered
as he struggled not to screech.

For all my weary battles,
For all my hours of woe,
At last, I've had my innings
And laid the Peanut low.

I Know I've still to suffer,
And run a weary race,
But oh! The blessed pleasure!
I've wrecked the Peanuts face.

Thus, the highest ranking United States officer on the Asian mainland, the Presidents appointed delegate to the largest country in the world, spent his time and energies for a substantial portion of his tour in China. It was discovered later that his hostile derangement included the preparation of detailed plans for the assassination of Chiang Kai-shek and Mme. Chiang. The contradictions and venom suggest, at the very least, something other than an orderly well-intentioned mind. Upcoming efforts to organize the discrediting of the Chinese government indicate more than personal antagonism was involved.

Although Stilwell used vile terms and slander in referring to the leader of America's ally, there is no record of Marshall ever taking issue with the insulting terms or the inconsistencies in the reports conveyed by Stilwell or his subordinate, John Davies. To the contrary, Marshall effectively covered Stilwell's backbiting and slander. When criticism of Stilwell was voiced, Marshall opted for the indirect defense, he attacked the critic. The President and Administration gradually gained an impression of Vinegar Joe as an upright American warrior fighting both a devious Chiang Kai-sheik and the Japanese enemy. Years later, Admiral Leahy who attended all top level meetings as Presidential Military Advisor wrote: "I was for a time sympathetic with Stilwell . . . The reasons for the Generalissimo's and Mountbatten's attitude toward him have been completely clarified by the publication, in 1948, of the Stilwell papers."[7] Although Stilwell apologists have presented the Chiang – Stilwell

7   Leahy, *I Was There*, p.256,272

relationship is one of mutual dislike and acrimony, there is no record of a Chiang Kai-shek discourtesy to Stilwell.

In July 1942, Roosevelt sent out an emissary, Dr. Lauchlin
Currie, to resolve differences between Stilwell and Chiang Kai-
sheik. By that time, the cost of Stilwell's Burma debacle was evident. Chiang told Currie Stilwell's failure to follow orders for
immediate troop withdrawal to Myitkyina and his personal flight
to India resulted in thousands dying from hunger and cold, and he
again stated Stilwell had falsely accused his Chinese subordinate of
desertion as he, Stilwell, headed out for India. Currie moved to resolve what he considered were ruffled feathers. Chiang had enough.
He kicked the issue back to Washington, and the War Department
answered clearly that Stilwell was Chief of Staff for Allied operations throughout the China theater and responsible for the planning
of Chinese Army operations. "He prepares plans as the directed by
the Generalissimo and when they are approved transmits them for
execution." Although these orders were very specific and came
from Marshall's office, Stilwell prepared no plans for the Chinese
Army. General Marshall took no action to remedy the lack of plans
for a major war theater and Stilwell suffered no penalties.

In March 1943, Chiang Kai-shek radiogrammed President
Roosevelt a status report and forecast. He cited Russian attacks
on China's western province, Sinkiang, and predictions that Mao's
Reds, rather than aggressively fighting the Japanese, were assem-
bling troops and resources to attack Sian, the government base of
operations for the Yellow River Valley. Chiang also predicted the
large-scale Japanese offensive that would emerge later as the Ichigo
offensive. Chiang Kai-shek's predictions rang true. Nothing was

done in Washington in regard to the Russian incursions in Sinkiang, Mao's Red threat on Sian or the upcoming Japanese offensive.

After licking his Burma wounds and maligning Chiang for nearly a year, Stilwell and Davies executed a plan to expand the anti-Chiang campaign and enhance the image of the Red Chinese. Stilwell, through Marshall, convinced a reluctant Secretary of State Cordell Hull to augment Davies ill defined mission. The proposed staff additions were justified as helping Stilwell conduct intelligence and subversive activities against the Japanese. The group would ostensibly "supervise political, economic, and psychological intelligence and warfare operations. The request was patterned after Communist Chou En-lai's earlier suggestion to Davies. (In Davies August 6, 1942 report to Washington, he openly reported that Chou En-lai advised him to send representatives to Yenan on the "pretext" of gathering intelligence.)[8] While the scope and purpose of the Stilwell-Davies proposal was vague in nature, Davies was specific on who should be involved, naming John Service, John Emerson, and Raymond Ludden. None had any serious background in intelligence work or psychological warfare. At that point, it should have been obvious to Washington that interference in the internal affairs of an ally was possible. The proposed expansion of Davies activities also overlapped other U.S. agencies in China. OSS and Navy Intel were already performing the tasks listed by Davies as justification for the added staff. Secretary of State Cordell Hull reluctantly agreed but directed that the group would report their movements and views to the highest local U.S. diplomatic envoy (i.e., the Ambassador.) A directive Davies and his new colleagues

---

8   Liang, *General Stilwell in China*, p.197

immediately ignored. In order to avoid contradiction and revision by objective observers, they funneled reports directly to associates in the State Department in Washington, who distributed them to key administration figures. Some reached the President. All who received the reports assumed the information was properly reviewed by the U.S. Embassy in China. Soon, the Stilwell and Davies propaganda supported by General Marshall and the State Department convinced President Roosevelt that Chiang Kai-shek was highly temperamental, heading a corrupt, inefficient government that had no sympathy for the abject misery of its people. There is no record of Davies or any of his colleagues producing any meaningful intelligence on enemy activities. All efforts were devoted to discrediting Chiang Kai-shek and the Nationalist Government and elevating Mao's CCP.

Many of the anti-government charges such as low Army morale and corrupt officers could be applied to even the most dedicated armies to some degree. Such conditions certainly existed where leadership was decimated by five years of total war. Davies learned from the early "hoarding" charge that quantifying and detailing charges could lead to his exposure. From then on, they made charges that were general in nature, charges that with sufficient repetition were difficult to completely refute. Most went unchallenged. While Davies charged fascism and vague secret police activities, Chiang recommended and the Chinese Government approved a habeas corpus act. Unlike America's Russian allies, who hauled off their citizens in the middle of the night, never to be heard from again, and unlike the tens of thousands of American citizens imprisoned in California without trial because of their

Japanese ancestry, the Chinese People were guaranteed against imprisonment without trial.[9] This momentous event went unnoticed in Washington circles and Davies baseless slander continued to be accepted.

The only defense against a Davies type campaign would have been to mount a higher volume campaign of factual information. Chiang had facts, but no capability for dissemination. The young revolutionary who fought, clawed, and united the largest nation on earth, had no exposure to western style PR campaigns. His efforts in that direction relied solely on the energetic efforts of his American educated wife. Unfortunately, Mme. Chiang came late on the scene; the slander had already taken hold in Washington. In that contest, volume, not substance, produced the desired effect on the audience and Davies had a receptive audience in the State Department.

Chiang Kai-shek's personal demeanor also made him an ideal target for Stilwell-Davies slander. All allied leaders who met with Chiang found him extremely courteous and sincere, qualities that did not serve him well in dealing with Stilwell. A second Chiang "defect" was his Chinese cultural background. He was raised in the ancient Chinese traditions and relationships derived from Confucianism that stressed support of family and friends. Chiang acknowledged he suffered from family, friends and bureaucrats in government who did not serve him well through either incompetence or dishonesty. His corrective measures consisted of isolation of family members who failed him. His brother-in-law, a key figure in the Chinese government throughout World War II, Foreign

9   Time Magazine, *The Bear's Paw, 7/31/44*

Minister Soong, was isolated for nearly 6 months during one crucial period. In non-family matters, Chiang tried to apply the esprit and discipline he installed at Whampoa Military Academy, but the Japanese had decimated the ranks of Whampoa graduates. Ancient Chinese traditions, the composition of the country, warlord provinces with varying degrees of loyalty to the Nationalist Government chain of command and devastating war losses made the concept of a tightly disciplined well-organized government impossible to achieve. General Chennault, in one meeting with Chiang, launched into a long harangue on the inefficiency of the Chinese Air Force. Chiang shrugged grunted a sentence and left. Mme. Chiang translated "he says he knows all about the things you have told him, and he knows the men are no good." Chennault exploded "if he knows all about them, why doesn't he do something to them?" Mme. replied "He says that these are the only people he has to work with, and if we get rid of all those people who were at fault, who will there be left?" Later, Chennault saw Chiang's dilemma as "He managed by playing off one against the other, getting what he could from them, and every now and then lopping off a few heads as a warning that there was a limit to his patience." Not the modern concept of executive management, but Chiang Kai-shek had kept warlords in line and moved the nation forward until his success aroused Japanese aggression.

Prior to 1942, Claire Chennault was the only American experienced in dealing with high level Nationalist government officials and the only American with intimate knowledge of China's situation. He'd seen Chiang Kai-shek in action during the dark days. "He traveled up and down the provinces of the hinterland, whipping up sagging morale." "We will fight for a hundred years if necessary" and "We are losing battles, but we need only to win the final battle. China will never yield." In regard to political corruption, as the American saw it, the line between legitimate squeeze, (similar to American suppliers entertaining customers), and elaborate gifts and outright corruption was often "hard for the oriental eye to discern." In Chennault's development of China's Air Force, he was given a fund for gratuities, large and small but found that pens and mechanical pencils were adequate... "[10]

Meanwhile, as the war wore on, Chiang became more remote from contact with western correspondents while General Stilwell thrived in contact with his favorite newsmen. Given the squalid living conditions in the over-crowded, war-torn capital, "desk" correspondents, conscious of their physical discomforts and fed anti-Chiang propaganda by Stilwell's office, focused negatively on Chiang Kai-shek. Although Chiang's posture and performance had remained consistent, one prominent correspondent, described his view of China's leader "He was a man I first learned to respect and admire, then to pity, then to despise."

No evidence has ever been presented to indicate Chiang was other than a patriot dedicated to the betterment of China, but stories of corruption involving his wealthy in-laws were heavily promoted. When a New York newspaper identified Chiang in-laws T V Soong and H.H. Kung as having "more than a billion dollars on deposit in this country ...." The President put the FBI on it. Director Hoover ordered the investigation be given "preferred and expeditious attention to immediately determine the extent of domestic

---

10   Chennault, *Way of a Fighter*, p.78

bank accounts of captioned individuals as well as industries, corporations or enterprises under their control... every possible lead to secure information should be pursued." The FBI came up with nothing.[11] Lack of any evidence should have killed the slander campaign, but the malicious gossip had a life of its own.

The bottom line significance of all the Red propaganda was zero when compared to the potential for American lives lost in the war. If all corruption charges were true, one overriding truth remained: Chiang Kai-shek's Nationalist army tied down the bulk of the Japanese army throughout the war with weapons from their own arsenals, at virtually no cost to the United States. Compared to that undeniable fact, none of the propaganda charges merited consideration. If China fell and the U.S. faced those hundreds of thousands of Japanese troops in battle, hundreds of thousands of young Americans would have died in combat. In the political climate of the forties, this core fact did nothing to limit U.S. meddling in Chinese affairs and nothing to interrupt a passionate romance with Mao's CCP.

---

11 Pakula, *The Last Empress, p.600*

10

BURMA STRATEGIST

ONCE EXPOSED TO scrutiny, General Stilwell's push for a new supply road, a "lifeline to China," as replacement for the Burma Road invited a flood of criticism. It also faced strategic obstacles. Initial planning called for amphibious landings by the British and commitment of American infantry divisions. Chiang wanted Allied amphibious landings to support any Burma campaign by his army. As a fallback position, he wanted the major Burmese port, Rangoon, be taken by U.S or British forces. When it was decided the designated amphibious forces and ground forces were needed in Europe, Chiang opted for a hold up of any Burma campaign until adequate forces were available.

Stilwell pushed for any campaign he could get. Through Marshall, he advanced the concept of a campaign without amphibious landings and with no involvement of British Army troops. U.S. Ambassador Gauss, one of the few Americans with experience in the area, raised sensible objections to all the plans under consideration. Gauss maintained that conquering Burma did little to help China. He saw the most pressing need of China was bombers and air transport. Bombers could be sent against the enemy immediately and raise flagging morale. Transport planes could carry equipment needed to produce more weapons for a Chinese army that was gradually being disarmed by reduced weapons production in China and lack of promised American weapons. He also felt that without sufficient naval and air strikes, a ground offensive was impractical. U.S. Naval Attaché McHugh, an old China hand and author of a Chinese-language textbook, stated that Stilwell's insistence on the recapture of Burma was a personal ambition resulting from his recent defeat and represented a diversion of supplies authorized for Chennault's Air war.

On May 23, 1943, the combined Chiefs of staff met with the FDR and Churchill for discussions on the grand strategy for the war. They agreed on all plans except Burma. Churchill believed a Burma campaign and the opening of a new Burma Road was not feasible at that time and Ambassador Gauss and Chiang Kai-shek's held similar positions. They were supported by warnings from the American construction and supply staff in India that the terrain of the planned route was unstable for road construction. One analyst, recognizing China's complete lack of truck fuel, produced a simple equation that should have resolved all controversy. It clearly showed that trucks negotiating a thousand mile mountain road from India to China and returning, would utilize much of their cargo space to carry fuel for the round trip. Simple logic demonstrated that trucks could not deliver worthwhile tonnage to

China. It should have doomed the project. Although, all who were knowledgeable about the situation in Burma objected to the road, General Marshall swept expert advice and simple truth aside and pushed for the "Lifeline to China" and a Burma military campaign for Stilwell.

Stilwell's plan for clearing the enemy from the planned supply line route called for the use of the two and one half divisions of Chinese troops he'd trained in India, supplemented by small contingents of British and American commando forces. Chiang believed, once the campaign began, Stilwell would demand troops from his China defense forces. He saw the time-consuming planning, military operations and road construction would extend China's supply miseries for several years. The final decision would be made by FDR and Churchill.

Stilwell's India based attack force consisted of the Chinese divisions that retreated to India after his earlier Burma debacle. These units were brought up to strength with reinforcements flown in from China. Since they were in India where supplies were plentiful, they were completely armed and outfitted with U.S. equipment and designated the X force.

In Chungking, Chiang Kai-shek struggled with the total American focus on Burma. A Burma campaign, even if effective, could provide the Japanese with an opportunity to attack China and force a weakened China out of the war. Chiang was baffled by the continuing strong support of Stilwell emanating from Washington. During his early conflicts and struggles to unite China, he'd used a number of foreign military advisors, when he had a problem with a Russian advisor; a simple request brought a replacement. Although

JAMES FITZGERALD

the British also felt Stilwell should be recalled, General Marshall blocked all such moves.

The only competition for Stilwell's focus on Burma came from the other conspicuous American military personage in China. While Stilwell had shown dismal failure in action against the enemy and generally poisoned the waters in China, Claire Chennault contributed significantly in China's desperate hours. Chiang first hired the 47-year-old retired U.S. Air Force Captain to evaluate a Chinese Air Force organized for him by the Italian government. At their first meeting, Chiang was confronted with news that the Italian's report of 500 operational planes was fraudulent. His Air Force chief reported 91 planes operational. Chennault confirmed it and went on with further bad news. Chennault later recalled "that session . . . established the tone of my relations with the Generalissimo. He came to rely on me for bald facts no matter how unpleasant they might be, and he always allowed me to have my way if I could convince him, whatever I proposed would help the war. In all my dealings with him that seem to be his sole standard . . . whether it would help the war. He even allowed me to deal directly with the Chinese Communists and the leaders of other dissident factions when I convinced him it was necessary for rescuing of American pilots and obtaining target intelligence."[1]

When Chiang contracted with the American Captain to form the Flying Tigers, Chennault recruited American volunteers with prior flying experience. After intense training in tactics tailored for the less maneuverable P-40 planes available, the American Volunteer Group, AVG, bested the Japanese in every encounter.

1 Chennault, *Way of a Fighter*, p.41

Chennault's air tactics produced the best kill ratio of any U.S. or Allied flight group in WW2, in aircraft considered distinctly inferior to the enemy aircraft they faced.

In Washington, Marshall and others considered Chennault an overly optimistic proponent of airpower, but none denied that he produced results with meager equipment and supplies. Chennault represented the only positive U.S. military presence in China. Yet, when his views of Chiang Kai-shek's' situation and performance conflicted sharply with the Stilwell and Davie reports to Marshall and the State Department, he was devalued in Washington. When a commander of China air operations was to be selected, Marshall presented Chennault as too close to Chiang Kai-shek and arranged the appointment of an inexperienced member of the establishment.

In early 1943, Chennault proposed an aggressive air offensive and Chiang Kai-shek approved wholeheartedly. It would be the first offensive effort by American forces in China. But, it would require supplies be drawn away from Stilwell's preoccupation with Burma. Stilwell resisted it, predicting the Japanese would respond with an offensive and capture the U.S. airfields. Marshall supported his friend and the issue was bumped up to higher levels. Stilwell and Chennault flew in from Asia for a high-level face-off where FDR would hear them out and make the decision. At the meeting, Stilwell shrank from confrontation. To the chagrin of his patron Marshall, he ". . . sat humped over with his head down and muttered something about China not fighting." Stilwell traveled halfway around the world and was unable to present his case to FDR. None at the meeting saw irony in Marshall and Stilwell opposing a U.S. offensive while claiming the Chinese wouldn't fight.

Chennault got his air offensive. When the decision went against Marshall, the ever formal dignified Chief of Staff went into a pout. "In his dealings with the President he took pains to be formal and official, would not let them see him smile when Roosevelt cracked jokes and sat frozen faced when others laughed . . . his annoyance in the matter of China extended to Hopkins,. . . they had ceased to speak to each other."[2] Stilwell adjusted. For his next meeting with FDR, he would bring supporting cast.

With the decision for Chennault's "Trident" plan, Marshall told Stilwell the problem had been to support him against constant pressure from almost everyone interested in China. Then Marshall reverted to the role of solicitous friend. He told Stilwell that he, Stilwell, had attained most of his goals for the Chinese,[3] a statement that raises questions on Vinegar Joe's goals for China and Marshall's complicity. Stilwell had failed dismally in Burma. Up until that time, his only successful effort was the installation of his anti-government propaganda program. Did Marshall's "attained goals" refer to the undermining of China? (It was Stilwell's only success.)

On July 14, 1943, Stilwell left Chungking and China to spend seven full weeks in India, ostensibly inspecting the two divisions of Chinese troops based in India. While there, he found time for a vacation in Kashmir. In Washington, although the decision was made for Chennault's Trident air offensive, Marshall had not given up. He warned again, as soon as Trident stung the Japanese, they would retaliate by attacking Chennault's air bases. Peculiar, but

---

2 Tuchman, *Sand Against the Win, p.370*

3 Romanus, *Stilwell's Mission to China, p.277,278*

unnoticed was the total lack of interest by Marshall and Stilwell in planning any steps to meet the Japanese retaliation they'd predicted. At that time, still working to discredit Trident, Marshall warned the President many influential Chinese wanted the United States to fight China's battles for her. Marshall's limited experience in China fifteen years earlier coupled with his remote personality provided him little knowledge of the wants and desires of any Chinese. It was a typical Marshall tactic. When quality information didn't support his purposes, he lent his lofty prestige to unsupported insights prejudicial to the opposition. When Chennault came up for promotion with achievements that exceeded all expectations and could not be challenged, Marshall hinted at disloyalty. General Marshall had no reliable information conduit from China. He drew on and parroted derogatory information furnished by the Stilwell-Davies conduit when it suited his purposes. In regard to Chinese wanting Americans to fight China's battles, as mentioned previously, the ratio of Chinese to American killed in action in the war against Japan was approximately 20 to 1 and unlike other war theatres, no American ground forces fought and died on Chinese soil.

The lack of overall China defense planning, by the U.S. Army officer assigned and repeatedly ordered to do it, has never been explained. Both the Chief of Staff in China and the Chief of Staff in Washington had done nothing on plans requested and promised numerous times. To the contrary, Generals Marshall and Stilwell would soon begin committing China's best trained, best equipped troops to a questionable campaign outside China. At best a costly sideshow, at worst an invitation for a complete Japanese victory in China.

In November 1943, FDR, Churchill and Chiang Kai-shek met in Cairo. Stilwell attended supported by John Davies. Although the sole purpose of the Cairo meeting was to agree on plans for prosecution of the war against Japan, Davies discovered on the flight to Egypt that his friend General Stilwell, Chief of Staff, of China's armies, had no plans to present at the meeting. Davies and Stilwell hurriedly sketched out a plan on hotel stationary and Stilwell's staff arranged it in the proper format.

During the meetings FDR repeated his pledge to return Manchuria to China and made further commitments to Chiang Kai-shek, promising to fully equip and supply 90 Chinese Army divisions and provide comparable air force expansion. Stilwell, supported by Davies, made a better impression than he had at his previous meeting with FDR. The British were less impressed.[4] Nevertheless, Stilwell gained official approval for his Burma venture and then reverted to tourist mode. He took a holiday and toured the land of the Pharaohs.

With Chennault's Trident air offensive stifled by limited Hump capacity and supply restrictions, Stilwell's "Lifeline to China" grew to become the focal point of U.S. efforts on the Asian mainland. The popular view in late 1943 was, only Stilwell's "Lifeline" would save China. Although road completion was at best a year away, the option of supplying China through the Soviet Union was not reconsidered.

The Burma plan consisted of Stilwell's force of two and one half divisions of India- based Chinese troops supplemented by a 3000 man American commando unit. A British commando

---

4   Heiferman, *The Cairo Conference*, p.67

unit, "The Chindits." that had been operating in Burma for some time, would make up the British contribution. Meanwhile, in Chungking, Chiang felt the Japanese threatening. He was increasingly reluctant to divert troops from the defense of China to engage in what he considered a futile and useless fight beyond China's borders against a minor fraction of the Japanese Army. But, Stilwell exerted enough pressure through Marshall and Roosevelt to keep Chiang on board with the plan. The British were not enthusiastic, they wanted the recovery of Southeastern Asia accomplished by British troops rather than by Americans or Chinese, who might hinder reestablishment of their colonial empire. In that obscure part of the world, Marshall was granted oversight that he no longer enjoyed in Europe and the Pacific. Since Marshall was unable to induce Stilwell to produce plans for the Chinese Army, and Trident was hobbled by supply problems, the "Lifeline to China" became the only American military plan for the entire Asian conflict.

Later, it was decided the 3000 American troops, christened "Galahad", would report to British General Orde C. Wingate, commander of the Chindits. Stilwell complained but Marshall's out of character reply seemed to put Stilwell in his place: ". . . their training must be closely coordinated with that of the British . . . we must all eat some crow if we are to fight the same war together. . . ." However, Stilwell was not to be denied. As with the earlier Chennault/Bissel command issue, Marshall soon reversed himself and Stilwell gained command of Galahad. Also, similar to his Chennault relationship, Stilwell immediately installed General Merrill, from his headquarters staff, as insulation between himself and the Galahad combat commander. Merrill was soon heralded by Stilwell's press corps as the leader of Merrill's Marauders. The "Merrill's Marauders" title was for public consumption only. Merrill was physically incapable of the task. Earlier, when he walked out of Burma with Stilwell's staff and nurses, he was found at one point lying face down in a stream. He had neither the physical constitution nor the jungle combat experience that would be needed in the upcoming campaign. The unit retained the tactical designation "Galahad" and was led through the entire campaign by Colonel Charles N. Hunter.

Stilwell spent the first half of 1944 in Burma, trying to get operations underway. Progress at first was slow and British planners pushed for abandonment of Stilwell's campaign in favor of an invasion of Sumatra. They doubted the town of Myitkyina and its airfield could be taken before the monsoon set in. Without Myitkyina, construction of the road could not be completed. Stilwell reacted angrily sending his own mission to Washington without notifying his British superior, Lord Mountbatten. When Marshall came out strongly in favor of Stilwell and against the British plan, Mountbatten cited Stilwell for violating the chain of command and requested that Stilwell be relieved. Marshall again stepped in and prevented Stilwell's recall.[5]

---

5   Bjorge, *Merrill's Marauders*, p.19

11

FIASCO

1944, AMERICA AND its allies are on the offensive. Rome is taken. Eisenhower's massive D Day invasion forces breach Hitler's western wall and threaten German soil. The German U-Boat fleet that threatened Atlantic shipping is decimated. In the Pacific, MacArthur launches his campaign to retake the Philippines, Marines take Wake Island, Guam, Tinian and Saipan. From Tinian, B-29 bombers begin mass raids on the Japanese homeland. On the Eastern Front, the Russians force the German Army into retreat.

On Feb. 2 Stilwell launched his small scale operation in Burma to push elements of the Japanese 18th division from the planned route of his "Lifeline to China" supply road. His Chinese forces and Galahad's 3000 Americans, fought well. After four grueling months, the combined force reached the airstrip at Myitkyina and captured it easily. The Galahad force, commanded by Colonel Hunter, had performed aggressively and completed all assigned missions in extreme conditions. So extreme that, after four months of jungle fighting, Galahad was spent. Lacking food, ammunition and medical supplies, many of the survivors were sick, all were exhausted. Stilwell's HQ appointee, Merrill, had promised Hunter and his troops immediate re-supply when they signaled the airfield was operational. Galahad's signal brought transport planes towing gliders by order of General Stilwell. On landing, the gliders disgorged construction engineers and materials to repair runways that were not damaged. Stilwell noted "Told them to keep going all night."[1] The following flights brought in a Chinese infantry regiment lacking commander and staff. The next day, Stilwell's personal airplane, "Uncle Joe's Chariot," touched down bringing Stilwell and a dozen correspondents. U.S. Army records described: "The brilliant seizure of the Myitkyina airstrip was the height of Stilwell's career and the grand climax of the North Burma campaign." The airstrip was taken easily, but the North Burma Campaign was far from over. The following day General Merrill arrived. Yet another day elapsed before the promised food and ammunition arrived. The lack of hands-on leadership worsened when General Stilwell and his entourage completed their photo op and flew out.

Although the airstrip was securely in Allied hands, some 300 to 700 Japanese continued to occupy the nearby village. Myitkyina had to be taken in order to continue road construction. At that point, a front line, "Fighting Joe Stilwell" of public image, with 30,000 Chinese troops at his disposal, could have led a surge on

---

1 Stilwell, *The Stilwell Papers*, p.296

the relatively few Japanese defenders and easily taken the village. Instead leadership disappeared.

When Chinese troops jumped off in their first assault on the village, they penetrated Japanese defenses and entered the town. Then, the lack of leadership surfaced. Confusion ensued as Chinese units fired on each other and retreated. In the following days, more attacks failed. The situation continued to deteriorate as the Japanese reinforced the village forces up to some 5000 troops.[2] When Stilwell ordered a Chinese attack on May 24, he seemed to revert to his earlier performance in Burma. He was unable to motivate his Chinese commanders to advance. As his campaign sputtered out, he relied increasingly on the few surviving Galahad troops. At one point, he brought in road construction personnel, conscripted civilians who had no combat training. Again, reminiscent of his first Burma campaign, Stilwell, under stress, seemed to disengage himself from his military goal. In the following weeks, he pondered his personal situation and made journal notes of his dinner menu etc., "Played checkers with Joe,[3] (his son and G-2 Officer), went for a swim", etc. Few of his notes addressed tactics to resolve the stalemate at Myitkyina. His brief visits forward included newspaper correspondents who reported him as leading the fight. None of his appearances at the front coincided with any changes in the situation. It seems he was totally relying on help from his patron in Washington. Stilwell demanded more Chinese troops, and Marshall forced Chiang Kai-shek to send China defenders out to

---

2 Tuchman, *Stilwell and the American Experience in China, p.575*

3 Stilwell, *The Stilwell Papers, p.293*

Burma by threatening, and in one instance, executing a complete cutoff of the meager trickle of war supplies to China.

Many aspects of the campaign troubled Galahad's leader. Colonel Hunter carefully drafted a letter to Stilwell, submitted it and then revised it on recommendations of Stilwell's deputy commander. He then presented it to Stilwell, who folded it, placed it in his shirt pocket, and never replied. Hunter commented later ". . . but I was never to have a free and frank discussion with this man who, to me seemed unapproachable though he was publicized as a soldier's soldier and cultured gentleman, masquerading under an acidulous demeanor . . . although I was with him constantly for two days at one time. I never saw him talk man to man with an American soldier or make any attempt to familiarize himself with their problems, personal or otherwise...."[4] Colonel Hunter wrote ". . . what was not understood and has never been adequately explained, is why it (Galahad)was expended to bolster the ego of an erstwhile theater commander such as Vinegar Joe Stilwell."

During the campaign, news correspondents had Stilwell in the thick of the fighting on the front lines. His personal papers paint a different picture ". . . commanders are uneasy for fear I get hit and they be held responsible, insistent that I stay back and let them do it." Stilwell had arranged for his son to be assigned to his staff as G-2, Intelligence Officer and two sons-in-law to be assigned as a liaison between himself and his Chinese divisions. Their level of fluency with the Chinese language, if they possessed any, is not known. Their presence on Stilwell's staff constituted direct violations of a Marshall General Order.

---

4   Hunter, *Galahad*, p.130

In addition to command inadequacies, in the course of his campaign, "Vinegar Joe" tarnished his carefully cultivated public image as the soldier's general. The American Galahad troops were volunteers; many were veterans of South Pacific island campaigns. All were promised a ticket home if they completed four months of extreme duty in jungle warfare. The four months expired when they reached the airstrip and fighting in mountainous jungle terrain had taken a severe toll. In addition to combat wounds, they suffered fevers and dysentery. Many cut the seats out of their trousers in order to relieve themselves while firing their weapons. When, the campaign bogged down at Myitkyina village, Col. Hunter, and the regimental and battalion Surgeons recommended removal of the few survivors to a rear area. Stilwell, not only rejected evacuation of the Galahad survivors, he ordered his medical staff to return Galahad troops to combat using medications to keep down fevers. He then halted all evacuations until a special medical exam was conducted by doctors appointed by his staff. A fever of 103° was required for evacuation. It follows that seriously sick or wounded soldiers in the field suffered and perhaps died awaiting arrival of the special medical inspector from General Stilwell's headquarters. He later justified his not relieving the seriously ill and wounded Galahad survivors because he needed their jungle skills and relieving them would have set a bad example for his Chinese troops. But the jungle fighting phase of the campaign was finished. The objective was a fortified village. In regard to Chinese morale, Stilwell's Chinese troops had suffered approximately 20% casualties and Galahad sustained over 80% casualties at that point in the campaign. Despite previous PR stories of Vinegar Joe's close involvement in the "front lines action," when Galahad's pitiful story surfaced, Stilwell floated a story through his media supporters maintaining he was unaware of the Galahad medical restrictions. One report had him weeping when he discovered the situation. A different view of "Vinegar Joe the soldier's friend" came from one of his troopers, "I had him in my rifle sights. I coulda squeezed one off and no one woulda known it wasn't a Jap that got the son of a bitch."[5]

While General Stilwell forced his sick and wounded and un-trained construction people into battle, and used Marshall to strip defenders from China, the nearby British 36th Division, was trained, equipped and available, but Stilwell decided against using it.[6]

As 1944, the third year of America's war progressed, Stilwell continued to divert all Lend Lease weapons coming into China away from China defense forces and Marshall continued to force Chiang to send China defense troops out to Burma. The draw-down of China defenders for Stilwell's Burma campaign did not go unnoticed. The enemy saw the Chinese Army divisions remaining in China lacking weapons, short of ammunition and declining in morale. The Japanese amassed a force of 1,500,000 including 650,000 frontline troops for "Ichigo," possibly their largest offensive of WW2. Japanese Imperial General Headquarters listed the first objective of the offensive as "To forestall the bombing of the Japanese homeland by American B-29s . . . ." The B-29s were based in western China, controlled independently of Chennault's 14th Air Force. Contrary to Stilwell/Marshall assertions, destruction of Chennault's airfields was not cited as an Ichigo objective.

---

5 Prefer, *Vinegar Joe's War, p.152*

6 Ibid, *p.147*

The other Ichigo goal was "to destroy the backbone of the Chinese Army and force increased deterioration to the political regime at Chungking."[7]

Chiang's spy system quickly detected Japanese mobilization efforts. Chennault, had developed his own grassroots intelligence network years earlier, but Stilwell ordered him to rely entirely on G-2 reports from young Stilwell's G-2 office. Chennault warned Stilwell on April 6, 1944 and again on April 7 and April 8, of the Japanese offensive. He stated his Air Force could not repulse Japanese air groups supporting the impending offensive, without increased supplies. Meanwhile, the State Department Davies group, officially assigned to gain intelligence, reported nothing on Ichigo and the purported widespread, aggressive guerilla forces of Mao Tse-tung neither reported on nor disrupted Japanese rail or over-the-road troop movements. Several days after Chennault warned Stilwell of the all-out enemy offensive, on April 10, young Stilwell's G-2 report stated "Japanese do not have offensive capabilities in Yellow River area." Six days later, the Japanese poured three infantry divisions and a tank corps across the Yellow River. Despite increasing reports from China of Japanese troop movements, Stilwell, in Burma, nearly 1000 miles distant, again refused to divert any Hump tonnage to help. He'd diluted his G-2 intelligence capabilities when he brought in and classified the Davies group as intelligence operatives, and further weakened it by the appointment of his son as G-2 officer. Gathering information on Japanese movements was not a high priority for General Stilwell. His son's G-2 reports conveniently supported his contention that

---

7   Liu, *A military History of China, p.219*

the great Japanese Ichigo offensive was simply a food foraging expedition. Stilwell pointedly told Chennault not to send a gloomy intelligence report to Chiang.[8] A few days later, Chiang, with dire reports from behind Japanese lines, requested an appraisal of the air defense situation. Chennault pointed out his previous assurances that his Air Force could successfully defend East China, no longer applied because most of his aircraft had been drawn off for operations far distant.

When the Japanese launched major attacks to take the central China Railway, Chiang refused to send more troops out to Stilwell in Burma. In Washington, General George Marshall, seen as the ideal image of the disciplined military man, responded by usurping the powers of his President. Marshall cut off all China aid. Without FDR's approval, he ordered the complete shutdown of Lend-Lease shipments to an ally under heavy enemy attack. Official Army history declares Marshall was: "making a logical extension of the President's views...."[9] Although such a shutdown would not immediately affect the besieged Chinese defenders who'd received no U.S. weapons, it would completely shut down supplies for Chennault's 14thAir Force and seriously impair the limited air cover they were providing the beleaguered Chinese. It also cut off of raw materials to the relocated Chinese arsenals. If continued, it would stop the last trickle of ammunition to troops defending the Capital and the Kunming supply terminal. The assumption of Presidential authority by the protocol conscious General Marshall, indicates the extent FDR had shifted his attention to Europe and

---

8   Romanus, *Stilwell's Command Problems, p.314*

9   Ibid, *p.321*

the lengths Marshall would go to support his friend's activities in Asia.

Chennault's situation report to Chiang stressed that his 14th Air Force, formerly 500 aircraft, had been depleted by 200 taken to defend the B-29 base in Western China and Stilwell drew off another 150 to support his Burma campaign. The former Flying Tiger leader concluded his remaining 150 aircraft could not adequately support Chinese defenders without additional fuel and Stilwell would not allow more fuel.

Ignoring the immediate military emergency, Stilwell moved against Chennault, citing disobedience of his order to not give Chiang a pessimistic situation report. He requested the War Department immediately relieve the only American military leader successfully fighting the enemy in Asia. Fortunately, General Marshall was away from Washington and the Deputy Chief of Staff warned Stilwell he would be blamed for any defeat that followed. Stilwell quickly withdrew his request.

Based on Chennault's situation report, Chiang requested the loan of the 200 idle aircraft based at the B-29 airfield. Since The B-29 base was the prime objective of the Ichigo offensive, logic suggests fighting the Japanese before they closed on the base would be advantageous. Stilwell denied the request. Chiang also requested 500 gallons (less than two tons) of gasoline. When Stilwell refused, Chiang took the request to FDR. By that time, Roosevelt was completely focused the European Theater. He'd delegated complete authority over China-Burma to Marshall. FDR signed Marshall's letter of refusal thus denying an ally a perfectly logical request for an insignificant volume of war material.

As Ichigo threatened, the gap between Chiang and Stilwell widened further. Stilwell dropped all pretense of working with Chiang Kai-sheik. Ambassador Gauss notified Marshall that Stilwell, suddenly, on his own initiative, moved his headquarters to India. When Marshall took issue with Stilwell, nothing changed. The farce of Stilwell acting as Chief of Staff for the Chinese Army ended.

Three months after warnings of Ichigo from Chiang and Chennault and the Japanese assault across the Yellow River into East China, on June 8, Stilwell, in Burma, declared an emergency in China.

At that time of crisis, Communist Mao Tse-tung, confined to his small enclave at Yenan, saw an advantage. On the pretext of safeguarding the city of Sian, the Reds persuaded the nearby Government troop commander to lift the blockade. The Reds then attacked the Nationalists from the flank.[10] The timing suggests the Red attack was coordinated with the Japanese offensive, but solid evidence is lacking.

In the midst of the dilemma posed by the massive Ichigo offensive in China and increasing pressure from General Marshall to send troops to Burma, Chiang Kai-shek conceded to what he considered a less harmful proposal from Washington. He allowed the Davies group to insert representatives into Mao's Chinese Communist Headquarters in Yenan. Ultimately, this decision would prove far more damaging than Ichigo.

As the long summer progressed, U.S media reported desperate battles and brave Chinese defenders, but decision-makers

10   Crozier, *The Man Who Lost China, p.257*

in Washington seemed detached from the realities in China. In mid-July, Americans read of "tired, half starved, miserably equipped Chinese suddenly burst into attack upon the enemy from all sides . . ," stopping an attack by 100,000 Japanese. Unfortunately, another Japanese force was converging in a pincer movement. The enemy threw 40,000 fresh troops with artillery and tanks against Hengyang and the threadbare Chinese troops resisted fiercely. Chennault repeatedly requested supplies and ammunition for air drop to the defenders and was denied.

The overall picture was beyond ridiculous. The Ally facing the major portion of enemy's army was engaged in a life or death struggle. Survival depended on the decisions of Joseph Stilwell located 1000 miles away. A strange preoccupied personality who'd refused to gain first hand knowledge of the crises and had moved his HQ out of the country he was assigned to defend.

Chennault's emergency requests met with successive refusals from Stilwell's office. The responses exposed a strange mindset:

-"It would set a precedent . . ."

-"He (Stilwell) is working on a proposition that will give this spot a real face losing and is loath to commit himself . . ."

Finally, as the defenders ran out of ammunition and died, Stilwell's office made the astounding reply- "In view of . . . Chinese misuse of equipment they have and improper employment of their forces . . . small arms and ammunition would be a waste of effort. . ." Stilwell's "proposition" was an upcoming move to take over China's armies. The lives of the Hengyang defenders were irrelevant.

By early September, the Japanese offensive threatened both China's capital and its sole supply depot. Kunming was the receiving point for Hump cargos and also the terminus of the new supply road to China. On September 17, six months after the Japanese crossed the Yellow River and launched operation Ichigo, Stilwell authorized his first air drop to Chinese defenders of Kweilin. It was based on glaring Intel errors. Engineers were demolishing the Kweilin base before the advancing Japanese.

Despite his belated recognition of the crisis in China, Stilwell again contacted Marshall to pressure Chiang to give up more troops for Burma. He told Marshall "Chiang is a crazy little bastard" for refusing him more troops. Marshall did not question the logic of risking loss of the supply terminal in order to acquire ground for a future road to that terminal. Although China's crisis was public knowledge in the U.S., Marshall continued to press Chiang Kai-shek to send troops out of China to Burma, while China faced the heaviest enemy assault of the war.

Marshall composed letters over FDR's signature and used words that were beyond his level of authority. He warned Chiang Kai-shek he would face "the consequences" if he did not provide manpower for northern Burma.[11] Chiang cared nothing for Marshall's consequences but Stilwell held the trump card, control of aircraft fuel. Chiang saw his besieged troops in desperate straits if Chennault's Air Force was grounded by lack of fuel. He had no alternative but to comply and further deplete his China defense forces.

---

11 Liang, *General Stilwell in China, p.254*

On the ground, the Ichigo offensive churned forward. When Chennault urgently requested Stilwell to increase supplies to defend East China and his remaining 14th Air Force bases, Stilwell's motives emerged. A year earlier at the Trident meeting with FDR, he and Marshall had predicted an air offensive would arouse the Japanese to retaliate against the 14th Air Force bases. As Ichigo advanced, Stilwell discarded his previous claim that Ichigo was a food foraging expedition and presented it as a punitive attack in response to Trident. The aberrant Stilwell, next, refused to allow Chennault to divert his U.S. Air Force portion of Hump tonnage to supply the beleaguered defenders. To Stilwell's thinking, Chennault was "trying to prepare an out for himself by claiming that with a little more, which we won't give them, he can still do it"[12] Stilwell's top priority was exposing what he perceived to be the Trident error in a meeting long forgotten by all others. In Stilwell's thinking, Chennault was trying to "duck the consequences of having sold the wrong bill of goods."

When Chiang further pressured Stilwell to release supplies to his beleaguered troops, Stilwell kicked it upstairs to Marshall who once again supported his friend. The tragic irony of this situation was that while the U.S. military denied supplies to Chinese troops fighting and dying, The State Department trumpeted the claims of Nationalist Chinese not fighting. Meanwhile, the Davies "intelligence" group in Yenan recommended aiding Mao's Communists, who, at that time, enjoyed an informal truce with the Japanese.[13]

---

12   Utley, *Last Chance in China*, p.58

13   Liang, *General Stilwell in China*, p.354

When Stilwell finally recognized Ichigo as a major offensive, he declared Chiang should use the Chinese Communists. Based on limited conversations with Red military leader, Chu Teh (Zhu De), Stilwell believed the Red Army numbered 500,000 armed, organized, experienced troops. During his tours in China, he'd not seen, much less inspected any substantial units of the Red Army. A more realistic figure emerges from Mao Tse-tung's statements. The Red Army, in 1944, consisted of something less than 18 divisions of troops. A force of possibly 200,000, who were, according to Mao's internal directives, responsible for planting, cultivating and harvesting their own food supply.[14] Mao's Red "Army" was essentially an impoverished militia. They lacked weapons and ammunition, they lacked recent combat experience against the Japanese and they were dispersed throughout the rural areas of Japanese occupied North China indoctrinating the peasantry and raising crops for their own survival. A Russian survey of Red Chinese forces found "no one engaged in combat training. ---Meetings are the only form of work carried on in the Army units. In the summer this is supplemented --- with the laying in of farm produce ---." "In the staff of the front line division, men killed time by playing cards and gossiping. Russian liaison Vladimirov found "the years of inactivity have had a degrading influence on the Armed Forces (of Mao's CPC). Discipline is slack and cases of desertion have become more frequent. The men neglect their weapons. Training in the units and staffs is not organized...."[15] From a military standpoint, Stilwell's Intel on Mao's forces was a par with his assumptions on Ichigo and his pre war reports on

14   Mao Tse-tung, *Selected Works of Mao Tse-tung, Vol. 3*, p. 19,192

15   Vladimirov, *China's Special Area*, p.35,58

Japanese Army capabilities. He was totally ignorant of the status of the forces he conveniently proposed for combat. Similar to the "lifeline to China," ploy that allowed Stilwell to pursue his Burma campaign, his proposed use of Red troops, was either a feeble effort to mask his failure to plan Chinese Army operations or a direct attempt to aid the overthrow of China's government.

The dual role of Mao's militia seemingly also escaped the eyes of the State Department "intelligence operatives" then residing in the Red enclave. If the Davies group knew of the Red militia's agricultural responsibilities they did not report it. Meanwhile, Marshall in Washington, had access to Navy and OSS intelligence reports that conflicted with the Stilwell/Davie reports. If he realized the Red troops Stilwell proposed for use against the Japanese were part time soldiers, he didn't act on that information. Marshall bought Stilwell's version of China and conveyed it to the President.

In the Burma Theater, in addition to gross tactical errors, there's no evidence of military leadership or basic management techniques being applied by Marshall. His communications to the subordinate, who ignored his direct orders and violated his published policies, were abjectly apologetic. On July 1, while Stilwell, in Burma, swam and played checkers with son Joe, a fawning Marshall apologized that the situation in China made it necessary "for me to trouble you in the midst of your terrific struggles with the jungle, Japanese, logistics and scrub typhus complications which beset you to a degree I do not believe any commander of modern time has experienced." By the end of that month, Stilwell accepted an invitation to sit in for Mountbatten who was called away from his Ceylon Headquarters. Until then, Stilwell had resisted requests from Chiang for his presence in Chungking, claiming he was tied down by his responsibilities in Burma. He found time for Ceylon. While his Burma troops continued to struggle to capture the village of Myitkyina and the Japanese Ichigo offensive in China threatened to take China out of the war, Stilwell flew off and enjoyed and recorded the delights of Ceylon for three weeks.[16] He found Ceylon "a paradise."

When Myitkyina finally fell on August 4, 1944, the initial, 3000 strong Galahad force was down 130 men. For the survivors, their promised tour of duty had been nearly doubled by General Stilwell, then enjoying plush accommodations in Ceylon. Stilwell noted in his diary "Boy will this burn up the limey's." It was sadly ironic that, after his many claims that China was waiting for Americans to win the war, Stilwell pushed his Americans past human limits. The two and one half Chinese divisions and 3000 Americans Stilwell commanded at the start of his Burma campaign was by far the smallest combat command ever led by a four star General of the U.S. Army. The 3000 man Galahad force represented Stilwell's only combat command of American troops during his entire career.

The town fell, two and one half months after the airstrip was taken. The defeat of possibly 5000 Japanese troops was presented to the public as a major victory with Stilwell as its heroic leader. When the village was finally captured, although the war in Burma was far from over, Vinegar Joe Stilwell reacted quickly to his sudden fame by moving to take over China's Army and the War in China. A war he had, until then, so

---

16   Stilwell, *The Stilwell Papers*, p.309-314

carefully avoided. If successful, his coup would catapult the former staff Colonel on the verge of forced retirement, from six months of "hands off" experience in Burma, to command of 325 divisions in China. Marshall went all out in support of Stilwell's quest for power. Both used ruthless deprivation of promised supplies to force Chiang's hand. Similar to Galahad at Myitkyina, lives on the battlefield were expendable.

With Myitkyina taken, military and road construction operations resumed and a decision was made that removed any possibility of a viable "lifeline to China." That decision negated all the U.S. efforts in Burma and all justification for withdrawing troops and resources from the defense of China. The road was narrowed to a single lane. In simple theory, it was a capacity reduction of 50%. In reality, the single lane, 1000 miles of it, had to be entirely cleared of one-way traffic before the return flow could begin. In ideal weather conditions, the road could possibly have been of some minor use. But as knowledgeable locals and engineers predicted, weather conditions were extreme. One summer rain deluge totaling 17 inches in two days washed out 300 River crossings and culverts. It loosened boulders weighing as much as six tons and sent them crashing on the road.[17] The two-year American ground war in Asia produced a supply road that would be declared useless soon after it opened. Meanwhile, although it was rendered useless by reduction to a single lane, construction continued and Marshall continued to pressure Chiang to draw more troops from the defense of China.

---

17   Sinclair, *Confusion beyond Imagination*, p.243

Official Army history later stated the town was taken "to make possible an intensified air effort . . ." The great supply road, "the lifeline to China" the sole justification for Stilwell's two-year adventure and America's total focus on Burma simply disappeared.

12

A New Face

"THIS JOB THAT I've got in mind, Pat, isn't one that just anyone can do. What we need is an adventurer, a man who loves to take chances. We're looking for a man with a little piracy in his blood."

"Mr. President,. . . why didn't you say so in the first place? Of course, I'll take the job. . . . You know Mr. President, while I will serve you loyally as a soldier; I'm against everything you stand for politically."

"I know, Pat, but right now I need a pirate."

"I thought you had them all in the in the New Deal," said Patrick Hurley, trouble shooter extraordinaire.

"All but one," Roosevelt answered.[1]

As the China-Burma situation worsened, FDR realized it was time to act. He turned to Patrick J. Hurley. Hurley was an American

---

1   Lohbeck, *Patrick J Hurley*, p.155

original. Born into poverty, he worked as a child coal miner and as a teenage cowpuncher. He grew up on Native American lands in Oklahoma, attended their schools and later defended their rights in court. Apparently, none of the reputed taciturnity of the Native Americans rubbed off on Hurley. He was a talker. FDR once remarked, "Pat Hurley was the only man he knew who could make Winston Churchill stop talking and start listening." Hurley was FDR's point man, useful when bad news had to be conveyed to Churchill or Stalin or when a dangerous mission needed close supervision. After one face-to-face with Stalin, the dictator, looking at Hurley, reportedly conceded "you're one tough baby." Newspapers presented Hurley as a rough and ready tough hombre. One reported, Hurley as a young boy had "killed a fractious mule by bashing its head in with a two by four." Hurley retorted "It is absolutely false to say that I ever killed a mule . . . I have never killed a mule. I have not even killed a career diplomat." At times, his attempt at humor got the best of him. After his first meeting with the Communist Chinese he opined ". . . the only difference between a Chinese Communist and an Oklahoma Republican is that the Oklahoma Republicans are not armed." His friend humorist Will Rogers advised him "Pat, you stop telling jokes. Let me tell the jokes, that's what I get paid for."

Hurley served in France in World War One and received a Silver Star for gallantry in action on November 11, 1918. On his return, he courted and married an admiral's daughter in Washington and returned to Tulsa, Oklahoma to begin a law practice. When he arrived, postwar Tulsa was descending into black-white confrontations. Violence reached a point where the locals requested the governor establish martial law and send in National Guard troops. While the governor deliberated, city leaders approached Hurley and asked him to take command of the situation.

He accepted and against the advice of the town officials, he walked into the barricaded black district alone, promised the rebels no further violence and persuaded them to surrender their weapons. By the time the National Guard arrived, the riot was over. When Hurley was acclaimed in the media, Republican leaders sounded him out for Congressional and Governorship candidacy. He refused saying he would not enter politics until he had sufficient resources for financial independence.[2]

Pat Hurley first met future President Herbert Hoover, in Belgium, during World War One. After Hoover's election to the Presidency, he summoned Hurley to the White House and offered him his choice of several governmental positions. Hurley selected Assistant Secretary of War. Beyond the borders of Oklahoma, politicians responded "Hurley from Oklahoma, who's he?" The void was soon filled by exaggerated episodes drawn from his colorful past. He seldom denied or corrected these stories. Before the year was out, Secretary of War James W. Good died and Congress unanimously approved Hurley to fill the post. Pat Hurley, 46 years old, was the first cabinet officer from the state of Oklahoma and the only Secretary of War to have served in the army with the rank of Private.

His first WW2 assignment from FDR was: smuggle supplies to MacArthur's beleaguered American and native troops in the Philippines. The U.S. Navy, crippled at Pearl Harbor, could not

---

2 Lohbeck, *Patrick J Hurley*, p. 79

penetrate the Japanese blockade. Several submarine runs and aircraft flights delivered a trickle of supplies, but cargo ships were needed to deliver meaningful volume.

Hurley organized a fleet of twelve cargo ships in the South Pacific and succeeded in getting three ships through the blockade. His blockade runners furnished the only meaningful aid the troops received before they fell in the worst U.S. defeat of World War Two. During his adventures in the South Pacific, Hurley was slightly wounded and on another occasion he flew the Japanese flag from one of his ships, confirming his credentials as a bona fide pirate.

Most of Hurley's assignments were in the diplomatic field where FDR bypassed his State Department and relied on selected individuals to carry out his personal diplomacy. When other Americans thought it improper to cite America's enormous Lend Lease program supporting Britain and Russia throughout WW2, Hurley would remind a Churchill or Stalin that America was supplying them with huge amounts of arms and equipment and he seemed to gain their respect by saying it. He reportedly hit it off with Stalin to the extent that he was the only American, perhaps the only foreigner, permitted to visit Red Army battlegrounds and other Soviet restricted areas.

On his 1944 China mission, Hurley was officially directed by FDR to "promote efficient and harmonious relations between Chiang Kai-shek and General Stilwell and to facilitate General Stilwell's exercise of command over the Chinese armies placed under his direction. Secondly, FDR, influenced by claims that Mao Tse-tung's militia was a formidable fighting force, directed Hurley to bring the Reds into the fight against Japan.

Hurley arrived in China in early September 1944, after a meeting with Soviet Foreign Minister Molotov in Moscow. Molotov had assured him the Soviets were not connected with the Chinese Communist Party. He told Hurley the Chinese Communists Were "radishes," red on the outside but white inside. With Molotov's assurances in mind, Hurley was optimistic about gaining an agreement between the Nationalist government and the Communists.[3]

His first meeting with Chiang Kai-shek introduced him to the ongoing controversy. Chiang related that the U.S. State Department and Stilwell were working against China's government and attempting to force him into an agreement with Mao's Reds. Stilwell, who'd disobeyed direct orders from Washington and ignored China's military problems for nearly two and one half years, believed "The cure for China's troubles is the elimination of Chiang Kai-shek."[4] Stilwell wanted complete control of China's Army and evidence suggests he drew down China defenses to weaken the Nationalist position to the point where he would be accepted and given the authority he desired. Stilwell's most extreme derangement had occurred when he'd ordered his staff to develop plans to assassinate Chiang. According to one plan, (he had several) Chiang's pilot, during a flight over the Hump would declare an emergency and all passengers would be forced to bail out. Chiang and Mme. Chiang would be given faulty parachutes. After FDR's death, Stilwell claimed the President authorized the plot at Cairo, but he'd worked on several assassination plots well before his Cairo meeting with FDR.

---

3   Wedemeyer, *Wedemeyer Reports, p. 309*

4   Stilwell, *The Stilwell Papers, p.321*

On September 16th 1944, Stilwell made his move to gain power. He sent a note to the Chinese Foreign Minister stating the Generalissimo must appoint him to command all of the Chinese forces, or he would recommend that the United States withdraw from China and set up its Asia base in the territory of the Soviet Union. At that time, the U.S. high command consisted of President Roosevelt focused on the dramatically changing European situation with General Eisenhower making the key decisions on the ground in Europe and General MacArthur and Admiral Nimitz running the Pacific war. Marshall had peripheral involvement in Europe and the Pacific, but in the China-Burma Theater he reigned supreme.

On September 18th, Marshall sent, over FDR's signature, an aggressively worded letter to Chiang Kai-shek. It warned Chiang, failure to send China defenders off to Stilwell in Burma would have dire consequences on the new supply road to China. It remonstrated with Chiang for resisting previous Marshall pressure to send China defenders to Burma. It seems implausible that Marshall, the strategist would pressure Chiang to send troops away from the big fight in China in order to prepare a situation where Stilwell could ride to the rescue. But no other explanations have surfaced for Marshall's continued illogical demands that Chiang must stop impending disaster in China by sending more troops out of China to Stilwell in Burma. Salvation would only be realized if Chiang placed "General Stilwell in unrestricted command of all your forces."

Chiang Kai-shek, once again cautious under threat of a supply embargo, didn't reject the proposal until "Vinegar Joe" overreached. Stilwell demanded full authority to use the Chinese Communist forces and refused an order from Chiang to pull in

Chinese troops from Yunnan to help stop the Ichigo offensive. Chiang Kai-shek had enough.

At 5 PM on September 24, Chiang Kai-shek called in Patrick Hurley and told him Stilwell must go and if necessary China would fight alone against Japan. At that point, an abashed Stilwell offered to drop the use of Communist troops and pledged to bring back troops from Burma as soon as possible. Chiang's patience was finally exhausted. He formally requested Stilwell be recalled. He provided a clear picture of the Stilwell-China-Burma situation and the strategy as he saw it, (he was not yet aware of the one lane lifeline.) He pointed out the misconceptions then entertained in Washington. He again questioned the concept of building a tenuous mountain supply road within easy reach of enemy forces in Burma. He'd predicted Stilwell would require additional forces, forces that could only be drained from Chinese armies protecting China. He pointed out the Japanese Ichigo offensive forces in China were vastly greater than the Japanese forces stationed throughout Burma and the consequences of defeat in China far outweighed any potential negative results in Burma. He pointed out Stilwell's failure to supply weapons and ammunition to Chinese armies fighting in China and the complete focus on Burma that resulted in victory at a village in North Burma and the loss of East China. The letter was bitter medicine for Marshall who thought he was successfully "managing" Chiang Kai-shek and expected continued compliance from him.

Hurley, on the scene, had come to believe Stilwell had no intention of cooperating with Chiang Kai-shek that his goal was to defeat him. He reported "Stilwell's fundamental mistake is the idea that he can subjugate a man who has led a nation in revolution and led an ill-fed, poorly-equipped practically unorganized army against an overwhelming foe for seven years."[5] On October 12 Hurley formally recommended Stilwell's recall and the long controversy was brought to an end.

Hurley prepared his letter of recommendation and in forthright style discussed it with Stilwell who thought the whole issue would blow over. Vinegar Joe, insulated from accountability by his patron, seemed to believe he was untouchable. Hurley reported to FDR ". . . Gen. Stilwell is not only in controversy with the Generalissimo. He is having difficulty with certain elements of his own command, and he is having other difficulties of an international nature . . . I respectfully recommend that you relieve Gen. Stilwell and appoint another American general to command all the land and air forces in China under the Generalissimo." FDR, realizing Chiang would not tolerate Stilwell any further, ordered Marshall to remove him without further delay.

When Marshall's strenuous objections to the recall failed, he switched to a radically different approach. He suddenly pushed for Stilwell's retention, but confined to Burma, a sector that was then being relegated to backwater status, a huge step down from his recent efforts to raise Vinegar Joe to command of all China's forces. A most peculiar situation had arisen. This was the period when the "Lifeline to China" was effectively killed by the narrowing of the roadway to one lane. But that demise was kept under wraps. Marshall's peculiar last-ditch efforts to keep full General Stilwell, then equal in rank to Eisenhower and MacArthur, in the backwoods of Burma correlated with

---

5   Romanus, *Stilwell's Command Problems*, p.270

the need to keep the lid on the Lifeline fiasco. With Stilwell retained in Burma, the foolish project could be covered-up until another crisis replaced it.

Suddenly, all mention of the all-important "Life line to China" disappeared from Marshall's letters to Chiang Kai-shek. His letter to Chiang on October 6,[6] (before Stilwell's recall was finalized), cited the tremendous value of the new supply road. Thirteen days later, when it was obvious Stilwell would not retain any authority in Burma, Marshall's. October 19 mail to Chiang omitted all mention of a new supply road. The "Lifeline to China" simply disappeared. Suddenly, the goal of America's sole military campaign and massive construction project in Asia was described as vital pipelines and a "low level flying route," Previously not worthy of mention, these suddenly appeared as the primary goals of Vinegar Joe's Burma campaign. The British stationed in Burma, christened Stilwell's lifeline to China "The White Elephant Road."[7]

In regard to the aborted "Lifeline to China", key questions were never asked. Who decided the road should be narrowed? Who ignored the impact on its capacity and pushed on with construction? More to the point, did Marshall know of the road capacity debacle and continue to deplete troops defending China for a useless project in Burma? Marshall's increasingly forceful letters to Chiang, over FDR's signature, his repeated references to the "lifeline to China," after it was narrowed to one lane, seem to indicate

---

6   Liang, *General Stilwell in China, p.264*

7   Sinclair, *Confusion Beyond Imagination, p.307*

an inordinate level of either ignorance or deception relative to the Burma situation.

Chinese casualties caused by the draw down of troops and supplies for Stilwell's Life line adventure were estimated at somewhere near a million. If the fiasco of the "lifeline to China" was publicized, the U.S. Army power structure would be shaken and Marshall's already eroding prestige could suffer fatal damage. His standing with Roosevelt was already in decline as reports from the front lines revealed the shortcomings of U. S. Army weapons and replacement systems. Damage control was needed. The War Department radioed CBI Theater HQ "The Stilwell Road must be presented as a success." One way convoys, (trucks would be abandoned in Kunming) were organized. To inflate tonnage figures, the weight of the trucks, trailers and personnel was added to lading reports. The Army created a motion picture acclaiming the road a great achievement and Kunming was left jammed with rusting trucks with empty fuel tanks. Tonnage on the "Lifeline to China" totaled 200,000 short tons, most of it dropped off in Burma for road maintenance. The one way stream of trucks that flowed into Kunming left 26,000 trucks abandoned in China while Eisenhower was deprived of adequate trucking in Europe. One month after the sham of activity, the Ledo Road, renamed the "Stilwell Road" was declared "logistically worthless."[8] In the welter of war reports from over the world, the U.S. Army public relations campaign effectively concealed information of Stilwell's second Burma debacle from the public. Today, any

---

8   Chennault, *Way of a Fighter, p.273*

Americans able to conjure up an image of the Burma Road retain a concept of a bountiful supply road to China. Although
FDR had become aware as the Stilwell situation unraveled and
Marshall's star was waning, it was not extinguished. Chiang
Kai-shek and Chennault knew the full extent of Marshall's involvement in the massive farce, knowledge that would, in the
future, prove costly for both.

Chiang continued to plead for increased airlift tonnage over
the Hump and after many empty promises, additional aircraft
were added and Hump supplies reached and then exceeded the
design capacity of the failed Stilwell Road.

Vinegar Joe Stilwell, a full General of the United States Army
and Chief of Staff of the Chinese Army repeatedly ignored direct
orders. He avoided planning or executing a single military operation against the million plus Japanese troops on Chinese soil.
He pursued a small, inconsequential military sideshow against a
fraction of the Japanese forces on the Asian mainland for two and
half years and constructed a useless supply road. Other than his
two Burma fiascos, the efforts of the Commander of U.S. forces
and Chief of Staff to the Chinese Army were subversive in nature.
His efforts to undermine Chiang Kai-shek did irreparable harm
to the government he was assigned to help. All evidence indicates
Marshall knowingly allowed Stilwell's malice, neglect and malfea-
sance. There is evidence of cover up of Stilwell's venomous behavior and his blind commitment to an unjustified military campaign
that consumed most of the aid intended for China. Stilwell's overall
commitment to advance the U.S. war effort in China can be gauged

from the contents of his diary where the Japanese enemy appears as a subject of minor interest.

While Stilwell displayed only malice toward Chiang Kai-shek, he strongly favored the Chinese Communists. In his final maneuver, he apparently saw no inconsistency in proposing to provide arms to Communist divisions,[9] while he deprived Government divisions of U.S. weapons. Stilwell's ignorance of CCP military strength and his apparent lack of awareness of the Ledo-Stilwell Road construction situation were simply two more in a string of situations not worthy of full commitment from Vinegar Joe Stilwell, serious blunders that, until Hurley appeared, did no harm to Stilwell's career.

Towards the end of his China tour, Stilwell remained unavailable when Chiang Kai-shek needed a Chief of Staff but found time for other activities including sightseeing and visits to the Russian Embassy, where he viewed their propaganda films and was impressed. Always upwardly conscious, he sent a letter personally congratulating Stalin and was pleased to receive a reply.

Hurley, subsequently declared "the record of General Stilwell in China is irrevocably coupled in history with the conspiracy to overthrow the Nationalist government of China, and to set up in it's place a Communist regime . . . and all of this movement was a part of and cannot be separated from, the Communist cell apparatus that existed at that time in the government in Washington."

Stilwell was ordered to leave China in 48 hours. He left in 26 hours, taking time for a leisurely meeting with reporters and

---

9 Liang, *General Stilwell in China*, p.257

a letter to Communist Chinese Army Chief, Chu Teh. He wrote to none of the Chinese generals who fought for him in Burma and left no information for the incoming American Commander.

In Washington, misinformation generated by the Stilwell/Davies group had reached a ready audience and Stilwell was pictured as a victim. Secretary of War Stimson viewed "the evil result," catastrophic as he phrased it, "that will come from Stilwell's recall." Contrary to prevailing Washington opinion, Stilwell's replacement would be a breath of fresh air.

For General Marshall, his unfailing support of Stilwell's performance in China Burma was costly. His standing in FDR's inner circle was gradually eroded by negative reports from the front lines on his early weapons and replacement decisions and indecisions. He was, passed over in favor of Eisenhower for command of the European, campaign and was further damaged as the "Lifeline to China" fiasco leaked out. His dedication to Stilwell remains a mystery. It was not the result of a friendship developed from long personal contact. It could not have been confidence in Stilwell's military abilities or dedication to duty. Marshall would soon develop another peculiar relationship with even more ominous results.

Unfortunately for the recalled Stilwell, Marshall no longer had the power to impose his friend on either Generals Eisenhower or MacArthur. Chief of Staff Marshall no longer had any real authority over War Theater Commanders. He'd been bypassed by Eisenhower, Wedemeyer was appointed over his objections and the third theater commander, MacArthur occupied a pedestal, above all Army authority.

Vinegar Joe was suddenly adrift. He related "Marshall had nothing to offer except that I could go and make my own arrangements." He toured the Pacific Islands and met with General MacArthur. Stilwell claimed he was offered the position of Chief of Staff and declined it "Told him no, I fancied myself a field commander." Apparently, others didn't see him in that light. Patton died in Germany, other command positions opened, changes were made throughout the Army. As the war moved toward conclusion, Stilwell whiled away eight months with no responsibilities. At the end of the Okinawa campaign, a few weeks before Japans surrendered ending WW2, he was appointed commander of the 10th Army and attended the surrender ceremonies.

In 1946, on Stilwell's death, the official publication of the U.S. Communist Party, the Daily Worker, published a letter written in Stilwell's hand "Isn't Manchuria a spectacle? . . . It makes me itch to throw down my shovel and get over there and shoulder a rifle with Chu Teh" (CCP Army Commander).[10] Whatever his motives and lack of commitment to his country's interests, Stilwell had set the critical wedge in China –America relations for others to exploit.

While C.O.S. Marshall gave General Stilwell complete support through his intrigues and escapades in China-Burma, it's significant that throughout Stilwell's career, spanning two World Wars, Joseph Stilwell was never assigned to command regular army troops in combat. During "fighting Joe's" long career, his only command of Americans in combat consisted of the 3000 Galahad volunteers in Burma.

---

10   Liang, *General Stilwell in China*, p.277

The connection between the seemingly correct, rank conscious Marshall and the caustic, abusive, insubordinate Stilwell is difficult to define. They shared one career trait; both backgrounds consisted of staff rather than line experience. They may have shared one behavioral trait. Marshall "preferred to manage rather than alienate." He used clever, circumspect methods rather than face-to-face confrontation. Stilwell, in stressful situations in Burma, seemed to have great difficulty in face to face confrontations with Chinese and American subordinates. The remote posture of one and the caustic demeanor of the other may have masked a common weakness. Both seemed to lack the force of personality needed to ensure their orders were accepted and executed by subordinates. Records also indicate that both were adept at ingratiating themselves with superiors. The insightful number two Red, Chou En-Lai who'd dealt with both, remarked later that Marshall reminded him of Stilwell.

The net effect of the Stilwell-Marshall impact in China was decidedly negative and evidenced a lack of positive commitment to America's interests. The ally fighting the bulk of the Japanese Army was disarmed in war time rather than aided with promised arm and ammunition. During Stilwell's tour, over the course of two and half years of war, the Chinese Army operating in China received 60 cannons, 50 antitank rifles and 30 million rounds of rifle ammunition[11]. The long term effect of Stilwell's propaganda program set the stage for the execution of Moscow's plans for China.

---

11   Taylor, *The Generalissimo, p.271*

Fallout from Stilwell's demise included a great injustice. As Vinegar Joe's fortunes faded, he exercised his penchant for shifting blame to others. Chennault was the prime target. Marshall, unable to help his friend, used his diminished influence to get Chennault. He'd previously admitted Chenault's excellent performance, but once the skies over China were swept clean of Japanese aircraft, Marshall intrigued a rearrangement of CBI air forces. Chennault's veteran squadrons were transferred to a favored "desk" commander. When the Theater Commander examined the plan he found it would result in a 50% reduction in combat capability and reported to Washington it was "impossible to adopt such a plan."[12] He was ordered to carry out the plan "regardless of the consequences." The leader who best represented America in China was banished from that theatre of operations.

Claire Chennault, who exceeded all expectations in combat, who's performance inspired America's ally and did significant damage to the enemy was missing from the final victory ceremony. But the "small fry colonel," who set forces in motion that seriously damaged our ally, attended the formal surrender in Tokyo Bay.

The compromises Marshall made in Stilwell's favor seemed totally out of character when compared to his early reputation and his early image as a "by the book" commander. Stilwell made no attempt to perform his primary assignment in China and his superior did not require it. An extremely unusual, if not unique, situation in military history. That Marshall failure, combined with his failures in weapons development, training and logistics strongly

---

12   Chennault, *Way of a Fighter*, p.348-350

suggests a Marshall lack of commitment to U.S. war strategy. Marshall's future efforts in the affairs of China and Korea would display a higher level of involvement and raise many more questions but also provide answers.

With the Stilwell controversy finally resolved, several replacements for Stilwell were offered to Chiang Kai-shek, over Marshall's objections. Chiang selected Lieutenant General Albert C. Wedemeyer, at that time Chief of Staff for the Southeast Asia command.

Wedemeyer took over on October 27, 1944. He differed from many nonmilitary Americans, particularly those in the State Department in that his views were strictly pro-U.S. and they extended to the post war situation. He saw Americans fighting the war similar to a football game where the winner celebrated and went home and contrasted that with America's allies who used wartime strategies to achieve postwar goals. As a result, some who he dealt with in the European theater considered him anti-British at a time when many tended to make blanket concessions to Churchill's views. Others considered him anti-Soviet, a very unpopular attitude in Washington at that time. His move to Chief of Staff Southeast Asia had put him directly under British Lord Mountbatten, where he resolved any suspicions of anti-British attitude.

While in India, Wedemeyer had looked into the lifeline to China supply road and traveled down the road as far as Stilwell's field headquarters. Among other negatives, he saw the risk of devastating landslides. His objections to the construction of the road and the associated North Burma offensive reached FDR's office, but nothing changed. The North Burma campaign remained the only U.S. strategy on the Asian mainland until he replaced Stilwell.

Wedemeyer's orders to duty in China included one new provision. He was directed to support the Chinese in the conduct of military operations against the Japanese but not against "civil strife." The Stilwell- Davies propaganda barrage was bearing fruit. War strategy was modified to benefit an insurrection in China.

Enroute to China, the new Commander stopped in India to meet with Stilwell's former second-in-command, General Dan Sultan. Sultan had nothing to offer in the way of plans. Stilwell, he stated, had been secretive about his tactical plans. On his arrival at U.S. Chungking headquarters, Wedemeyer found no trace of information or plans to stop the critical threat posed by the Ichigo offensive. He thought the officer in charge was joking when he said he was not familiar with operational plans because "the old man had carried such information in his hip pocket."[13] Stilwell, after lengthy meetings with reporters, had simply abandoned the scene without bothering to leave even a memo for his successor.

Wedemeyer soon found his view of China and Chiang Kai-shek contrasted sharply with the picture Stilwell had created and communicated to Washington. He recalled his first meeting with Chiang Kai-sheik, ". . . I went there prepared not to like him from things I had heard . . ." After Wedemeyer sorted things out, he found that cultural differences diminished Chiang's influence with Americans. Some Americans had taken to blaming Chiang Kai-shek for the pitiful conditions created by seven years of Japanese style total warfare. Wedemeyer cited ". . . Chiang's old world,

---

13   Wedemeyer, *Wedemeyer Reports, p.294*

behind the scenes, diplomacy which took very little or no account of democratic means to influence public opinion. His reasonable attitude, of course, got him nowhere in a world where public relations, propaganda, or blackmail was the means adopted by other nations to secure maximum American aid." He'd previously compared China to India and found stark contrasts. "Amid the squalor and deprivation was the smiling good nature of the Chinese, particular the children. Ding hao they would shout with the thumbs up. This was such a contrast to what I had experienced in India, where everyone looked at the white man through eyes of burning hatred." He saw the many areas demolished by bombing. "The Japanese would come up the Yangtze River . . . drop their bombs just about sundown and fly back. The Chinese had no heavy anti-aircraft guns, only .30 caliber machineguns, scattered around the perimeter of the city. The early warning system consisted of fires that would be lighted from hilltop, much as in the days of cavemen or the early Indians in America."

As 1944 ended, Hump flights were disgorging increasing volumes of arms and supplies in China. The war in Europe was winding down, and American war production reached amazing levels. Supplies were becoming abundant, and planes were available to fly more tonnage over the Hump. However, the Japanese Ichigo offensive threatened Kunming, the sole supply terminal for air and ground shipments. Unless Ichigo was stopped, none of the suddenly available supplies would reach China's frontlines. Wedemeyer also faced supply bottlenecks on the ground. The exclusive concentration on Burma ignored the primitive road system in China.

From the Kunming supply depot out to combat areas, drastic road improvements were needed.

One week after Wedemeyer arrived in Chungking the Japanese Ichigo offensive surged forward threatening the capital. Chiang scraped together local remnants and brought in army units from distant areas. Most were under strength, ill fed, ill-equipped and dispirited. After seven years of warfare, Chiang Kai-shek was reaching the bottom of the barrel. But some fought bravely. At Henyang, an important rail center, 16,275 Chinese defenders aided by Chennault's 14th Air force fought off six Japanese divisions (60,000 troops) for 47 days.

Where Stilwell considered the Japanese Ichigo offensive as vindication of his earlier prediction and refused aid to China's defense efforts, Wedemeyer, acted as an ally. As Japanese pressure increased, Wedemeyer began to realize the futility of the entire Burma campaign. He brought in two divisions from Burma and convinced Chiang to release two divisions then blockading the Chinese Communists. He removed restrictions on Chennault's air operations and flew in 23,000 reinforcements from the northwest and ordered an attack in the north to tie down Japanese troops in that area. The Wedemeyer-Chiang Kai-shek cooperative effort stalled the Japanese drive.

The new Chief of Staff then shifted incoming supplies to equip China defense forces for an offensive against the Japanese. Within a few months of his arrival, reports from all sources agreed Chinese armies were better organized, more sensibly located and the command at both staff and field was much improved. A system of supply in charge of an American General was beginning to work.

Wedemeyer later wrote "as the weeks passed I began to understand that the Nationalist government of China, far from being reluctant to fight as pictured by Stilwell and some of his friends among the American correspondents, had shown amazing tenacity and endurance in resisting Japan. He said "As I learned more about the situation, I realized that it was part of China's tragedy that we Americans, for the most part, had been indifferent to her self sacrificial efforts to stop Japan before 1941. Pearl Harbor alerted the Americans to the real situation. But China by then was already exhausted and was no longer capable of any such military effort as she had made in 1937 and 1938. Few Americans even knew that it in the summer of 1937 the troops of the Chinese Nationalist government had resolutely fought for three months at Shanghai against the Japanese invaders in the "bloodiest battle that the world had seen since Verdun." (Infamous field of slaughter in World War One.)

Washington, consistent with the Stilwell-Davies image of Mao's Red Army as a formidable fighting force, had also directed Wedemeyer to pursue involvement of Mao's forces in the fight. The agile enablers in Washington had successfully bridged the gap between the Reds "fighting furiously" and "getting them in the fight."

Wedemeyer met with Mao Tse-tung and Chou En-lai and became enlightened when the Great Teacher slipped and seemingly undermined his propaganda program. Mao frankly dispelled several well promoted misconceptions. Among them, the concept then popular in Washington, that the Chinese Communists were simply "agrarian reformers." Mao declared "Chinese revolution is an integral part of world revolution against imperialism, feudalism, and capitalism. We are definitely committed to the struggle for political and economic revolution in China . . ." In regard to reports of the Reds fighting furiously, Mao stated that military moves against the Japanese would only ensue after they received American equipment, guns and ammunition.[14]

By January 1945, the entire Asian situation began to change rapidly. Japan's days were numbered. How China fared, after the enemy's demise, depended on decisions made on the other side of the world.

---

14 Wedemeyer, *Wedemeyer Reports, p.286,287*

13

MASQUERADE

WHILE WEDEMEYER, CHIANG Kai-shek and Chennault staved off the Japanese Ichigo offensive, words, more than bullets threatened China. Mao Tse-tung with increased outside support, sharply escalated his propaganda program. Admiring news correspondents and authors presented favorable images of Mao's movement to America and the Davies group continued to feed Red propaganda directly to high circles in Washington. However, Mao, despite his successful propaganda efforts, had two other obstacles to overcome before he could achieve his goal of U.S. recognition. The Reds, although perceived by many as more virtuous than the National Government, had to be seen as completely disconnected from Russian Communism and, most difficult, Mao Tse-tung, confined to his small barren wasteland and presiding in a cave village of 30,000, had to be seen as governing a significant portion of China's huge population.

Mao supporters worked diligently to present the Reds as simple rural reformers, even promoting the concept of a semi-democratic Chinese Communism. In regard to the Russian connection, Mao simply stated his Reds had no connection to the Soviet Union. Adhering to the party line on this required ignoring Mao's many prior declarations. ". . . and mankind can free itself from suffering only by the road pointed out by Stalin and with his help." Mao also warned against false friends saying "However, there are friends of another kind, friends who have real sympathy with us and regard us as brothers. Who are they? They are the Soviet people and Stalin." And again, "Stalin is the true friend of the cause of liberation of the Chinese people. No attempt to sow dissension, no lies and calumnies, can affect the Chinese People's wholehearted love and respect for Stalin and our genuine friendship for the Soviet Union."[1] Earlier, when Mao joined the Government-sponsored United Front and motivated his followers against the Japanese, he stated the goal as ". . . and by these means to assist the Soviet Union." Most damning should have been Mao's reaction to the 1941 Russian-Japanese neutrality pact. In that pact, Soviet Russia approved Japanese sovereignty over Chinese Manchuria. But Mao, rather than protesting the loss of China's richest provinces, declared, "It marked a major victory for the Soviet Union's peaceful foreign policy."[2] All this negative evidence was conveniently ignored, and despite an absolute lack of supporting evidence, the faithful raised the volume of their declarations, subdued all dissenting voices and positioned Mao's Reds as independent rural reformers.

---

1   Mao Tse-tung, *Selected Works of Mao Tse-tung, Vol. 2, p.335,336*

2   Ibid, *p.468*

During the early years, Mao Tse-tung wisely cultivated the few Western writers who filtered through the Government blockade of his sanctuary and he prepared for a greater influx. In 1944, when Chiang Kai-shek allowed foreigners access to Yenan, Mao handled the flow of impressionable visitors in masterful fashion. The guests dined and held lofty discussions with Mao and Chou En-lai and other Red leaders in a model community.

They had no concept of the dire living conditions existing outside city limits and little awareness of the domiciles of the seemingly cheerful, obedient citizens of Yenan. Throughout the period from 1942 to 1945, unreported by the Davies group, Moscow's liaison, Petr Vladimirov, resided in Yenan and met regularly with Mao and top level Reds. His diary provides valuable insights on Mao Tse-tung's Yenan masquerade.[3]

(Although public areas were dressed up for visitors, living conditions of the residents were primitive.) "Our caves are a row of large burrows in the mountain. The entrances boarded up with a cloth curtain in place of the door and the windows pasted up with paper.... It's noon, but it's raining and so I have to light up a candle."

On rare occasions, a glitch in the efficient Red curtain gave an outsider a glimpse of peasant life in the countryside. In 1940, Stanton Lautenschlager, an educator, fluent in Chinese, arranged a visit to Yenan. When guides failed to meet him at the border, he took his first meal in Red territory at a small village. His dinner was "noodles boiled in river water seasoned with a pinch of salt and a spoonful of bean oil. When his chagrined guides arrived, they

---

3 Vladimirov, *China's Special Area, p.499*

quickly whisked him away to more sumptuous arrangements among the well-fed citizens of Yenan. Russian liaison, P. Vladimirov, recorded a more detailed, stark, picture after a 10 day trek in the hinterlands of Mao's domain "Poverty and illiteracy are astounding... They sleep naked... and cover themselves with lice ridden rags. There is hardly a family that does not stupefy itself with opium.... We bypassed regions swept by smallpox and typhus." He reported "support of the population for the CCP is feeble...."[4]

However, visitor's movements were controlled and the Red propaganda program made few mistakes. All visitors to the Red community were impressed with the make-believe village. The New York Times headlined "Yenan, A Chinese Wonderland City." (Reference: *NY Times 11/14/43*.) In their pilgrimages to magic Yenan, visitors strutted about in Red Army uniforms and were suitably impressed by the citizens and their well rehearsed stories of great Red victories over the Japanese. A few visitors noted a curious uniformity in the demeanor of the citizens but dismissed such impressions and considered more weighty issues. They accepted the most extreme Communist exaggerations, and the fortunate crowned their visits with an interview with "The Great Teacher." They wrote glowing reports of Communist social successes and admiration for Mao exceeded all limits. Most visitors came wanting to believe, avidly pursuing their romance with the new political religion and its leaders.

Even sceptics were converted. A pair of Dutch diplomats en route to Yenan said they hoped to expose a Russian plot in China. When they arrived at Yenan, twenty thousand townsmen cheered

---

4   Vladimirov, *China's Special area*, p.54,55

and sang songs for them at the gates of the town. They were taken to a tailor shop, fitted with Communist uniforms, into a shoe shop for sandals. They were hurried from one meeting to another invited to make speeches for the military academy, the art school, and the Political Institute. And when they left Yenan, after a three-day visit, they felt like a pair of schoolboys returning from the greatest adventure of their lives. On their return to free China, they seemed to be changed men.

Gushing descriptions of Mao Tse-tung exceeded all limits. Mao was seen as a legend in his own time. "An Olympian figure who made pronouncements like a Delphian Oracle," "the most selfless man ever encountered", "a genius living 50 years ahead of his time," "incomparably the coolest most balanced mind in China," "an immense intellectual force, a mind as sharp and flexible as steel." Mao's presence even gave one enthusiast "a fleeting glimpse of eternity."[5]

Soviet agent Vladimirov, during his years of exposure to Yenan and countless face-to-face meetings with Mao and Red leadership, saw a different Mao Tse-tung "… He is truthful only when this is in his interest. Moral standards are not for him. If you have strength or possibility to achieve something (even through the most unseemly means), do! Justification will be found later! He saw in Mao a conviction that cruelty is the result of justice, and that, properly speaking, there is no cruelty at all! There is justice and only justice! He never questions the justice of his own decisions. And then this conviction in cruelty turns into violence." He saw Mao as "in behalf of socialism Mao betrays socialism, in behalf of the Communist

---

5   Shewmaker, *Americans and Chinese Communists, p.186*

Party he destroys the Communist Party, in behalf of democracy imposes terror..."

Vladimirov continued "Mao Tse-tung, master propagandist, had created a new reality. Claims and pronouncements of top Red officials were treated with reverence. Actual verification of Communist claims was prevented by restrictions on visitor's movements. Mao successfully muted curiosity about outlying areas by conducting selected individuals on guided tours of carefully prepared sites. No information leaked out against Mao Tse-tung's will, from this little closed world. Even now when Yenan is visited by numerous foreign correspondence, military and political leaders, the strict control of Mao Tse-tung and Kang Shang (Mao's enforcer) over every party member and soldier makes it possible to successfully continue misinformation activities."[6]

One Red agricultural program presented a problem in relation to visitors. Vladimirov noted "...vast stretches of land are sown to poppy, a very unpleasant and shameful fact." Army brigades were sent to destroy (opium poppy) plots along the roads into Yenan."[7] The CCP, in its struggle for survival, turned to expanding the opium trade. One official told Vladimirov selling salt to nationalist areas only produced "an undernourished purse." "Now we send along an undernourished bag of opium and bring back a caravan loaded with money". In September 1943, the Russian noted although soldiers were sent to tear up the poppies along the roads used by American visitors, it was impossible to conceal the scale of opium production, A separate study showed in 1943 nearly 1,000,000

6   Vladimirov, *China's Special area, p.491*

7   Ibid, *p.198*

boxes of opium were exported at a value of $2 billion a year later the income had gone up 10 times and opium profits rose to 40% of CCP income.

Meanwhile Russian Vladimirov saw Mao "looking for his victories in the victories of the Japanese which would help achieve his goal, collapse of Chinese government forces. Chiang Kai-shek must be weakened by any means." "Let the Japanese seize Chinese land and burn towns." Troops in the field told the Russian "We are told not to touch them." All CCP units are strictly ordered not to undertake any vigorous operations or actions against the Japanese. In a word, not to engage in any combat actions, down to retreating under attack, seeking, if possible, a truce." When Vladimirov came across a telegram that left no doubt that Mao's was in regular contact with the Japanese command, Mao attempted to explain the "shameful fact" to the Soviet liaison.[8]

In their zeal to create a model city, the Reds omitted all unpleasant aspects of a normal community. The aged and infirm, the occasional mentally ill or social dropouts were not to be seen. Enthusiastic visitors saw nothing unusual. A Yenan consisting almost entirely of young, well fed, uniformly motivated citizens was accepted as proof of Red success. Occasionally, in their rapture, the guests revealed the pitiful magnitude of Mao's resources. One raved over the unrationed gasoline for Mao's "ten trucks." Others reported handicrafts and workshops as "Industrial achievement."[9] A few visitors, usually those who had prior experience with Communism reported more realisti-

8   Vladimirov, *China's Special area, p.483*
9   Tuchman, *Sand Against the Wind, p.476*

cally. Novelist Ernest Hemingway, who knew the Communists in Spain, found the Chinese Reds were expert propagandists and was impressed by Chou En-lai's intelligence and enormous charm but was substantially in agreement with Chiang Kai-shek's view of the Reds. Hemingway, on return to the U.S., was dissuaded from publishing his views by presidential aide Dr. Lauchlin Curry. Hemingway's wife, journalist Martha Gellhorn, who "would have followed Chou to the ends of the world had he beckoned" was encouraged to publish her views freely on return to the U.S.

Author Freda Utely, whose Russian husband was taken from their Moscow apartment in the middle of the night and never seen again, also marveled at Chou En-lai's charm but maintained an objectivity gained by grim experience. Unfortunately most Westerners couldn't recognize the core Communist principle that the end justifies the means. They couldn't fully grasp the concept that truth and accuracy were irrelevant when not useful to the cause, that the value of a communication rested entirely in its effectiveness.

The prime Communist tool for control of its subjects was terror. Terror was the most cost effective method and it produced complete control. It was not applied indiscriminately or by whim, but strictly as a means to achieve the end. Only a missionary who worked directly with the peasants could tell of the calculated acts of barbarism displayed in public in order to terrorize peasants into the orderly, disciplined workers so admired by western journalists in Yenan. One missionary reported: they would find a good man, a patriot, one who had expressed sentiments favorable to the government, and would tie him by his hands to the topmost branch of the tallest tree in the neighborhood. Then they would gather below and shout up at him derisively, "Now do you see your friends from the national government coming to help you?" If he said yes defiantly, a Red in the tree would lop off the branch and the victim would be dropped to the ground to his death, if he said no truthfully, they would mock his patriotism, revile the government, and drop him to his death anyway, with the excuse that he was a traitor! . . . In the winter, for a seasonal change, they would break the ice of the river in two places. They would drop their victims in one hole into the freezing waters and then tease him by showing him the other hole, a little distance away, as he came up gasping. "You can come out here," they would shout as the man made a supreme effort and struggled under the water to the other hole in the ice. As soon as he came up his captors would push him back into the water. Now he knew there was another opening and he would make for that one, hoping they would relent, but as soon as he came up, they would push him back in. They did this over and over until the man froze or drowned. They were but a few of the public tortures calculated to terrorize the peasants and thereby make them compliant."[10] In order to be of value, these "means justified by the end" had to be made widely known to the peasantry being indoctrinated. Secluded acts of cruelty constituted wasted effort. All applied terror was, of course carefully hidden from foreigners.

In June 1944, Chiang Kai-shek entertained two Americans who could never be accused of holding anti-Communist views.

---

10   De Jaegher, *The Enemy Within, p.125*

Vice President Henry Wallace was a great admirer of all things Soviet, (he was later characterized by then President Truman as a Communist.[11]) Wallace was accompanied by John Vincent, one of the "bright young men of the State Department." Vincent thoroughly analyzed issues from all angles but invariably seemed to conclude in favor of Red causes. The two came to China with a purpose, and left with Chiang's agreement to allow John Davies and his State Department colleagues access to Mao's Yenan. U.S. official justification to Chiang was: "gathering intelligence on Japanese forces." Any visit of U.S. officials to Red headquarters conferred a semblance of U.S. recognition on the Communists and conversely implied diminished regard for China's National Government. The move coincided with a pro-paganda drive by the American Communist Party calling on the U.S. government to pressure Chungking to allow an American mission to Yenan.

A U.S. Army Observer Group headed by Colonel David Barrett made up the military component of the American delegation, the "Dixie Mission" to Yenan. The Dixie mission was also assigned to "Investigate the strength of Chinese Communist forces." On June 29, 1944, Mao convened a special meeting to discuss the upcoming American mission. Moscow's agent Vladimirov attended the meeting "Mao Tse-tung de-manded the alteration of all information on the New 4th Route Army and the 8th Route Army as well as on the puppet and field Japanese armies (figures are being currently juggled in the

---

11   Truman, *Dear Bess*, P.539

most unscrupulous manner."[12] Dixie mission Intel reports on their prime assignment, investigate Red military strength, were conveniently lost or destroyed. The State Department's John Service provided the input on Red strength. Typically, the Reds would claim an army or population size totally out of proportion compared to existing information and Service would present the inflated figures to Washington as solid information by prefacing the numbers with "there's no logical reason to doubt . . . ." He carefully avoided reporting any personal observations of Red troop numbers. Dixie's military component, seemed to be another Stilwell type intelligence operation, verbiage substituted for hard data.

There exists no record of Dixie officers inspecting Red formations of any substantial size, no reports of the Red Army's subsistence farming responsibilities and no reports of opium production. More serious, Dixie produced nothing on Japanese preparations for the massive Ichigo offensive. The lack of objectivity and professionalism of this U.S. Army group is betrayed in a Yenan photo of a foolishly grinning group of U.S. Army Officers dressed in Red Army uniforms[13] in flagrant violation of U.S. Army regulations. Colonel Barrett admitted later Communist "sweet talk" might have taken him in. Barrett's successor in Yenan, Colonel Yeaton, the only Dixie Commander with Intel background, said the Communists did not fight the Japanese at all. He regarded the Dixie Mission "a great big farce."[14]

---

12 Vladimirov, *China's Special Area*, p.205,206

13 Tuchman, *Stilwell and the American experience in China*, p. 430 (photo)

14 Carter, *Mission to Yenan*, p. 202

John Service was the prime generator of information from Yenan to Washington. He sent firsthand, on-site reports that assumed an all knowing, all seeing attitude and pictured with absolute certainty the unblemished virtues of the Chinese Communists. His reports fell into a pattern designed to determine the level of exaggeration acceptable in Washington. An initial report would test the water with the claim of great magnitude. If rejected outright it would be followed up with a less exaggerated claim and if necessary the process would be repeated until an acceptable level was determined. The mindset in Washington included a substantial gullibility factor such that the magnitude of an initial rejected quantity or quality did not affect the credibility of the final accepted claim. Service first displayed the process on July 28, 1944 when he described Yenan as a "democracy." Apparently, that was too much for acceptance in Washington. Thus on July 30, he backed off reporting the Reds were "capable of promoting democracy." Then on August 3, he reported the Reds "had a real desire for democracy." In all, fourteen reports from the Davies group conveyed the concept of Chinese Communist government apparatus as a quasi-democracy, but none reported any evidence of political opposition.

Stalin's representative, Petre Vladimirov, held a different view of the life of ordinary citizens in Yenan, "... once they find themselves in the special area (Yenan) people are compelled to sever all family and social ties. Correspondence is frowned upon and, in fact, very few people would dare to correspond with their relatives. Family attachments are regarded as something to be ashamed of and are carefully concealed. With time, men grow out of the habit of associating with women. The sight of a man walking and conversing with a woman is an extraordinary occurrence here. Married couples don't live together, for each of them is registered at the place of work. They can meet only on Saturdays and often by special permission of the party organization."[15] Communists were required to reject the concept of privacy. "Small Broadcasts" and "Speaking Weird Words" were programs that required reporting casual conversations or humor. Failure to report resulted in being labeled as a spy. With this Mao gained complete control and essentially turned his subjects into robots. John Service had noted "In their thinking and expressions there is a noticeable uniformity." But he saw the remarkable homogeneity of thought in Yenan was a positive if mysterious trait. While Service touted Red democracy, Mao conducted purge campaigns in his pursuit of absolute power. The U.S. State Department mindset is also apparent in that Service, ostensibly on a mission to gain intelligence on Japanese military matters, received no criticism for completely ignoring the Japanese. With one exception, his reports denigrated the National Government or elevated Mao's Chinese Communists. That exception occurred on September 1944 when he abruptly urged support for the Communist Party in Japan. Strangely, this unprecedented interest in Japan coincided with Japanese Marshal Hata's later statement that his representative was stationed in Yenan in September 1944.

When Service lacked Yenan material for his reports, distance seemed to increase his insight on Chungking affairs and his rants against the Chungking government. On August 29, 1944

---

15   Vladimirov, *China's Special Area, p.45*

his telegram from Communist headquarters opened with a tirade against the National Government ". . . weak, incompetent and uncooperative. . . politically blind and thoroughly selfish . . . lacking popular support . . . miserable and dispirited conscript armies . . . " He followed with a specific recipe for the solution of China's problems. High on Service's list of recommended cures for Chiang's Government was inclusion of more political factions and more freedom and democracy. Chiang had already instituted a council that included Communists and other factions. The Council was meeting in Chungking while total political suppression was underway before Service's eyes in Yenan. Nevertheless, Washington soon adopted Service's view and pushed Chiang Kai-shek for more inclusion of political opposition. It was America's first meddling in the internal politics of an ally. It was justified as pursuit of the war effort. Later, at war's end, the State Department created a new justification for vastly increased meddling.

Service, joined at times by Davies and Ludden, thoroughly enjoyed life in Yenan after living in humid, bomb torn Chungking. They saw Yenan as a small, clean, orderly village. It's obvious they were visiting Yenan both for propaganda purposes and as a pleasant escape from war-torn Chungking.

According to John Davies, his colleague John Ludden immersed himself in the "mass of a mass movement." When Davies referred to a "mass" movement based in Yenan, with a population the Reds claimed was 30,000, questions may have arisen. It was decided that Ludden would venture out from Yenan and verify "all of the reports we had on the Communists . . .

indicating that the vitality and discipline of the center (Yenan) permeated to the far-flung outlying parts of the movement."[16] "All of the reports they had," were unsupported claims fed them by their hosts. Ludden set off on an escorted tour of carefully prepared CCP sites ostensibly to gather information on Communist strength. He spent four months in the hinterlands, much of it in the so-called "liberated" areas where the Japanese allowed Red Chinese occupation. He attended selected village indoctrination meetings and was suitably impressed as he had been in Yenan. According to Davies, Ludden reported orally on his return. It's significant that a four-month intelligence survey produced nothing worth putting on paper or information not wanted in the records. There is no record or evidence of the huge populations the CCP claimed they governed, and although Ludden alluded to the much-heralded Eighth Route Army, during his four month tour, he saw no sign of a standing army. He saw none of the fortifications that should have existed to protect the Communist capital from Japanese retribution for reported furious Red attacks. Throughout the four-month sojourn with "guerrilla forces" they incurred no contact with the enemy. Worldly wise Ambassador Hurley, who was initially impressed by the Reds, interrogated Ludden on his return to Chungking and dismissed the Red Chinese claims of population and troop strength as exaggerations. However, no alternate numbers were presented and, in the existing State Department climate, Ludden's tour succeeded in conveying an air of authenticity to Yenan's claims.

---

16   Davies, *Dragon by the Tail,* p.402

While the Communist Chinese enjoyed peaceful coexistence with the enemy and Davies, Service and Ludden enjoyed the safety and collegiate atmosphere of Yenan, the Japanese attacked free China with fiendish abandon distributing plague, cholera, dysentery, typhoid and anthrax microbes in reservoirs, major cities and rivers in Government controlled territories. In addition to horrendous military casualties, Nationalist Chinese opposition to the Japanese resulted in non- combat situations as described in a report to the British medical Journal in August 1944 by H. T. Laycock a fellow of the Royal College of surgeons who doctored hundreds of Chinese. He wrote of pitiable human beings debased by the Japanese, then "repatriated" into government held territories. ". . . without warning some hundreds of harmless pedestrians, hawkers and beggars are rounded up in the streets of a Japanese occupied city . . . then systematically starved in one of the worst sort of concentration camps. From the camp, victims considered sufficiently weakened are transported in overcrowded junks to the coast of free China, where those that have not died on the way are left totally destitute, on their own resources . . ." This was one of many imaginative Japanese tactics designed to weaken the Nationalist economy and will to fight.

As Red sympathizers idled in Yenan, other correspondents sought the scene of action. They reported on China's desperate fight against Japan's great offensive and brought a more accurate picture of China's crisis to the American public. Time magazine reported on Government troops defending Loyang "For weeks the enemy inched closer to Loyang. But, every day from the city's radio station a calm Chinese voice spoke of the firm will to resist. Men built barricades, fought behind them as the Japs drove into the 2,700 year-old city. . . Far greater warnings of danger came this week from central China: four strong Japanese columns had plunged southward towards the thrice captured, (twice recaptured) ruins of Changsha." On July 17, Time reported "Hengyang holds out. About 100,000 Japanese fought down 100 miles from Changsha past Hengyang. In bypassed Henyang the Chinese 10th Army held out with desperate courage. It fed on the city's rice stores, kept up the fight with well-worn guns, and ammunition parachuted by the 14th U.S. Air Force. (Chennault disobeyed Stilwell's orders in order to make the air drop). . . Then the Chinese army turned on counter pressure. New troops came in from other districts, attacks grew sharper. In the face of that opposition the Japanese apparently began to withdraw." On July 31, Time reported "China's ragged army had fought a critical campaign under appalling hardships." While Americans on the street became aware of China's struggle, Washington made decisions based entirely on the Davies group's ludicrous scenario where only the Red Chinese opposed the Japanese. Decisions were made that actually depleted Chinese defenses and aided Japan's Ichigo offensive. It seemed no volume of newspaper reports from the front lines could offset the Davies group's propaganda program.

The most durable of the Davies group charges against Chiang Kai-shek's regime was exposed by the new Presidential Representative to China. Patrick J. Hurley stated "In regard to the hoarding and selling charge, all the propaganda going on about China selling Lend Lease supplies is absurd. All Lend Lease supplies going to China had been handled by our own establishment and given directly to the troops . . . China has had very little Lend-Lease either to use or to sell. There have been abuses of lend-lease supplies in other parts of the world...."[17] Hurley knew the key corruption existed within the State Department itself. In his previous assignment in Iran, he found the allies were selling lend lease supplies for profit. He also found the Soviets, who were receiving enormous quantities of American rifles, other weapons and supplies, had in turn sold 50,000 rifles and quantities of tanks and airplanes to Iran. The evidence was undisputed. All agreed these situations existed. Hurley recommended U.S. take control over Lend Lease supplies in the Middle East, and FDR agreed. But future Secretary of State Dean Acheson held a different view. He approved a State Department assessment that the Hurley proposal was "hysterical, messianic globaloney." It seemed Acheson and his State Department associates regarded the selling off of lend lease supplies acceptable if practiced by favored allies and yet a useful slander to be applied against China. FDR's approval of Hurley's recommendation was ignored, the Iran arrangement remained undisturbed. Hurley's forthright exposure of the false corruption charges in China and the misappropriation of lend lease in Iran won him no friends within the State Department and was not received well in a Washington enamored by courageous defenders of Stalingrad.

The Reds addressed their last hurdle on the road to legitimacy in direct fashion. Mao had to convince the United States he governed a substantial portion of China's population. From remote Yenan, he floated trial balloons. His initial claims were

---

17   Liang, *General Stilwell in China*, P.271

over-the-top. His first claim of governing 200 million, nearly half of China's population stretched the imagination of even the most ardent Red admirer. Gradually, through trial and error the Reds settled on a claim of governing 80 to100 million, approximately 20 percent of the population. A far cry from reality and a claim that could have easily been refuted. Somehow the concept of 80 to 100 million people governed from a cave village of 25,000 or 30,000, escaped the outright rejection it deserved.

Red population could be broken down into two geographic areas. The base area governed directly by Yenan and the so called "liberated" areas, rural areas lying within Japanese occupied China but claimed to be governed by the Reds. Admiring western journalists and diplomats supported bizarre Red claims of 54 million base area population. (Mao reported 1.5 million base area population to his 1942 conference of Senior Cadres.)

Estimating population in the "liberated areas" was near impossible. These areas were thinly populated, marginal crop lands not worthy of Japanese attention, definitely not the densely populated breadbasket or rice basket of China. Population centers in liberated areas were small towns and villages where inhabitants devoted their lives to subsistence farming. After eight years of war, these inhabitants wanted only peace and had little allegiance to any party. There was no reason to believe the Reds, in 1944, commanded the allegiance of more people in these hinterlands than in the Base Area. When the Japanese abandoned these areas, varied groups of all political persuasions filled the void. A visitor to one locality reported it governed by a board of nine, three followers of the local nationalist warlord, three Communists, one Nationalist party representative, one former Shanghai newspaper editor and one schoolteacher.[18]

One solid indicator of population could be projected from the relative troop strengths of the Red Army and the National Government Army. Assuming the Red citizenry at least equaled the patriotism level exhibited by the people of free China, the ratio of mobilized troops to population should be roughly the same for each. The government fielded some 350 divisions from a population of 450 million equaling slightly over three quarters of a division per million population. Mao's statement in late 1942 claimed four divisions and at a special meeting on 6/29/44, in Yenan, Mao set a goal of gaining weapons for four divisions. Applying the above ratio of population to military strength points to a Red population of slightly over 3 million in 1943. Other Red claims also defied logic. Newsweek, in 1945, reported the CCP claimed an army of 600,000 operating in the so-called liberated areas. If such an army existed, Mao would certainly have broken the 200,000 man government blockade enclosing his Base Area. The blockade remained in place until the Japanese surrender in late 1945.

The United States was not the only recipient of false Red claims. Mao also sought to raise the CCP image in Moscow with "far-fetched" troop totals. Soviet liaison Vladimirov concluded "overstatement is the modus operandi of all responsible Army

---

18   Hanson, *Humane Endeavor, p.244*

and party workers without exception."[19] Since these distortions occurred at all levels, counts were inflated exponentially.

All available evidence indicated the Reds were an extremely aggressive but very minor factor in China at that time. The most damning evidence of Red insignificance was the lack of attention they received from the two who knew them best. Stalin considered them hardly worthy of support until the U.S. sent the Dixie Mission to Yenan and Chiang Kai-shek bottled them up in a wasteland area with a fraction of his army and ignored them for years. In more normal times, Mao's figures would have been dismissed as ridiculous. Unfortunately for China, America was focused entirely on the war in Europe and in the Pacific. While all information, regarding Germany or Japan was carefully dissected and examined, information favoring a political faction in the far-off China escaped critical attention. The Davies group reports from Communist Chinese headquarters were accepted as accurate and Washington thinking was evolving towards believing the Chinese Communists had a fair claim to a sharing of power with China's National Government. Mao's threadbare Red faction, headquartered in a remote cave village, had come a long way.

---

19   Vladimirov, *China's Special Area, P.272*

14

SHEER OSTRICH INFANTILISM

IN DECEMBER 1943, President Roosevelt and Prime Minister Churchill met with Soviet dictator Stalin in Teheran, Iran, the first face-to-face meeting between Roosevelt and Stalin. Before the meeting, FDR directed a reluctant State Department to have Patrick Hurley, who'd dealt with Stalin, attend with the rank of Major General of the Army, the title of Special Representative of the President and the rank of Ambassador. The Department sent Hurley's orders to its offices in Chungking and New Delhi while Hurley was meeting Department people in those cities. But his orders were withheld. Hurley discovered the petty intrigue at the last moment. He hurried to Teheran, arrived just in advance of the meeting and found the State Department had assigned a replacement. A minor incident, but one that indicates the ease with which the U.S. State Department ignored Presidential orders and partially explains how Soviet Agent Alger Hiss appeared on FDR's staff at the crucial Yalta meeting a year later.

Stalin's first ploy at Teheran succeeded when FDR accepted residence in the well-bugged rooms of the Soviet Embassy. In the course of the meetings, FDR proved to be most accommodating. He conceded the Baltic States, Lithuania, Latvia, and Estonia to Soviet rule. These were independent countries before the Soviets invaded in 1939. This gift was a direct violation of the Atlantic Charter created and signed by FDR and Churchill a year earlier. All FDR concessions at Teheran were premature. Stalin's Army was still struggling to push the German Army from Russian soil and, at that time, unable to occupy Poland or the Baltic States.

Although Chiang Kai-sheik was not invited to Teheran, subjects vital to China were raised. Stalin moved to regain old Tsarist rights in Manchuria. Rights renounced by the Soviets a quarter of a century earlier when they sought influence with Sun Yat-sen. At Teheran, Stalin indicated he wanted the Manchurian city of Dairen (Dalian) declared an international free port, and wanted the privilege of moving Russian trade over the Chinese Eastern and the South Manchurian railroads. Roosevelt did nothing to dissuade the aggressive dictator. On other matters, FDR seemed to playfully side with Stalin over Churchill. At one point, the conversation touched on India. FDR told Stalin he thought the best solution of the Indian problem would be reform from the bottom, somewhat along Soviet lines. For Churchill, the realist, the discussions were more serious. At that time, the British were battling a Communist insurrection in Greece. Roosevelt urged Churchill to yield to the "inevitable." Churchill had a different view. "We are an old ally of Greece. We had 40,000 casualties in trying to defend Greece against Hitler, not counting Crete. The Greek king and the Greek government have placed themselves under our protection. It would be quite easy for me, on the general principle of slithering to the left, which is so popular in foreign policy, to let things rip when the king of Greece would probably be forced to abdicate and the EAM (Red insurgents) would work a reign of terror in Greece. . ." Later when challenged by his House of Commons on the Greek issue he proclaimed. "Democracy is no harlot to be picked up on the street by a man with a Tommy gun...."

FDR's posture of carefully avoiding any issue that might offend Stalin was a dramatic change from his previous position. When Roosevelt, negotiated with Stalin for U.S. recognition of the Soviet Union in 1933, he found that every promise Stalin made was soon broken. Only three years before the Teheran meeting, in 1940, FDR declared "The Soviet Union, as everybody who has the courage to face the fact, knows, is run by a dictatorship as absolute as any other dictatorship in the world." He knew Stalin's record, as a breaker of treaties and outright aggressor. He'd been so angered by Stalin's attack on Finland that he used his influence to have the Soviet Union expelled from the League of Nations. But at Teheran, he came away from the meeting confident he could work with Stalin. He was developing a novel negotiating strategy for his next meeting with Stalin.

In China, Hurley, with increasing skepticism, pursued his mission of involving Mao's Reds in the war. He met, discussed, debated and came away with essentially the same proposition the Communists had pushed all along. They wanted American weapons. Hurley then invited the Red leaders to Chungking for further negotiations. In the end, all efforts failed.

While Hurley dealt directly with CCP leadership, the Davies group continued their underground propaganda campaign. In addition to bypassing the U.S. Ambassador in Chungking, they now concealed their reports from Hurley, the President's Official Delegate to China. When Hurley learned of the unauthorized flow of misinformation, he moved to have Davies and his colleagues recalled. But Stilwell's replacement, the newly installed General Wedemeyer, unaware of the group's propaganda activities, forestalled Hurley's move and the Davies group survived to continue their campaign.

Three months into Hurley's China assignment, FDR asked him to take over as Ambassador to China. Hurley declined, saying the duties he performed in China were his most disagreeable ever. He felt his support of the Nationalist government aroused opposition from un-American elements in the State Department. But FDR could not be denied. Hurley accepted the post.

In Hurley's reassessment of the Government-Communist impasse, he focused on the Davies group, noting they violated specific directives and evaded normal scrutiny from the Ambassador's office. He also came to believe they undermined his mission by furnishing information to the Reds and otherwise encouraging them towards noncooperation. (One of Davies colleagues was later cited for passing classified documents.) Hurley, at one point, succeeded in dispersing the group only to find them later occupying more influential positions.

1944 was a year of great Allied advances that sealed the fate of both Germany and Japan. The Russian Army, forced Hitler's Wehrmacht into retreat along the eastern front and Eisenhower's Normandy landing and drive across France assaulted Germany from the west. In the air, American and British fighter planes decimated the proud Luftwaffe that had earlier attempted to bomb Britain into submission. American bombers blasted German industry in daylight raids, and British bombers rained destruction on German cities in night raids. The U.S. Navy mounted combined air and surface attacks on the German U-Boat fleets that had nearly strangled Britain. The Battle of the Atlantic reduced Germany's undersea naval offensive to a few suicidal U-Boat attacks.

Japan, with her largest troop contingent tied down in China, lost control of her Pacific empire. Exemplary cooperation between General MacArthur and Admiral Nimitz brought the combined force of the US Army, Navy and Marines on Japan's island empire. By the end of the year, Americans were closing in on Japan's home islands and powerful, new, B-29 bombers pounded the Japanese homeland unmercifully from the air.

On the Asian mainland, America's presence had been clarified. The bizarre Stilwell/Marshall Burma fixation that nearly lost China was over. However, the supply situation though improved was still pitifully inadequate for China's bloody but unbowed infantry divisions.

Possibly, the most important new factor in the Asian-Pacific theatre was the condition of Japan's cargo fleet. Japan, an island empire, similar to Britain, depended on sea going supply lines. By the end of 1944, most of Japan's cargo ships were on the bottom of the ocean. American submariners overcame dud torpedoes and suffered the highest fatality rate of any U.S. service branch and essentially cleared the Pacific of Japanese shipping. The vital raw materials that motivated Japan's attack on Southeast Asia ceased to flow to the home islands. Along with that, Chennault's 14th Air Force had control of the air along the Chinese coast and reduced shipping to the point of isolating the millions of Japanese then in China. The Japanese homeland was slowly strangling.

There was no longer any question of who would win World War Two. The remaining issue was the final cost. The great challenge was subduing a Japanese homeland that appeared near impregnable. Successive assaults on the Japanese held Pacific islands, Iwo Jima, Okinawa, resulted in shocking increases in casualties as the U.S. forces closed on mainland Japan. In Japan, the government encouraged all citizens, from the youngest to the oldest, to fight to the death. Time was running out for Japan, but estimates of the cost in American lives for an assault on the Japanese homeland and final victory reached horrifying levels.

In Washington, the Navy proposed blockade and slow strangulation, Nationalist China, slandered and deprived of munitions by early limitations on Hump tonnage, was, despite Wedemeyer's improvements, no longer considered an offensive force in the war on Japan. The U.S. high command looked to Soviet Russia and pushed for an early Soviet invasion of Manchuria. The logic seemed inescapable but, in reality, a Soviet takeover of Manchuria would have no effect on the huge number of American casualties expected in the direct assault on the Japanese home islands. The American Navy had already blockaded the Japanese home islands and Chennault's air force controlled the China coast. None of the million and one half Japanese troops in China/Manchuria could return and strengthen the defense of the home islands. Manchuria itself could have been bypassed and left for the newly armed Chinese divisions. Washington, strategists prepared two estimates of Japanese capabilities in Manchuria. The estimate showing Japan's weakness was pigeonholed. Navy Secretary Forrestal had a separate analysis prepared. It explicitly advised against Soviet involvement. It too failed to reach the decision makers. With only one staff opinion in hand, the decision went for Soviet entry into the war. Thus the Russians would invade and occupy China's richest provinces.

The greatest failure at that critical time was one of diplomacy. The Japanese were ready to concede to anything short of exposing their Emperor to war crimes prosecution. Their attempts to contact and resolve surrender terms through Moscow, and through a captive American educator failed.[1] The obstacle was the Churchill-Roosevelt surrender terms requiring "Unconditional Surrender." To the Japanese "Unconditional" meant their God-like Emperor would be prosecuted for war crimes. The final surrender terms exempted the Emperor, but Asia was completely redefined by that time.

In February 1945, a debilitated FDR met with Stalin and Churchill in Southern Russia to resolve the major postwar issues of

---

1   Stuart, *Fifty Years in China,* p.150

Europe. Before leaving for the Yalta conference, FDR had shocked his friend, former Ambassador to Russia, William Bullitt. He told Bullitt of his intent to convert Stalin to his plans for the post war world. To attain that goal, Roosevelt listed four items:

1. To give Stalin without stint or limit everything he asked for the prosecution of the war and to refrain from asking Stalin for anything in return.
2. To persuade Stalin to adhere to statements of general principles such as the Atlantic Charter. (As noted, the Atlantic Charter was already violated at Teheran by FDR's gift of Latvia, Estonia and Lithuania to Stalin.)
3. To let Stalin know that the influence of the White House was being used to encourage American public opinion to a favorable view of the Soviet government.
4. To meet Stalin face-to-face and persuade him into an acceptance of Christian ways and Democratic principles.

When Bullitt objected and portrayed Stalin in the realistic light Roosevelt himself had seen earlier, FDR replied: "Bill, I don't dispute your facts, they are accurate. I don't dispute the logic of your reasoning. I just have a hunch that Stalin is not that kind of man. Harry (Hopkins) says he is not and that he doesn't want anything but security for his country, and I think that if I give him everything I possibly can and ask nothing from him in return, *noblesse oblige*, he won't try to annex anything and will work with me for a world of democracy and peace." Bullitt termed FDR's new approach, "sheer ostrich infantilism."

Harry Hopkins, an FDR favorite who'd served as emissary to Stalin, had been enthralled with the Soviet leader. In a typical report to the President, he gushed "no man could forget the picture of the dictator of Russia as he stood watching me leave – an austere, rugged, determined figure in boots that shone like mirrors . . . he's built close to the ground, like a football coach's dream of a tackle." Roosevelt apparently had complete faith in Hopkins' impressions.

The new FDR approach to diplomacy was unprecedented in world affairs for good reason. Subsequent events indicated FDR's failing health was at least a partial factor, but it was also evident FDR's view of Stalin had changed radically in only a few years. At Yalta, he gave as he told Bullitt he would and Stalin reaped a bountiful harvest of territory and people. FDR and Churchill conceded control of Poland and all of Eastern Europe to Russia. FDR formalized the gift of the neutral Baltic States to Stalin, although Russia had invaded these small countries when Stalin joined with Hitler to carve up Poland. The concessions were later excused as a "fait accompli" due to the Russian army's occupation of Eastern Europe. But, the decisions were actually made earlier at Teheran, before the Russian Army advanced into these Eastern European countries.

At Yalta, FDR then expanded his magnanimous approach, applying it to issues beyond the agenda of the meeting, issues vital to China, although Chiang Kai-shek was not included in the Yalta meeting. Roosevelt and Stalin discussed the Manchurian situation they had touched on at Teheran. While Roosevelt envisioned the concepts as discussed at Teheran, Stalin had decided, in the interim, to press for more. Rather than open access, he wanted a principal interest in Manchuria's principal ports and railroads.

Concessions that would give him a choke hold on the economy. As discussions progressed, FDR essentially gave away Manchuria by awarding the Russians "Preeminent" interest.[2] FDR first qualified his agreement by stating that it was all subject to China's approval. Then, before the meeting was over, a written agreement was prepared, signed, and the deed was done. Control of China's most industrialized provinces was freely given after only recently assuring Chiang Kai-shek at Cairo they would be returned to his authority. Months later, when Chiang Kai-shek was finally made aware of the secret concessions, his Foreign minister asked for a definition of "preeminent" interest. The State Department's answer was "ask the Soviets."

With one stroke, FDR surrendered his support of China's sovereign rights and diminished the nation he had proposed as one of the four decision makers of the post war world. FDR also contravened his own fervent dedication against imperialism and contradicted his position that Japan's invasion of Manchuria and China was unacceptable, a posture that precipitated Japan's attack on Pearl Harbor. It's significant that none of FDR's staff took exception to the sudden inclusion of Asian issues to the agenda and they raised no objection to the blatant gift of China's sovereignty to the Soviets. It's also significant that one member of the U.S. delegation was later proven a Soviet agent. (For decades Alger Hiss was defended with righteous indignation until Soviet records were opened during Pestroika.) FDR's waning grasp of the situation and the State Department's usurpation of control are further evidenced by the amazing fact that Hurley, Chiang Kai-shek and the U.S. war

2   Tsou, *America's Failure in China,* p.249

theater commanders had not been advised that the Yalta conference was being held.

British signature on the secret Manchurian agreement has been presented as proof of approval by Churchill and Foreign Secretary Anthony Eden. Chiang had impressed both British leaders at the Cairo meeting. Eden thought. "His strength is that of a steel blade." Churchill thought Chiang a calm, reserved and efficient personality. In private, they objected to the treaty. While Churchill did not agree with FDR's previous plans for China to be one of the "Big Four" that would guide post war world affairs, he also objected to any Soviet presence in China. He believed it was the opening that would bring sufficient Soviet aid to the Chinese Communists for a successful assault on China. Foreign Secretary, Anthony Eden, was adamant against signing the treaty but Churchill looking towards other battles he considered more crucial for the British Empire, reluctantly signed the agreement.

At the end of the Yalta meeting, the shameful Manchurian giveaway was classified secret. Thus China was further damaged by depriving them of knowledge of the situation they faced with the Soviet Union. There is evidence FDR did not realize what he had done. Ambassador Hurley, then in Washington, heard rumors of the agreement and discussed it with a confused FDR who professed little knowledge of any such agreement. Together they searched and established that the agreement existed. Hurley pointed out that the concessions were a serious blow to the strong, independent, China FDR had envisioned and a violation of Roosevelt's firm plans to prevent a postwar return to colonialism and imperialism. He proposed and gained Roosevelt's agreement to pursue revisions with the Soviets. Lucid FDR motives for the surprise giveaway, if such motives existed, remain a mystery. Why the meeting on European issues was extended to include crippling concessions for an Asian ally not represented in the meeting seems beyond explanation. FDR's lack of prior discussion with his top people and his avoidance of discussions with Chiang Kai-shek indicate a possibility of hidden bias. America's China policy as implemented throughout the war had done nothing to refute Ghandi's earlier warning to Chiang that China would not be treated as an equal. China was obviously a second-class ally. One that could be bullied and deprived of supplies at will. Only China was subject to slanderous, unproven U.S. recriminations. All of which were eminently more applicable to the Soviet Union. Was Chiang's final rejection of Stilwell too "uppity" for the hubris of the only four-term President in U.S. history? Was it another surfacing of a subtle undercurrent disfavoring Asians? The undercurrent that had resulted in tens of thousands of American citizens interned because of Japanese ancestry while the American offspring of other World War II enemies were undisturbed? Or was it simply a result of FDR's declining mental capacity and his dependence on impressions conveyed by an impressionable Harry Hopkins?

FDR's confusion was evident in his last public address, the report on the Yalta conference delivered to Congress on March 1. Roosevelt said: "It cannot be a structure complete. It cannot be what some people think . . . a structure of complete perfection at first. But it can be a peace . . . and it will be a peace . . . based on the sound and just principles of the Atlantic Charter."

In an afterthought, the Administration's remedy for the Soviet encroachment on Chinese sovereignty was a friendship treaty to be signed by Chiang Kai-shek and Stalin. Ostensibly, the treaty would cement a solid relationship that would benefit China in their efforts to rebuild after the depredations of the Japanese Army. The Soviets were "to render to China, moral support and aid and military supplies and other material resources, such support and aid to be given entirely to the Nationalist government as a recognized government of China."[3] In reality, the treaty was pure window dressing. The State Department continued to develop flimsy excuses to hold off notifying Chiang Kai-shek of China's loss of sovereignty in Manchuria. Meanwhile, Chiang proceeded to negotiate a treaty with the Soviets unaware the Soviets across the table controlled the future of his most valued territory. Stalin had at various times aided, violently opposed and later again aided Chiang Kai-shek, they'd known each other since 1923. Stalin had voiced a high opinion of China's leader. ". . . knew that Chiang Kai-shek was "selfless," a "patriot" and that "the Soviet in times past had befriended him."[4] Words that in no way affected Stalin's actions toward China. China had been in the Communist crosshairs since Lenin's time.

Four months after Yalta, Hurley notified Chiang Kai-shek that control of his Manchurian ports and railroads was awarded to the USSR. But, by signing a friendship treaty, the Soviets would support China's Government and would deny support to the Chinese Communists. En route to China, Hurley met with Churchill and Stalin and received confirmation of British and Soviet support

---

3   Wedemeyer, *Wedemeyer Reports, p.347*
4   Rose, *Dubious Victory, p.130*

for the concept. However when he reported these commitments to Chiang Kai-sheik, the State Department began backing away. American Ambassador to Russia, Averill Harriman, felt Hurley was "too optimistic." Secretary of State Stettinius betrayed the sham declaring ". . . if China were not unified at the time of Russian entry into the Asian conflict, Stalin would have legitimate option of siding with Yenan rather than Chungking." The U.S. Secretary of State granting a legitimate option to the Soviet Union to break a treaty so recently proposed by United States shows clearly how little the State Department was committed to support of the Government of China. With Russia then about to declare war on Japan, the key word uttered by Stettinus "unified" meant that any-thing less than the immediate inclusion of the Communist Chinese in the Nationalist government would justify Russian aid for a Mao insurrection.

FDR's grand plan for the postwar era had envisioned the Soviet Union as a good neighbor to China. He pictured the treaty between the two nations as cement for a solid relationship that would benefit China in their efforts to rebuild. At wars end, the U.S. was the dominant power in the world. A healthy FDR of sound mind could have forced Soviet compliance with China's restoration. That was not to be.

One month after the Yalta meeting, Franklin D. Roosevelt died and left a void in the leadership of America and the world.

15

MOMENTOUS EVENTS

D URING WORLD WAR II, the United States advanced from a series of demoralizing defeats on land and sea to become recognized as the most powerful and richest country on earth. FDR's
successor, Harry S Truman, was the first American to assume the
Presidency of a United States that had reached world supremacy.
That level of power and prestige, used wisely, could benefit the
entire world. Unfortunately, Franklin D. Roosevelt left a woefully
unprepared Vice President to assume the Presidency. Truman had
served only a few months as VP when FDR died and during that
brief tenure, the new Vice President had, inexplicably, been ex-
cluded from all top-level war meetings. HST faced extraordinary
challenges. The end of the war was in sight, but the expected death
toll for invading Japan far exceeded WW2 killed in action prior
to that date. He also had to resolve multiple, formidable domestic
and international challenges as the world and the U.S. entered an

era of redrawn national boundaries and struggling postwar economies. The new President also led a nation that, after fighting to save Europe in two world wars, was heavily committed to Europe's future. Except for the recent war with Japan, Americans saw Asia as distant and obscure. Facing a post war cauldron of worldwide proportions, President Truman was forced to delegate authority and he delegated China relations to one he'd acclaimed as "Greatest living American."

Harry Truman approached his responsibilities in a forthright manner. On April 23 in a meeting on recent hostile Soviet moves in Eastern Europe, HST took a strong stance "if one part of the agreements, which they (the Russians) had entered with President Roosevelt at Yalta, were breached, he, (Truman) would consider the entire Yalta agreement no longer binding on any of the parties interested." This could have voided much of FDR's "give them everything and ask nothing" concessions. However, advisors persuaded the new President to back off, a pattern that would be repeated.

HST had given his view of China "Chiang's government fought side by side with us against our common enemy, that we have reason to believe that the so-called Commies in China not only did not help us but on occasion helped the Japs. We're not mixing in China's internal affairs." He sent Patrick Hurley to Moscow in an attempt to revise the Yalta Manchurian giveaway. Hurley hoped to use his past warm relationship with Marshal Stalin to gain concessions. He was unsuccessful.

The baffling array of problems facing the President each day would challenge the most experienced, most talented executive. Quality of character and mind and Congressional experience did not provide adequate preparation for the enormous job at hand. Harry S Truman, with only 82 days experience as Vice President had a tenuous hold on the Presidency. On the international scene, he was completely unknown and he had no experience in foreign policy issues. As an unelected President, he'd done none of the foreign policy study required of a candidate in a presidential election campaign. More importantly, he had none of the supporting cast an elected President brings into office. HST had to rely on the existing administration, an establishment that had been in office 15 years guided loosely from the top. Some Departments operated with a peculiar lack of accountability and developed questionable goals. While FDR largely bypassed his State Department, using Harry Hopkins, Currie, Hurley and others as delegates when important issues were at stake, Truman was forced to rely on a State Department bureaucracy eager to join the fray and push their own agenda.

As Truman groped for policies to meet the myriad of new situations he faced, one of his first moves was the appointment of James F. Byrnes to Secretary of State. Byrnes was a person of considerable ability whose management of the civilian war effort won him the unofficial title of Assistant President. At the recent Democratic Convention, Byrnes was held in higher regard than Truman, but characteristic of that era, he was bypassed for the Vice Presidential nomination because he was both a Catholic and a Southerner. With Byrnes appointment to Secretary of State, the new President satisfied party faithful but placed a domestic politician with no foreign policy experience as Secretary of State serving a President with the same lack of qualifications. This insured HST"s complete dependence on the State Department and raised State bureaucrats, long ignored by FDR, to the level of unchallenged experts in foreign policy issues. From that point on, contrary to HST's declaration that "We're not mixing in China's internal affairs." the State Department concentrated on serious interference. State previously justified their wartime meddling in Chinas' affairs as aiding the war effort. They quickly shifted gears and voiced concern for the freedom and living conditions of the Chinese people. Within weeks after WW2 ended, State demanded a major restructuring of China's government. The new President had discovered that "being a president is like riding a tiger. A man has to keep on riding or be swallowed." Much later decoded espionage messages and exposed Soviet records would prove that HST's tiger had a distinctively pink tint.

Soon after HST took office, events accelerated. On May 4, 1945, Germany surrendered. Europe's death struggle ended leaving national boundaries to be redrawn, displaced millions to be resettled, hungry millions to be fed, and a myriad of other problems yet to be defined.

On July 16, 1945, after years of research and development the U.S. successfully tested a nuclear bomb. Secretary of War Stimson and the Joint Chiefs of Staff reviewed U.S. strategy and advised the President "Soviet entry into the war was no longer considered necessary..." Truman, ignored the Stimson-JCS advice, he wrote later, "I was reassured to learn from Hopkins that Stalin had confirmed the understanding reached at Yalta... Russian entry into the war against Japan was highly important to us."

In late July, Truman, Churchill and Stalin met in Potsdam, Germany. It was HST's first exposure to high-level negotiations. On meeting Stalin, Truman wrote, "I like Stalin. He is straightforward. Knows what he wants and will compromise when he can't get it...."[1] A quick, neat summing up of the Machiavellian leader who climbed from obscurity through multiple levels of Communist thugs to lead one of the most murderous regimes in history. Top Administration staff in Washington began referring to Stalin as "Uncle Joe." As the Potsdam meeting progressed, Stalin received confirmation of Russia's "preeminent" position in Manchuria and more. All of it without China's attendance, consultation, or approval. Truman rejoiced, ". . . and it (the Russian/Chinese Friendship Treaty) is practically made . . . in a better form than I expected. Soong did better than I asked of him." The USSR-China, (Sino-Soviet) friendship treaty created to benefit China and offset the Manchurian giveaway, would soon prove worthless.

The concessions made by FDR at Yalta gave Stalin much to digest, but at Potsdam, he gained more. Secretary of State Byrnes pointed out. "Under the agreement President Roosevelt had entered into at Yalta, China was to retain control of the Manchurian port of Dairen which historically handled 70% of Manchuria's imports/exports. Truman then relinquished control when Stalin promised to maintain it as an open port. Two years after Potsdam, Dairen remained closed to American ships and the U.S. State Department absolved the Russians of any fault. The status of Manchurian ports would play a key role in China's upcoming struggles.

---

1   Truman, *Dear Bess*, p.522

Truman urged Stalin to follow through on previous promises to declare war on Japan and promised huge supplies of lend lease. He left his first "Big Three" meeting feeling he had done well "I've gotten what I came for . . . Stalin goes to war August 15 with no strings on it." HST left Potsdam satisfied. He assumed that Stalin's agreements and compromises at the conference table would be reflected on the ground. Stalin, as usual, harvested whatever was available. It's ironic that the Soviet dictator walked away the big winner in three successive meetings with Roosevelt, Churchill and Truman while Chiang Kai-shek, the only leader with proven ability to deal with Stalin, was shunted off to the sidelines.

On August 6th, America shocked the world. A single US Air Force B-29 dropped one bomb on Hiroshima, Japan and obliterated the entire city. Stalin took notice and invaded Manchuria before his promised attack date, before Japan could surrender.

Three days later, the U.S. devastated Nagasaki with a second atomic bomb. Five days later Japan surrendered on condition the Emperor would be protected from war crimes prosecution. After the surrender, the Soviet Army continued to roll across and envelope China's Manchurian provinces.

Meanwhile the world rejoiced. The slaughter was ended. The world was saved from Fascism and Imperialism, or so it seemed. It was a time for celebration. For some who'd fought the fight and suffered greatly, victory would not be sweet. The Poles and other Eastern Europeans fell under Communist dictatorship. The Chinese, who'd fought the longest and suffered the most, now faced their most critical test.

China needed massive reconstruction after eight years of brutal Japanese style warfare. At the same time, she faced the prospect of insurrection leading to civil war. War waged by a foe supported by a neighboring superpower, a foe who'd concentrated on gaining power, while China bled. A foe completely unrestricted by ethics. Sabotage of critical infrastructure was a prime strategy of Mao Tse-tung.

By August 14, 1945, when the Japanese surrendered, China's government and people, after eight years of total warfare, had lost much of the fervent patriotism that had enabled it to subdue warlord armies, unify a huge population and fight the Japanese to a standstill. One third of China was totally devastated. The food supply was severely reduced, and cropland in important rice growing areas had eroded and deteriorated. City people bought produce at escalating prices in black markets. The families of soldiers were suffering from the loss of prime breadwinners for eight years with no end in sight. Tax collections fell unevenly. Government revenues were far below expenditures. In addition to the direct cost of fighting the war, the U.S., while denying many of China's loan requests, had asked China to provide great sums of Chinese paper dollars to pay for the wartime construction of airfields and supporting roads. The government met the deficit by printing huge volumes of paper money, which bought less and less. The value of Chinese currency in terms of the U.S. dollar fell month by month. Inflation seemed to be spiraling out of control. But the immediate challenge was the urgent need to take over control of Japanese occupied China and restore the tens of millions Chinese displaced by invading Japanese.

Despite near overwhelming problems, a few weeks after Japan's surrender the Chinese celebrated the 34th anniversary of the Republic. "In Shanghai, the populace went wild with joy. The city fathers spent 5,000,000 Chinese dollars, on street decorations. In Chungking, cheering crowds sang the unifying words of the new China's national anthem. For the first time in a decade, they were not futile words. Peace had brought back a vision: a reunited China."[2]

Chiang Kai-sheik set the tone for post war recovery by removing wartime press censorship. Time magazine reported. "The high, earnest voice rang with new confidence. Generalissimo Chiang Kai-shek was sure his government, having survived the war itself, would overcome the ravages, dislocations and internal disturbances of the war's aftermath. In Chungking, before the Supreme Economic Council, the Generalissimo struck a significant, realistic note. He called upon his counselors to lean primarily upon China's own resources for China's revival. "Our problems cannot be entirely solved by aid from other nations. We must help ourselves. Our entire national future hinges on our ability to tap within ourselves the forces of constructive energy which are the key to the greatness of any people."

From Washington, came assurances of U.S. co-operation in the government's drive for internal order and security. Vast aid was again promised to help resolve China's huge problems. With peace in the air and the U.S. promise to revamp and supply a modern Chinese Army, Chiang made a crucial decision against rebuilding

---

2   Time Magazine. *One Goal, 10/22/45*

arms manufacturing capacity lost in the war. America would rearm China. Chiang Kai-shek would devote China's limited resources to restoring peace time industries and the economy.

From Moscow, the Soviets pledged cooperation and a quick return of Manchuria to Chinese rule, but noted Russian troops scheduled to exit Manchuria on December 3 would leave on January 3. The Russians promised to bar Chinese Communists from major cities and expressed a general willingness to help.[3] With the full support of the United States, and the USSR, perhaps Chiang Kai-shek could once again exhibit the leadership that unified China and fought the Japanese to a stalemate. With U.S. aid, perhaps he could lead his loosely unified nation to stability and prosperity. The last four months of 1945 would be crucial.

One incident seemed to contradict recent U.S. promises to rearm China; Lend lease shipments to China through India were halted. It was not a cost saving move. Huge quantities of munitions and equipment were destroyed. The hasty "Operation Destruction" cost the lives of 25 Americans and 125 Indians. The destroyed munitions were included in the lend lease totals charged to China.

While declarations of support came from national capitals, change was underway in China. Chiang Kai-shek saw early indications of CCP hostility and knew the Reds were moving into Japanese occupied China. His immediate problem was in the far north. There had been no Red Chinese troops in Manchuria when the Soviets invaded, but with the Russians in charge, that could change. Wedemeyer, considering Chiang's limited resources, advised against attempting a move into Manchuria when the Russians

---

3   Time Magazine. *We Must Help Ourselves, 12/10/45*

departed. But Chiang knew Mao's Communist Chinese troops would fill any vacuum, and if the Reds gained possession of huge supplies of Japanese armaments and arsenals existing in Manchuria they would be transformed into a real threat. At the risk of overextending his military forces, he decided to move in as the Russians pulled out.

With Mao's Reds threatening and his Army depleted by eight years of war, Chiang believed the time had come for fulfillment of previous U.S. pledges. At that time, as a result of the U.S. training and supply efforts, the Chinese Army contained a small core of American trained and equipped divisions. The remainder, perhaps 90%, of the Army was desperately short of ammunition, weapons and even footwear. The years of grinding warfare had thinned the experienced leaders and troops of combat units and morale and discipline had declined. At this point, Chiang requested the U.S. train and equip the remainder of the 90 Chinese divisions pledged by FDR at the Cairo meeting. Secretary of State James Byrnes recommended America proceed with the aid considering China's present situation. A frugal and misinformed President rejected his Secretary of State's recommendation. It's likely the new President was presented with costs for manufacturing new weapons and supplies rather than war surplus stocks. Truman, in political form, stated that a careful search a records did not disclose anything relative to the promise. Hopkins recalled the commitment by FDR, but Truman then sidestepped, pleading Congressional resistance to spending. Thus, while huge stockpiles of U.S. war surplus arms and ammunition lay decaying around the globe, another promise was broken.

Months earlier, while China fought the Japanese for survival, a situation arose that told much about America's internal resistance to arming China. The 7.92 mm. Chiang Kai-shek rifle, manufactured in China's war-depleted arsenals, the primary weapon of China's soldiers in the war against Japan, was an exact replica of German Army standard issue Mauser rifle. After years of devastation from the Japanese onslaught, China's weapons production was drastically cut. From 1940 onward, more than half of China's troops went into battle unarmed, waiting to grasp the rifle of a fallen comrade. By 1942, nearly all existing rifles exhibited barrel grooves worn smooth, rendering them increasingly inaccurate. By 1945, when Germany surrendered, the Chinese soldier was essentially disarmed but China remained committed to a long deadly fight against Japan.

In early 1945, the American Army captured huge quantities of Mauser rifles and ammunition when Germany surrendered. Easy fulfillment of American promises to arm the Chinese Army became immediately available with quantities sufficient to equip nearly all Chiang's divisions for remaining fight against the Japanese. General Wedemeyer immediately arranged shipment of German rifles and Ammunition to China. However, an order on White House stationery stopped the shipment. It was signed by Presidential Assistant, Dr. Currie, (Currie was later exposed as a Soviet agent.)[4] It seemed a frugal President was not the only obstacle to arming China.

On the ground, in China, Wedemeyer recognized that a race was on between Government forces and the Chinese

---

4   Utley, *The China Story, p.36*

Communists to move into and accept surrender of Japanese held territories.

In Yenan, Mao Tse-tung and his Peoples Liberation Army, the PLA, faced a sudden reality. Propaganda claims of a strong army would no longer suffice. Army chief, Marshal Chu teh, addressing the Reds Seventh National Congress in the spring of 1945 called for a transformation of the PLA to prepare for "regular warfare."[5] On August 6, 1945, Chu was more specific. The modest goals he set for the coming year indicate the then existing state of the Red Army. "During the year ahead, we should provide each full-strength regiment with a mortar battery and each under strength regiment with a mortar platoon in order to better cope with the enemy." A comment from the ranks of the Soviet invaders of Manchuria describes the condition of some of Mao's irregulars. A Russian gunner reported, "I saw some men coming down from the mountains. They were in rags, many were barefoot. They carried no weapons, but each carried a stick with a bundle on its end. So this was the heroic 8th Route Army."[6]

At wars end, Mao had no organized military forces in Manchuria. His major challenge was have an army, trained and ready and in place, before the Russians pulled out. That required training masses of people rather than simply seizing territory and terrorizing the population. Below Manchuria, in North China, the CCP had the advantage of already occupying some rural areas behind Japanese lines. Russian liaison agent, Vladimirov put

---

5   Bjorge, *Leavenworth No. 22, p.38*

6   Hastings, Retribution, p.532

total People's Liberation Army, PLA, troop strength, including guerrillas, in August 1945, at 380,000. Most of it dispersed into small local core organizations. These needed exponential growth to reach the levels needed if Mao was to be a force in China. To accomplish this, Mao put aside his agricultural collective program. His early policy of kangaroo courts and executions had disrupted production. He announced that, in the liberated territories, the new policy would initially avoid land confiscation. Collectivization would be held in abeyance until victory was achieved.

Mao either enjoyed an insight into the future or had inside information from the enablers in the west. In an August 13, policy statement, he advised that for a time, the upcoming civil war may be restricted in scale and localized. The CCP was in dire need of an extended breathing spell in order to create the army they'd claimed existed. The Chairman announced a new strategy. Develop toward the north and defend in the south. Take advantage of the Russian comrades in Manchuria and avoid, as much as possible, arousing the Government in the south.

The National Government's immediate challenge was taking control from the Japanese and then protecting and maintaining cities, railroads and utilities. The Red foe had no inhibitions on using sabotage, no concern for human survival.

Although the Chinese Nationalist Army was far superior to Mao's militia, in 1945, Government forces traveled by foot unless U.S. transportation was available. In Manchuria, the Russians possessed 375,000 GMC trucks and the capability to move large numbers of Red troops. China had none and the few Chinese trucks that survived eight years of war were worn out. Wedemeyer mobilized all available U.S. Army transportation to move Chiang's troops into position to accept the surrender of the Japanese, but as he moved forward a new policy emerged from Washington contradicting the U.S. commitment to move the necessary troops. Instructions precluded any actions that tended to support Government forces engaged against "civil strife." This granted the Chinese Communists veto power over any U.S. transportation of Nationalist troops. When Mao Tse-tung decided to move on a village, city or province, any attack on the defending government troops would create "civil strife" and prevent the U.S. moving government troops into the area. Wedemeyer interpreted the new policy liberally and continued his efforts with the resources available. Chiang's first move to regain Manchuria was a request to Wedemeyer to transport five Chinese divisions to Manchuria in anticipation of the Russian pullout.

Unknown to Chiang Kai-shek or the U.S., Stalin, aware of Washington's confused China policy, decided to upset the fragile balance in China and Manchuria. While China fought the Japanese for eight long years, Soviet Russia overran crumbling Japanese defenses in Manchuria in ten days. Within weeks, the Russians stripped Manchuria bare of industrial and utility equipment indicating they planned an early pullout. Days later, Stalin suddenly adopted a bolder strategy. On August 11, He cabled his Chinese Communist brethren: "the task of the Red (Russian) Army is to liberate the Northeast. Your task is to construct the Northeast.

Await orders."[7] Full aid for Mao's long ignored PLA became the new Soviet strategy.

The Russians, from that point on, dedicated their efforts to blocking movement of Government troops into Manchuria while aiding Mao's infiltration of Red troops from North China. The Soviets had no use for Japanese caliber weapons and ammunition, they left the former Japanese armament factories in place and intact. As Mao's troops arrived in Manchuria, their perennial shortage of armaments turned to abundance.

Suddenly, Moscow, Vladivostok, and Yenan radio blared anti U.S. propaganda. "Americans were in the Far East to exploit and conquer. The Nationalist government leaders were collaborators with imperialists and exploiters of the common people." Imaginative tales of Nationalist cruelty and corruption were beamed throughout the Far East, and repeated in the American press. Some claims seemed to mirror word for word the slanders in the Stilwell/Davies campaign to discredit Chiang Kai-shek.

In Manchuria, the Soviets not only violated their freshly signed treaty with the Chinese, but also the Yalta and Potsdam agreements with the United States. In October, an American convoy delivering Nationalist troops to Dairen, Manchuria, found on entering port, several thousand Chinese Communist troops busy digging entrenchments. The American commander, Admiral Daniel Barbey, was refused entry by the Soviet Port Authority. Dairen was an open port per agreement of Truman and Stalin at Potsdam. Barbey retreated, thereby setting a precedent for future blockade

---

7 Gorcharov, *Uncertain Partners,* p.10

confrontations in Asia and in Europe. At other Manchurian ports, Navy troopships found the Communist Chinese entrenched under Soviet port supervision and their entry blocked. In one encounter, the Reds fired on the U.S. Navy commander. With the ink barely dry on the U.S. sponsored China-Russia friendship agreement, China was barred from use of Chinese ports.

Barbey disembarked the government troops in South China. They undertook the long march back to Manchuria only to find Red Chinese, fully armed by the Russians, occupying prepared fortifications at key locations.

The port of Dairen was a specific issue at the Yalta and Potsdam "Big Three" meetings. According to Secretary of State Byrnes, FDR and Stalin had agreed at Yalta, China was to retain control of Dairen as a free port. Then at Potsdam, Truman acquiesced to Soviet control with Stalin's assurance it would be maintained as an open port.[8] It would be neither. The Soviets defied the Truman agreement and the U.S. timidly retreated thus breaking another promise to Chiang Kai-shek. Later, it was revealed the former Japanese armory in Dairen was a principle supplier of arms and ammunition to the Red Chinese build up of forces in Manchuria.

A U.S. complaint on the rejection of U.S. vessels from the "open" port was answered with a ridiculously flimsy Soviet explanation that Marshall and the State Department treated as legitimate. The Russians declared Dairen was closed under "wartime restrictions" because, although Japan had surrendered, end of war formalities had not been completed. (During

---

8 Byrnes, Speaking Frankly, p.205

that recent war, thousands of U.S. vessels, delivering American aid, had entered Soviet ports.) The issue was shuffled off to the American Ambassador in Moscow who responded "Soviet Government...has done everything possible for the exact execution of these (the Potsdam and Sino/Soviet) agreements".[9] Department records show that, rather than confront the farce, General Marshall busied himself for more than a year with details of establishing a courier service to Dairen in order to comply with additional Soviet red tape. Meanwhile, the Chinese Government remained blockaded from their Manchurian provinces.

Dealings on the ground with Mao Tse-tung and his militia were typified by Ambassador Hurley's August 31, 1945 report on a conference with Mao Tse-tung in Chungking. ". . . Have just concluded a conference . . . in regard to the killing of the American Captain J. M. Birch, Allied Commission, on August 29, at the railway station of . . . Tungshan, approximately 100 miles from . . . (here). . . "

Mao apologized for the killing. Wedemeyer insisted the Communist High Command had not indicated a desire to prevent such clashes. He cited four OSS officers held by the Reds since May and Mao had not replied to his inquiries. Mao claimed he did not receive any letters or dispatches. He would send the Americans back and investigate and punish the guilty. This meeting, only two weeks after the Japanese surrender, set a pattern. The Reds would confront, kill or wound Americans who were not involved

---

9 Foreign Relations of the U.S. 1947, vol.7. p.495 Amb. Smith to Sec. of State

in hostilities and then promise to investigate and punish. But nothing changed.

When Truman assumed office, four months before Japan surrendered, he voiced full support for the Chinese government and noninterference in China's internal affairs. On August 17, three days after the Soviets signed the treaty committing their support Chiang's National government, the Nationalist Foreign Minister, T V Soong, told Truman the Russians would reverse this policy if China remained weak. HST agreed and promised aid.

At wars end, mainstream America's views of China's Communist problem were summed up in an August 27, New York Times article, "The Chinese Communists . . . are in open rebellion against President Chiang Kai-shek and his Government. They repudiate his orders . . . which they are pledged to obey . . . They want domination. They're not a political party, they are a conspiracy to seize the Chinese government. And they consider the victory of the United Nations, (the allies in World War II) in which they played a microscopic role, as their great opportunity." President Truman and many in government and media voiced sympathy for Nationalist China, but the United States State Department was not deterred. They voiced concern for the Chinese people, but they repeatedly came out against programs of financial aid to China and ignored ruthless Communist sabotage of the infrastructure that supported China's delicately balanced food and fuel situation. The Reds focused their destruction on the railroads that carried rice and coal to the great cities of a China then existing on the edge of famine. In the China situation, the State

Department was in the position of supporting the saboteurs whose goal was cutting the critical flow of fuel and rice to the very people State declared were a major concern. This contradiction went unchallenged in the near chaotic Washington climate at wars end. Within weeks, a prestigious individual would join the cause and raise State's immunity to criticism to a higher level.

A U.S. War Department report dated July 1945 concluded: (1) the "democracy" of the Chinese Communists is Soviet democracy. (2) The Chinese Communist movement is part of the international communist movement sponsored and guided by Moscow. The report warned: China needed Manchuria, and there was reason to believe the Soviets had designs on it. The report was naïve in that it accepted CCP claims of troop strength because they "were reflected in their propaganda." Other than that, the report took a negative view of Mao's Reds. For background it quoted the American Military Attaché in China, in 1943, "In point of fact, the Communists could be crushed by force of arms. . . Nevertheless, no general offensive against the Communist areas has been launched, each crisis has been resolved through the moderating influence of the Generalissimo and others affiliated with Chunking...."[10] The report pointed out the many agreements broken and falsehoods propagated by Mao's CCP. It should have demolished the carefully laid scenario broadcast by Stilwell and the Davies group. But in the Washington political climate of 1945, the State Department managed to suppress the War Department Report. Despite several months of reports from the U.S. Ambassador and military per-

---

10 U.S. War Dept., *Report on Chinese Communist Movement, p.105*

sonnel in China corroborating the War Department report, State clung to the position that there was no connection between Mao Tse-tung and Stalin. The only source of this fiction was a June, 1944 Mao statement "There has been no connection between the Communist Party of China and the Communist Party of the USSR, either in the past or now." Other than one propaganda statement, all other declarations by Mao Tse-tung clearly stated his allegiance to Soviet Communism and his warm feelings for comrade Stalin. Wedemeyer commented on the political climate at that time, despite continuing aggressive Soviet and Red Chinese actions "it was taboo for any American in an official position to expose or openly oppose Stalin's aggressive actions and sinister aims."

On the international scene, its possible Stalin would have curtailed his aid to Mao's PLA and lived up to treaty obligations if pressured by the sole possessor of the atomic bomb. But the Truman Administration had decided to side step. The new Sino-Soviet treaty, signed at Potsdam, an offspring of U.S. policy, was suddenly labeled as strictly China's affair. State Department "help" would be confined to meddling in China's internal situation.

While declaring no policies were changed, the State Department cast China adrift on the world political scene and, at the same time, increased U.S. interference in China's internal politics in favor of Mao's Communists. Harry Truman's stated intentions going into office would have provided a simple, forthright policy of fulfilling prior commitments and halting interference in China's affairs. A policy that would have allowed Chiang Kai-sheik time to complete the transformation of China that was well underway until interrupted by the Japanese attack in 1937. Instead, the State Department implemented steps to impede, disarm and abandon China. Once the change in American support of Chiang Kai-shek was evident, Stalin discarded the new Sino-Soviet treaty and directly supported the Chinese Communists. All reports of Russian transgressions were quickly stifled or excused by the faithful Red enablers in Washington who staunchly maintained that Mao's Chinese Communists had no connection to Moscow.

America's unwritten China policy was beginning to emerge. Postwar China received food and medicine through UNRRA, the United Nations Relief organization, most of it financed by the United States. Food and medicine could not be fired at the Reds, but aid in cash payments could buy ammunition. When China requested $200 million left unspent from an American loan in 1942. Although previously approved, it was denied. Dexter White, Assistant Sec. of the U.S. Treasury played a key role in denying the Chinese request. White was later identified as a Soviet agent.

Following that, the State Department placed a choke hold on aid to China. Simply stated, aid to China's National Government could not be used for "fratricidal warfare" and China must have "political stability." Therefore, the Chinese Communists, could any time they chose, cut off U.S. aid to the Chinese Government simply by attacking and initiating fratricidal warfare. The "Political Stability" requirement could be construed to mean China could receive aid only when they didn't need that aid. Further aid restrictions followed.

As autumn leaves turned in Washington, meetings were held, papers were prepared and it seemed nothing happened. But the conflict between Truman's pledges to support Chiang Kai-shek's government and the State Department's push for a coalition government in China was coming to a head. On November 10, 1945, Wedemeyer conveyed Truman's assurances "guarantees to support you and the Nationalist Government" to Chiang Kai-shek. That month, in Washington, Truman wrote ". . . We are not mixing in China's internal affairs."[11] While the President's guarantee of support went forth the State Department decided to break another pledge. The U.S. Army would transport no more Chinese Government troops to Manchuria.[12]

On November 26, Secretary of the Army Patterson and Secretary of the Navy Forrestal issued a memorandum to then Secretary of State Byrnes on the issue of support for China. It concluded that any situation likely to arise from supporting China was a lesser threat to the U.S. than the results to be incurred by not supporting China. But Truman and Byrnes were well on the way to adopting the State Department's unwritten goal of forcing inclusion of the Communist Chinese into China's government. Less than three weeks after Wedemeyer conveyed HST's guarantee of support to Chiang Kai-shek, Truman "mixed in China's affairs" by publicly calling for "Fair and effective mediation leading to a new Constitution." Thus, the Chinese Communists achieved their goal of informal recognition by the United States. Stalin immediately shed all restraints on aiding the PLA and all pretensions of abiding by treaty obligations. He turned to full support of Mao's forces.

The Chinese National Government found their new treaty with the USSR evaporating. Chinese Ambassador Soong met with

---

11   Truman, *Off the Record, p.74*

12   Forrestal, *The Forrestal Diaries, p.109*

Secretary of State Byrnes after waiting unsuccessfully for an appointment with President Truman. He told Byrnes that chances for compromise with Mao's Reds were declining, that the Russian attitude had great effect on Mao's attitude. The Treaty terms had bound the Russians to help China and he mentioned that the Soviet Commander in Manchuria had promised he would not allow Communist troops into Manchuria. By that time, even the State Department had to admit the Reds were in Manchuria, in force. Byrnes tried to evade, asking if the Russian commander's promise was in writing. The Ambassador said the specific promise by the Russian Commander was oral but, the Sino-Soviet Treaty required the Russians to assist, not obstruct the Chinese National Government. The Ambassador also pointed out the blatant, violation of the U.S. - Soviet Yalta and Potsdam agreements by the continuing Russian block of American shipping at Dairen and other Manchurian ports. Byrnes showed no interest in the obvious violations of any of the treaties. "The Secretary stated he wished the Chinese had the Soviet promise in writing." Adding he would look at a previous note and "keep the Ambassador's thought in mind." Obviously the President and the Secretary of State were turning away from China's problems.

A few days later, in a State Department meeting on November 27, Secretary Byrnes proposed ". . . perhaps the wise course would be to force the Chinese Government and the Chinese Communists to get together on a compromise basis, perhaps telling the Generalissimo we will stop the aid to his government unless he goes along with this." Byrnes did not specify a force to be exerted on Mao's CCP. He ignored recent Russian transgressions and proposed to "tell Russia . . . to try to line them up with this policy." Dean Acheson was able to tell Byrnes the Department was already working on the approach he suggested.[13]

Ample evidence of Communist aggression arrived at the State Department from China daily. On November 28, the military attaché's report stated " . . . there seems to be little doubt that Communist troops will vigorously continue attacks on both Paotou and Kueisui as well as other strategic place(s) along . . . the Railway . . ." And in regard to Russian-Red Chinese connection "Communists have been moving into the vacuum created by evacuation of Russian troops and seem to be well entrenched with an estimated strength of 100,000 in many sections of Manchuria.

On December 12th, the Department's Charge' in China reported "Coal trains guarded by U.S. Marines and Marine plane (s) have been fired on." Meanwhile, the State Department appeared ready to completely ignore the Chinese Government. State admitted on December 12, that a November 23 cable from China's Head of State had lain for three weeks unanswered.[14]

Memos flew in Washington. Where China was concerned, logic was not required. The State Department had decided to restrict transportation of Government troops to Manchuria. The Department suggested it would serve as a lever not only on the Government but somehow also a lever on the Communist leaders. Even Secretary Byrnes took issue with this Department position. Byrnes found ". . . the State Department is, in effect, blessing the existence of autonomous armies in China probably for some time."

---

13 U.S. State Dept *Foreign Relations, 1945, Vol.7, p.686*
14 Ibid, *p.697*

The firm view of the U.S., until that date, had been autonomous armies meant civil war, there must be only one army in China. The push for Coalition government was justified by the perceived need to incorporate Red forces into the Government Army. Theory was civil war would be prevented by eliminating contending armies. Apparently, the Department enablers tried to slip one past their inexperienced Secretary.

Under mounting pressure to do something on the China situation, the new President and new Secretary of State assisted by the State Department were developing a new U.S. policy for China. Truman called in the Ambassador. The aging, fatigued Patrick Hurley had returned to Washington believing his health and financial situation were failing. Both had suffered during his tenure in government service. Both Byrnes and Truman had refused his attempts to retire.

The year had been an active one for Patrick J. Hurley. In Chungking, after resolving the Stilwell crisis, Hurley initiated diplomatic feelers to the Reds and met with them in Yenan. His first impression of the Reds was positive. But after months of fruitless negotiations, he took a more realistic view. He told Truman the Reds were much weaker than reported. Military strength, areas of territory under Red control and populations owing allegiance to the Reds, had been exaggerated. He pointed out that State Department officials, newspaper reporters and writers accepted unsupported Communist statements without question. Hurley saw the public posture of the Soviet Union as the critical determinant in resolving conflict in China. Six months earlier, on June 9, Truman had told Hurley that Stalin pledged "he will do everything he can to promote unification of China under Chiang, including Manchuria."[15] Since then, Russian activities in Manchuria contradicted those assurances, Hurley believed nothing less than a public statement from Stalin could change the situation. As he phrased it, once the Communist Chinese "saw the handwriting on the wall, they will be ready to read." Earlier, when Moscow radio announced the Sino-Soviet Treaty, Mao was apparently shaken because he announced he would go to Chungking in person.[16] A public statement by Stalin would have had a substantial impact. Stalin continued to declare his support for the treaty in private, but made no public statement and the U.S. did not request one.

Underlying Hurley's immediate situation was the fact that, in that time of great crisis, he'd returned to Washington seeking direction, but received none from either the State Department or the President's office. When pressed, Secretary Byrnes told Hurley "there is no change, there has been no change in policy.... But Hurley saw near total abandonment of prior commitments. On his return from China, Hurley, once again, told HST he wanted to retire. Truman persuaded "the old man" to rest at home and then continue as Ambassador. On November 25, before returning to China, Hurley met with the President. HST assured him that U.S. policy supporting Chiang's government remained unchanged. On Viet Nam, he told Hurley that FDR's anti-colonial policy would be continued. But, Hurley knew the China situation and he saw the French returning to South East Asia. He was not reassured and came away with a foreboding that he would oversee further damage to China.

---

15   Buhite, *Patrick J Hurlwy and American Foreign Policy, p.224*

16   U, S, State Dept. *Foreign Relations, 1945. Vol. 7 p.775*

He also found that stories appearing in the Communist Daily Worker and in the Chicago Sun contained information that could only have been sourced from inside the State Department. On the day following his meeting with the President, a left-leaning Congressman publicly criticized both Hurley and Chiang Kai-shek. Hurley determined that Congressman DeLay had special and unpublished information and took it as one more proof that his classified reports to the State Department were being passed on to Communist supporters.

Ambassador Hurley decided against another private submittal of his resignation that could again be refused. On November 26, the day after his meeting with the President, Hurley resigned publicly and issued a statement of crashing criticism of the Administration and State Department officials who promoted Communist Chinese interests.

The Administration was shocked and embarrassed, HST had only recently persuaded "the old man" to return to China. Administration supporters reacted by thoroughly abusing Hurley in print.

Hurley had objected to a disastrous policy change but, resigned in a clumsy manner that muted his objections. His career was long and varied. His favored position with world leaders resulted in concessions to U.S. goals. Hurley made the decision to recall Stilwell when others were paralyzed. He was a whistle blower when others went with the flow. Hurley was the last strong voice against the return of Viet Nam, Hong Kong and Indonesia to their former colonial masters. Hurley's failures were in delicacy of style. His contributions were many but his public resignation embarrassed politicians in power and he had to pay. The payment was massive ridicule. The authors of demeaning caricatures have never explained why he was valued by the Secretary of State and the President of the United States to the point where his privately submitted resignations were repeatedly refused.

His move to not be involved in damaging China had a reverse effect. Had Hurley stayed on as Ambassador, China might have had some chance of weathering the coming storm.

16

COMPLIANT MEDIATION

"We have faith in you. Much that we have done...has been
based almost exclusively on that faith."

(U.S. Mediator George C Marshall to Red Chinese negotiator Chou En-lai at
conclusion of U.S. sponsored Government-Communist mediation)

THE AMBASSADORSHIP TO China, vacated by Hurley, had to
be filled quickly, preferably, with a well-known name.
General George Catlett Marshall was available. Other than the
accolades he collected, Marshall's record of specific positive
accomplishments in WW2 was slim and there were serious
negatives. Acclaimed early on as the "Organizer of Victory",
he'd lost influence in FDR's circle of advisors during the
war. However, in the eyes of the new president and the public, Marshall's image was undiminished. The General, who
preferred that subordinates make decisions and who meekly

accepted outright disobedience of his orders during WW2, would soon demonstrate a new level of commitment and develop a peculiar "regard" for an insurrectionist leader.[1]

HST's appointment of and relationship with General Marshall displayed the new President's management style. Select the best available and fully support the appointee. A sound, logical approach, but HST exerted little direction on his appointees, a practice that would prove costly. In Marshall's situation, the General had full authority to decide and execute as he saw fit. He reported to the President and controlled the reports of others. The President heard no alternate or conflicting information from Marshall's sphere of influence. Truman's initial directive authorized Marshall to tell Chiang- no unity, (with Mao's Reds), would mean no aid. It was a negotiating ploy at that point, Marshall was clearly directed that if negotiations failed, aid would flow to China.[2]

In preparing for his assignment, early on, the new appointee seemed to have no illusions on Communist tactics. He raised the bottom line issue, if the mediation failed would the U.S. support Chiang? Truman and Byrnes replied yes.

Unfortunately for China, before setting out, Marshall again came under the influence of his intimate friend and former quasi subordinate, Joseph Stilwell. After a meeting with Stilwell, it seemed Marshall's attitude hardened. He immediately halted all negotiations for sale of U.S. surplus property in China,

---

1   U.S. State Dept. *Foreign Relations, 8/14/46. p.33 (Chou in a unique position in Matrshall's regard...)*

2   U.S. State Dept. *Foreign Relations, 1945. Vol. 7 p.765*

calling it a potential bargaining chip with the Nationalists,[3] this, while he carried no chips for bargaining with the Reds. One week, later in Chungking, when he met with General Wedemeyer, his former assistant in European war planning, he rejected Wedemeyer's views of the China situation. Wedemeyer had the most recent and most relevant experience in China and knew the current situation there. He'd experienced the chaos and trials of a China attempting to transform from devastating warfare to uncertain peace, and he'd dealt directly with Mao Tse-tung and Chou En-lai. When Wedemeyer said any coalition with the Reds was unlikely, Chiang would not relinquish power and Mao would not settle for less than complete power, Marshall erupted angrily saying he was committed to his mission and Wedemeyer was going to help. Two years later, Marshall would declare "I thought that (coalition) was an impractical proposition."[4]

In his memo on his farewell meeting with the President on December 14, Marshall noted he was instructed ". . . in the event that I was unable to secure the necessary action by the Generalissimo which I thought reasonable and desirable, it would still be necessary for the U.S. Government, through me, to continue to back the National Government of the Republic of China...."[5] It is impossible to explain his actions relative to execution of this Presidential Order or to the attached statement of

---

3   Marshall, *The Papers of George Catlett Marshall, Vol V,* p.443

4   U.S. State Dept. *Foreign Relations, 1948. Vol. 7* p140

5   Marshall, *The Papers of George Catlett Marshall, Vol V,* p.770

U.S. Policy toward China. That policy reaffirmed prior pledges of aid by FDR and HST "U.S will continue to furnish military supplies and assist ......in the further transportation of Chinese troops... re-establish control over the liberated areas of China, including Manchuria."

On December 21, in Nanking, Marshall launched his China mediation in a meeting with Chiang Kai-shek, Mme. Chiang, General Wedemeyer and other lesser officials. He used a favorite ploy, attributing a negative attitude to the American public and media in order to present veiled threats in regard to aid and troop movements. Mme. Chiang, educated in the United States, questioned him on the posture of the press and he promptly backed off citing Congressional attitudes. In reality, in December 1945, the American public, Congress and press were still elated with the end of WW2 and concerned exclusively with bringing the troops home. Unfortunately for China, the only "attitude on China" in existence in America lay within the U.S. State Department.

While Marshall began his mediation in Chungking, Secretary of State Byrnes was in Moscow listening to friendly, cooperative remarks from Marshal Stalin. Byrnes was apparently another impressionable American mesmerized by the Soviet dictator. His Moscow trip records show no evidence of his earlier proposal to have the Russians apply pressure on the Chinese Communists. Instead, Byrnes, passive and compliant, avoided unpleasantness. He volunteered to Stalin, that in order to pressure Chiang Kai-shek, the U.S. was withholding the ships China needed to transport Government troops to Manchuria, Byrnes raised no questions, much less objections, to Soviet blocking of American ships from Manchurian ports in violation of the Yalta agreement or Mao's troops flooding into Manchuria in violation of the Sino–Soviet Treaty.[6]

On December 28, with the Manchurian situation at a tipping point, Marshall was advised that during Byrnes' Moscow visit, Stalin ". . . spoke of you (Marshall) in terms of the highest admiration and respect and said that he would be strongly predisposed to agree with any recommendations regarding the Chinese situation which had your approval..." Marshall found no reason to use Stalin and then minimized the Manchurian crisis. He told Truman he'd convinced Chiang the "embarrassments" in Manchuria were "common to Russian procedure everywhere...."[7]

Despite continued Soviet control of Manchuria and increasing Russian aid, Mao's infiltration of Manchuria was experiencing problems. One Communist officer recalled "the thing that gave us the worst headaches were desertions. All of us Party members, squad commanders, combat team leaders, had our own wobblies to watch. We would do everything, sentry duty, chores and errands together... When the wobblies wanted to take a leak, we would say I want to have a piss too... Some of us were so desperate we adopted the method the Japanese used with their laborers... Collected the men's trousers and stowed them in the Company HQ at night." Mao's Peoples Army, similar to his Great March required forced "volunteers".

---

6   U, S, State Dept. *Foreign Relations, 1945. Vol. 7 p.849*

7   Ibid, *p. 825*

As the Soviets neared their revised date for departure from Manchuria, they claimed technical difficulties and refused to leave. They'd trained and installed Mao's recruits in the major cities, but Manchurian commander Lin Biao warned Mao "there is no great likelihood of holding onto the cities. He also reported "people are saying that the 8th (Red) Route Army shouldn't be fighting the government Army ... They regard the Nationalists as the Central Government."[8] Clearly the Chinese Communists needed more time and Russian aid.

In America, several weeks earlier, on December 5th 1945, the New York Times had reported "U. S. backing China, Byrnes Declares: Secretary restates policy." Five days later, Time Magazine reported, "The policy is expected to be unequivocal: open, forth right cooperation with Chiang Kai-shek's National government, serving notice on the Chinese Communists that the U.S. will not be deterred from carrying out its promise to assist the Chungking government in taking over North China and Manchuria from the Japanese." But the Time article was already outdated. The day before Byrnes had written of broadening the Chinese government to include Communists and stated the U.S. should "encourage" concessions by the Nationalist government.[9]

The abandonment of Nationalist China was taking shape. Less than two weeks later the New York Times reported "Truman Says Aid to China Hinges On Ending Of Strife And

8   Chang and Hilliday, *Mao: The Unknown Story, p.288*
9   Utley, *The China Story, p.9*

Unification Of Nation...."[10] The President, in a complete turn-around, succumbed to the State Department supporters of Mao's "Agrarian Reformers" and abandoned his previous declarations of firm support and intent to carry out his and FDR's promises to Chiang Kai-shek's National Government. Truman's latest statement to the public seemed to contradict his and Byrne's instructions to Marshall that U.S. aid would continue if "unification" failed. Was this merely amplification of the empty threat ploy? Public statements not withstanding, Marshall's official orders to support China's government if all else failed, remained in force.

The State Department drive for Red inclusion in the National Government continued in the face of mounting evidence of Communist transgressions. On December 20, The American Consul in China reported emergency repairs to one critical rail line "that suffered, in every possible way, damage from the Communists." It cited other Communist activities "wrecking railways, requisitioning foodstuffs and enforcing compulsory conscription." There was no reason to expect any form of Red cooperation in China or anywhere else. Communist coalitions invariably resulted in Communist takeovers. In China, there were increasing indications the National government of China would not survive a coalition with the Communists.

Wedemeyer soon discovered the internal staff situation Hurley had faced while dealing with Mao Tse-tung. The Davies group and other people in the State Department were obstructing his efforts to move Government troops to accept

---

10 NY Times, *12/16/45, p.1 Truman Says Aid...*

surrendering Japanese. The use of American ships to transport government troops was being restricted and shipments of ammunition and other supplies were held up, waiting the State Department approval. Behind the scenes, Marshall quietly cut the Joint Chiefs of Staff's China Military Advisory Group from 3880 to "a few hundred".[11] MAG effectiveness was then completely curtailed by orders preventing any visits to combat areas.

Entering 1946, China faced near impossible obstacles. The country ravaged with tens of millions of displaced persons, an armed insurrection and campaign of sabotage underway and a neighboring world power poised to move against her. Meanwhile, Chiang Kai-shek saw signs of abandonment from his only external asset, the United States. Chiang had formulated a broad plan, and he evidenced great confidence in the "enduring strength of the people". During his "War of Resistance" against the Japanese, he wrote *China's Destiny*, his view of the country's history and its future based on Sun Yat-sen's Three Principles. He wrote "We must . . . lay the foundation for national reconstruction before we can determine our destiny as well as carry out the Three Peoples Principles. If we are hesitant, servile and indolent, . . . then our lost rights may not be recovered . . . In summary, China's destiny will be decided by the ability or inability of the Chinese people to be strong and independent, and to fulfill the mission of the War of Resistance and national reconstruction." He again stressed ". . . China must first become self-reliant. In order to become self-reliant, she must seek freedom and independence, and . . . progress and development

---

11 Dept of State, *Foreign Relations of the United States, 1946, p. 614-617, 639-643*

in national defense, economics, politics and culture."[12]   The sudden end of his War of Resistance against the Japanese upset many of his plans and exposed horrendous problems. But on January 10, Chiang lived up to previous promises; he opened the People's Consultive Conference with a keynote speech announcing immediate freedom from wartime restriction of speech, the press, religion, and assembly. Political prisoners would be released, and all political parties would henceforth be equal before the law.[13]

Veteran China hand, Claire Chennault returned in January 1946 and was shocked by the devastation and famine. "In the former Japanese-held corridor running south from Hankow, every major city except Changsha had been completely destroyed. Half of Changsha was in ruins... All the smaller villages and towns had been burned to the ground... The Japanese had stripped the countryside bare of food during their retreat. Now Chinese were stripping bark from trees and eating boiled weeds. —Japanese slaughter of oxen and water buffalo for food and gobbling of surplus seed stores left Chinese farmers without the means to start a new crop . . . all this was in an area that normally produced surplus rice to feed half of China." He saw transportation as the most acute need. "United Nations relief supplies were flowing across the Pacific into a bottleneck in Chinese ports. Vital goods were piled high in coastal warehouses unable to move inland while millions of people in the interior died of disease and starvation."   China marshaled its pitifully small resources and plodded ahead.

---

12   Chiang Kai-shek, *China's Destiny andChinese Economic Theory, p.233*
13   Taylor, *The Generalissimo, P.335*

Faced with Mao receiving increasing support from the Russians, Chiang's only option was to continue his shaky reliance on the U.S. and hope Moscow's tilt toward the CCP was not beyond correction. He had no faith in Mao's good intentions and believed only Stalin's intercession could avert civil war. To gauge Stalin's intentions, he sent his son, a long time Moscow resident who knew the Soviets, to meet with Stalin. Chiang saw no other prospects for a peaceful solution. Meanwhile he had to cooperate with Marshall's mediation efforts in order to keep the door open for U.S. aid.

On the domestic scene, Chiang addressed economic problems. He banned the sale of foreign currency and gold bullion, set a ceiling on interest rates, froze all wages and prices for essential food items and postponed government projects in an effort to control inflation. These economic measures along with a relaxation of wartime restrictions on civil liberties brought Chiang Kai-shek and his party to their highest point of internal and international acclaim. To correct landlord excesses and respond to Red propaganda on land reform, a law reducing land rentals to 8% of land value was passed and a land distribution program was launched. In it, the landlord set a price on his land at which he would sell to the government for distribution to the peasants. If the price was out of line, taxes would be adjusted upward to penalize the excess.[14]

As the new year of 1946 opened, China's delicate balance continued to tilt toward mass famine and disaster. Its huge cities required rice from distant rice growing areas and coal from

---

14   Utley, *Last Chance for China,* p.322

North China. The rail system was vital for survival. Although the Nationalist Army was far superior to the Communist militia at the beginning in 1946, the government's first responsibility was to ensure the flow of food and fuel to the millions of city dwellers struggling to recover from the depredations of the Japanese. In contrast, the Chinese Communists rejected any responsibility for the welfare of China's people. Government defense against the Red campaign of sabotage, destruction of rail lines, dikes, dams, bridges and other infrastructure tied up much of Chiang's army and slowed Government occupation of Japanese held areas. When General Wedemeyer requested a substantial U.S. Army force to guard the food and fuel supply lines and prevent disaster in the cities, two U.S. Marine divisions were sent to guard the railroad line from Peking (Beijing) to the sea. Protection of all the remaining rail lines and infrastructure would have to be accomplished by Government troops.

Marshall began his mediation by raising the minority Chinese Reds to equal voice with the Nationalist Government in all negotiations and then using leverage only on the National Government. The mediation also suffered from a vast difference in the skill levels of the participants. General Marshall, a career military man who favored a formal aloof posture, had no experience in give and take negotiations. He considered himself a manager of people and his correct, icy manner served him well enough to gain advancement in army staff positions. However, his tendency to delegate decision making and negotiation tasks to subordinates left him ill-equipped to deal with the charming Chou En-lai. The Communist Chinese representative was a master intriguer and negotiator who soon penetrated Marshall's fragile social barriers. Marshall took Chou's charming manner as an indication of sincerity and a desire to cooperate.[15] But sincerity was a foreign concept to the charming Red, a lifelong true Communist whose engaging manner was only one of many tactics, a means to an end. In dealing with Chou, Marshall became the managed one. At the outset, Marshall broke one of the first rules of negotiation: deal only with decision-makers. After he accepted Chou as representing Mao's Communist movement, Chou, when in need of a delay, would request time to travel back to Yenan to get a decision. It seems, going in, Marshall took the Reds at face value. One reporter who was frequently invited to General Marshall's residence noted Chou En-lai had succeeded in captivating Marshall and "any doubts he had about the State Department's view of "progressive" Communists or doubts that they would bring democracy to China were soon dispelled." Soon after meeting with Chou En-lai, Marshall adopted the red-speak term "reactionary" in reference to elements in the Nationalist Government.

Entering 1946, Manchuria (Man zhou) loomed as the most pressing problem for China. All agreed China needed strong, prosperous northern provinces, but FDR's secret agreement giving Soviet Russia preeminent rights loomed against China's prospects. However, if the Soviets performed to the new treaty conditions and evacuated their occupation troops in orderly fashion, Manchuria might be saved. Wedemeyer advised Chiang to attempt an international arrangement to govern Manchuria and concentrate his military efforts on the remainder of China. But events were

---

15   Sheng, *Battling Western Imperialism,* *p.129*

accelerating. There was no time to develop international arrangements. Chiang had no alternative. He was forced to base his planning on American aid promises and the recently signed treaty with the Soviets. He committed his armies to the takeover of Manchuria from the Soviet occupiers, as outlined in the Sino/Soviet treaty sponsored by the U.S.. He hoped for U.S. pressure on Moscow that could resolve Russian support of Mao's Reds then flowing into Manchuria. His plans did not provide for the impact of George Catlett Marshall.

Marshall's first moves in China gave the Red Chinese precious time. Time needed to organize and train hordes of newly conscripted troops in recently occupied areas. Marshall used the embargo of munitions shipments to pressure the government, into a truce. According to the truce, all hostilities would cease immediately. But also all troop movements would cease. Meanwhile the Soviets continued to organize and arm their Red Chinese comrades then flowing into Manchuria. While Mao's Reds scrambled to organize and train the masses, the Russians filled the void. They reinforced the weak, newly recruited Red Chinese forces with "Union Communists", Korean, and Chinese exiles trained in Russia and also with Japanese POWs. Ignoring the niceties of the Geneva Convention, the Soviets gave recently captured Japanese prisoners of war the choice of fighting for Mao Tse-tung or death.

The U.S. denial of transportation followed by Marshall's embargos and truces restrained and weakened Government forces while the Soviets armed, supported, and directed rapid Chinese Communist takeovers in Manchuria. Below Manchuria, in North China, the Reds were no match for Government forces. They set up small governing bodies in the backwater areas of the Japanese occupation zone, but effective training and mobilizing of manpower was nonexistent. Mao's tiny government in Yenan had no experience dealing with great masses of people. Suddenly, they were faced with millions of new subjects. Above all, they needed time. Time to absorb and mobilize the millions of "volunteers" in the so called "liberated areas" of North China and millions more offered up to them by their Soviet comrades in Manchuria.

On January 15, only three weeks in country, General Marshall prepared a schedule for the demobilization of the Nationalist Chinese Army during the next six months. He pressed Wedemeyer for a "Rush reply" of supporting information that he could quote to Chiang in his next "mediation" session. When Wedemeyer replied, he was not aware of Marshall's arms embargo and other pressures Marshall brought to bear on Chiang Kai-shek, conditions that would normally be considered in developing recommendations for the demobilization of Nationalist troops. There is no evidence of a parallel Marshall concern with control of the Red forces that were then expanding exponentially.

Within days, the government moved to occupy Jehol and Chahar, two provinces flanking the overland route from China to Manchuria. State Department transport restrictions had prevented prompt occupation after the Japanese surrender. Government occupation of Jehol and Chahar would seriously impede Red ability to attack government forces moving into Manchuria when the Soviet army pulled out. Now, with Marshall on the scene, Chou En-lai objected to this latest Nationalist troop movement. Marshall pressured Chiang Kai-shek to concede the gateway provinces he needed to march his troops north. Marshall noted in a report to Truman: "the Communists claimed that their troops have already occupied those places."[16] If so, it was a blatant violation of Marshall's mediation agreements. The Government requested a truce team be sent to investigate but Marshall complied with Chou En-lai's request for no action[17] and the government's attempt to protect their route north was thwarted. A scenario that would be repeated a few weeks later when mediator Marshall again succeeded in blocking Government moves to assume control over Chinese territory.

Chiang Kai-shek's concessions brought no reward. When the Chinese Government protested that the State Department had disapproved export licenses, preventing purchase of small arms ammunition, Marshall told Chiang this move had been made without reference to him. On January 18, despite the cease-fire, Red troops attacked and took two cities in Manchuria, one an important port city, Yingkou. Marshall ignored the violations in his report to Washington, an omission that disturbed Chiang. Two weeks later, despite many such violations, Marshall told Truman "affairs are progressing rather favorably."[18] HST had every reason to believe the China situation was under control.

---

16   Marshall, *The Papers of George Catlett Marshall, Vol. V, p.416*

17   Ibid, *p.430*

18   Taylor, *The Generalissimo, 342*

Records indicate General Marshall was well aware of joint Russian/PLA activities in Manchuria. On January 14, 1946 he conveyed to his field observer Col. Byroade "information here, stated as being from a reliable source, indicates presence in Chihfeng, North China, of approximately 10,000 troops . . . organized by the Chinese Communists into a military force. A certain Japanese by name Tanaka is responsible for training this force. Armament for this force is supplied by the Soviets including 20,000 rifles, 150 heavy machine guns and 25 field pieces... Same source indicates presence of Soviets . . . who exercise command over previously referred to local force."[19] One week later, he learned the Soviets were not only aiding, but were actively participating in hostilities against the Government forces in Manchuria.[20]

On January 23, 1946, Marshall told Truman of Russians in Manchuria firing on Nationalist troops rather than aiding them as agreed in the recent treaty. The Soviets were actually increasing local garrisons and pressing for permanent Russian joint participation in the operation of the heavy industries they'd not already dismantled. Despite an increasing number of reports of direct Soviet aid to the Chinese Reds, Marshall would later declare the Russians were "aloof" in Manchuria, that he had no shred of evidence the Soviet Union was aiding Mao's forces. Invariably, Marshall's solution for China's problem of Red insurrection and sabotage was: bring the Communists into government "at an early date."

---

19   Marshall, *The Papers of George Catlett Marshall, Vol. V, p.421,422*
20   Ibid, *p.427*

Marshall's aid cut off meant the U.S. was reneging on Truman's promise of equipping of 39 divisions and 8 1/3 air groups, (in itself, a drastic cut back of FDR's promise to equip 90 divisions). More importantly, it meant that unless ammunition shipments resumed, the Chinese divisions already equipped with American weapons would soon be put out of action. Chiang's Chinese arsenals were not equipped to manufacture U.S. 30 caliber ammunition. For the majority of China's divisions, her war-depleted arsenals could produce only a fraction of the 7.92 mm. Chinese ammunition needed for their worn, inaccurate weapons. Chiang had relied on FDR's pledge to equip 90 divisions and had turned China's limited resources away from rebuilding his depleted arsenals. Now he was deprived of ammunition for his small U.S. equipped force and lacked capacity to supply the bulk of his army equipped with Chinese weapons. Marshall regularly used the prize of resumption of ammo shipments to gain concessions from Chiang Kai-shek. Although Chiang was a shrewd negotiator, after making concessions, he would find supplies held up by obscure red tape at lower levels.

When Chiang's son, Ching-kuo, returned from his Moscow meeting with Stalin, he reported a drastic change in attitude. Where Stalin had told Byrnes he was not concerned on how long U.S. troops remained in China, one week later the dictator warned Ching-kuo that the U.S. was trying to use China for its own purposes. He required not "a single American soldier" in China before the USSR would tell the CCP to come to an "understanding."

Before the month was out, the Soviet Commander in Manchuria, General Malinovsky, informed Chungking his army could not meet the new February deadline for Soviet pullout from Manchuria, due to "technical reasons."

On February 9, 1946, Stalin shocked Washington with a speech declaring World War II was the "inevitable result" of "modern monopoly capitalism and the next war would result the same." Truman reacted ordering Byrnes to "play compromise" no longer. The U.S. should "rehabilitate China and create a strong central government there. We should do the same for Korea . . . I am tired of babying the Soviets." But once again, the President was dissuaded from following through on his intentions.

In China, as peace unraveled, Chou En-lai kept General Marshall on course. Marshall's attitude was the only element that remained unchanged in China. But his reports to President Truman varied dramatically. Six weeks after Marshall dismissed Soviet transgressions in Manchuria as "embarrassments" and three weeks after reporting "affairs are progressing rather favorably", he told Truman "Manchuria is a festering situation." His solution, again, was bringing Mao's CCP into the Government "at the fastest possible pace and thereby eliminates vulnerability to Soviet undercover attack."

On February 25, The Reds generously agreed to a troop ratio in Manchuria of fourteen Government divisions to one PLA division. At that time, there were 30 Communist divisions in Manchuria. It was an agreement they obviously had no intention of keeping. However, General Marshall accepted it as a valid and generous concession and it further enhanced his image of Chou En-lai and the CCP.[21] Chou next agreed to a national ratio of 90 National government divisions to 18 PLA divisions, Marshall was immensely pleased. He believed the Communists would give up a huge and growing army if "reactionary" KMT factions in the National Government could be quieted. Elated, Marshall visited Yenan, and enjoyed the full treatment. He was received by wildly cheering crowds and had long talks with Mao and others. Mao complimented Marshall on the fairness of the ceasefire and told him Chinese democracy "must follow the American path." Chou reported to Mao that Marshall told him he trusted the sincerity of the Chinese Communists but was having difficulty persuading the Kuomintang leaders. Chou told his secretary that Marshall "reminded me of Stilwell."[22] General Marshall thoroughly enjoyed his visit to CCP headquarters and was immensely pleased with what he saw as progress.

In China proper, south of Manchuria, tension was mounting. The public was newly exposed to the inflammatory aspects of a free press, and the latest news was bad. As the Soviets continued to violate their pledge to move troops out of Manchuria, indignation increased to the point where Chiang Kai-shek was getting resistance from within his party. Then, in April, FDR's high-handed Yalta giveaway of Manchurian assets to the Soviets was revealed to the public in China. Seven high government officials signed a denunciation of the Yalta

---

21   Taylor, *The Generalissimo, p.343*

22   Ibid, *p.343*

pact as "a dark stain" on American and British relations with China. Concurrently, word reached Chungking of new Russian depredations in Manchuria. Demonstrations and riots erupted in the streets. Marshall somehow construed these several days of civic unrest in reaction to Red aggression as a serious offense to Red sensibilities, serious enough to justify excusing Red violations of his ceasefire.[23]

As the situation in China slid towards civil war, General Marshall raised questionable international concerns and displayed a curious naïveté. He saw an improvement of China's image on the world scene if the two divisions of U.S. Marines, then protecting the Peking railway from Red sabotage, were removed. He'd told Truman on February 9, his belief was ". . . time was running against the Soviet, since the longer her troops remained in Manchuria the more clearly she becomes a deliberate treaty violator in the eyes of the world." There exists no evidence that Stalin entertained the slightest concern for "the eyes of the world" at any point in his career.

When Marshall lacked solid data, he resorted to insights on world opinion, U.S. public opinion and Chinese public opinion in his efforts to persuade. Stiff and formal, Marshall had minimal exposure to any of it. Marshall's Appointments Secretary, who controlled contact with individual Chinese citizens, was later proven to be a Communist agent.

Marshall invented new reasoning in order to urge that China must speed up inclusion of the Communists into government.

---

23 Taylor, *The Generalissimo,* p.344

"We must clear our hands out here as quickly as possible in order to avoid the inevitable Russian recriminations . . ." Throughout his tenure, Marshall stated great concern for Soviet criticism and extraordinary concern over the U.S. image in the United Nations and the world. He also contradicted earlier assertions with the inexplicable declaration that he found no evidence whatsoever of Soviet aid to the Chinese Communists. He said ". . . it seems apparent to me that the Soviets were bending over backwards...."[24] But on May 13th, Chou reported to the Red Central Committee that Marshall said he was aware of "Soviet support to us in the Northeast."[25] It seemed Marshall's report to the President was a simple recitation of Chou En-lai's version of the situation. When specific, indisputable evidence of Russians aiding the PLA was presented to him, Marshall dismissed it as the work of local Soviet commanders, activities unauthorized by Moscow, or passed it off as Russians merely acting as they normally did. Chiang worried about a Marshall who thought "he knew Chinese politics very well, but . . . does not." In particular Marshall's remarks about Communist good intentions bothered Chiang, who had seen every trick the Reds had to offer. Marshall's next move defied reason.

When General Marshall pursued the primary purpose of his mission, the incorporation of Red troops into the National Army, Communist chief negotiator, Chou En-lai, insisted the Communists needed more time. Marshall stated later he was puzzled, but then had a "flash." His "flash" was a bizarre plan

---

24 Tsou, *America's Failure in China,* p.368,369
25 Taylor, *The Generalissimo,* p.349

to train Red officers and arm Red troops before they joined the National Army. Marshall claimed he initiated the scheme by asking Chou if it would speed things up if American officers taught the Communists the fundamentals of modern military staff work. (It may have been Chou testing how far he could move Marshall). It got worse. Marshall claimed the CCP was embarrassed by the condition of their troops compared to the segment of the Government Army trained and equipped by the U.S. and therefore the Reds needed arms as well as training.(Previously, when the Reds sought U.S. recognition, their troops were touted as vastly superior to government troops.) Now in true Communist dialectic fashion the super soldiers of a year earlier needed training to avert serious embarrassment of their hard-bitten leaders. The logic of training and arming the insurrectionist army before it joined the national army was not questioned.

Marshall proceeded rapidly with his absurdity. In order to set up a Red "West Point", he brought officers in from the U.S. to serve as instructors. He then expanded his "training" program to include the equipping of Red Army divisions. He saw no contradiction in arming Mao's Reds while he denied the Government promised munitions. Rather than pressing the Reds to adhere to the previously agreed upon schedule, Marshall then awarded the ultimate carrot, more time to digest the manpower and resources handed them by the Soviets in Manchuria. Marshall moved decisively to start his school for Red division and corps staff officers and commanders. He declared "it is of great importance to get the first courses started without delay. He contacted General MacArthur in Tokyo for aid in staffing the school, and he arranged with Dean

Acheson in Washington to get funding for weapons and ammunition for the Reds.[26] It seemed Joseph Stilwell's goal of arming the Reds would be realized.

On March 22, Marshall held forth on the integration of Nationalist/Communist forces. He calculated that Government units should not need much equipment in order to downsize to 50 divisions, although he had already blocked the U.S. pledge to equip 39 divisions. In a gesture of supreme trust, he decided the Reds should be equipped "before" integrating into the government forces. Equipment for ten divisions was on hand in Japan and Marshall was quite definite, it should be awarded to the Communists. He doubted any of it could be delivered to Government forces under the Lend Lease Act and he'd already blocked surplus sales to the Chinese Government. On March 27, the material that could not be lend-leased to China was reclassified. Marshall stated "I am trying to rush the provision of equipment . . . for the important 10 Communist divisions. This has to be managed if possible within lend lease provisions."[27] The Reds, by that time assured of full Russian support, ended the farce. They were well aware of the plight of the U. S. armed nationalist divisions then deprived of promised ammunition.

During these negotiations, Marshall's declared goal was bringing the Communist Chinese into the government of China under the label of "political unity". He induced the National

---

26 Marshall, *The Papers of George Catlett Marshall, Vol. V, p.465,466*
27 Ibid, *p.516*

government to take steps to ensure democratic civil liberties, promote local self-government, curb the "secret police," (China's FBI, CIA), grant equality to all legal parties, and release all political prisoners. Marshall, conditioned by Chou En-lai, was apparently not aware that Chiang Kai-shek had already granted freedom of press and other civil rights. There is no record of any comments by Marshall, during or after his visit to Yenan, in regard to civil rights in Red controlled areas. Rather than set requirements for the Reds, General Marshall seemed to follow Chou En-lai's advice. When Chou advised against a loan to the Chinese Government "it would make reactionaries more arrogant and government reform and military reorganization more difficult."[28] An insurrectionist advising on aid to a U.S. ally was not considered incongruous. Marshall ostensibly advocating a loan for China, recommended conditions that effectively negated such aid.

On March 11, a showdown was impending. Marshall had set up three-man truce teams to oversee his cease-fire as Chiang's government troops replaced the Russians in Manchuria. S. Herbert Hitch, an American on Marshall's staff, noted later it was strange that none of the American members of the teams spoke Chinese or had any familiarity with Chinese matters.

The agreed upon troop move was the decisive test of the Red commitment to drastically reduce their forces in Manchuria. Chiang Kai-shek quickly agreed with all conditions but the always agreeable Chou En-lai now objected. Suddenly, all the resolved issues were rendered meaningless. The Manchurian crises, the "festering situation" worsened. In this stalemate, Marshall

---

28   Sheng, *Battling Western Imperialism, p.138*

abruptly left for Washington, where he amazingly reported both sides "are now engaged in the business of demobilizing vast military forces and integrating and unifying the remaining forces into a Central army."[29]

Demobilization and integration became more unlikely as each day passed. While Marshall reassured President Truman in Washington, the situation in Manchuria degenerated into wide open warfare, and fighting also broke out in North China.

Ambassador Stuart voiced a more objective view of the truce violations "...The most serious of these was the Communist entry into Manchuria where the Soviet Union turned over to him very large stocks of Japanese military equipment. After this flagrant disregard of the terms, the Nationalists felt naturally justified in any form of retaliation."[30]

In Washington, Marshall blandly declared that a key difference existed between the Red insurrections in Greece and China. He told the Committee on Foreign Affairs: "In Greece you have a force which is being supported by bordering states, now in China, we had no concrete evidence that it is supported by Communists from the outside." He contradicted his Ambassador's very recent report and his own previous reports. He also defied simple logic. He did not explain where the Reds obtained the arms required for their massive buildup of forces after the Japanese surrender.

General Marshall then raised his trust of the Reds to new levels. In the past, news correspondents and authors visiting

---

29 Taylor, *The Generalissimo, p.345*

30 Stuart, *Fifty years in China, P.161*

Yenan accepted Red restrictions on their travel and then accepted Communist claims as confirmed information because they had no access to conflicting information. General Marshall completely accepted Red claims despite evidence and logic to the contrary. He ignored the Soviet's blocking the U.S. Navy from Manchurian ports and Navy reports of Red Chinese entrenched in those ports. Marshall's subordinate, Lieutenant. General Gellem reported from Manchuria "the Communists are definitely the aggressors." He pointed out that Communist strength in Manchuria, upon the Japanese surrender, was 30 to 40,000 but since had grown to 300,000. This, while Marshall's cease-fire agreement stipulated that only Government forces should move into or within Manchuria. Meanwhile, Chou En-lai pressed for a halt in further Nationalist troop movements into the area. On April 3, Mao directed Chou to use Marshall to reach a truce and thereby gain time to prepare to fight.[31] Mao christened this his "talk with fight" strategy.

The situation in Manchuria was deteriorating rapidly. In the far north, the Soviet Army was evacuating Mukden, Manchuria's largest city, leaving stunned, hungry Chinese and skeleton factories picked clean of machinery. Fires raged throughout the city as National Government troops moved in to take control and masses of Chinese Communist troops moved into position on the outskirts. On April 14, The Russians evacuated Changchun, the former Japanese capital of Manchuria and 20,000 waiting Red Chinese troops fully armed with Japanese weapons, immediately attacked and slaughtered 7000 Government occupation

31   Sheng, *Battling Western Imperialism, p.138*

troops. It was reported tanks operated by Japanese were used. It seemed logical, since at that early date, Mao's rural militia were incapable of operating motorized vehicles. Marshall was deeply puzzled by the attack. He evidenced no hint of awareness that his friend, the reasonable and agreeable Chou En –lai was the point man for a Communist "talk with fight" strategy. The State Department later decried the Changchun massacre as a" flagrant" cease fire violation. But they objected not for the 7000 slaughtered Nationalist troops, they complained the attack strengthened the hand of "ultra-reactionary" groups in the Chinese government. The use of Japanese POW tank units was ignored. By April 1946, the bulk of the Government's Manchuria occupation force had sat for months on the Manchurian border, waiting for the Russians to live up to the treaty obligations and pull out.

At that point, Marshall returned to China from Washington, and faced the realities he had denied in his Washington report. He criticized both sides but, took no issue with Chou over the Changchun massacre. Instead, he pressed Chiang to order a cease-fire and allow the Chinese Communists to retain occupation of the huge territories in Manchuria the Russians had ceded to them. Areas Marshall had designated as Chinese Government areas in his first truce.

On April 20, when Marshall addressed the Changchun situation with Chou En-lai, he ignored the massacre. His sole request to Chou addressed the safety of the U.S. military attaché, his assistant and five correspondents. He proposed no truce for Changchun. No criticism of Red aggression was voiced. Instead, on the same day, he wrote a lengthy communication to Chiang Kai-shek to explain and smooth over his planned supplying of arms to the Communist divisions included in his "Red West Point" project. He noted he made a special effort to arrange shipments to arrive in Shanghai before expiration of the lend lease act on June 30, the expiration date that precluded shipment of that material to the government. Two days later, April 22, Marshall met with General Yu, China's Vice Minister of War. He essentially blamed Yu and Chiang Kai-shek for the Manchurian situation, citing what he considered to be truce violations outside Manchuria, in China proper, and claiming Chiang's speeches had "murdered" his efforts to get a large loan for China. Marshall's "efforts" consisted of recommending restrictions that negated the benefits of a loan that China had requested from the Export-Import Bank.[32]

As the CCP continued to aggressively expand into new areas, Marshall asked Chou En-lai what it would take to pacify them. Chou responded by demanding an increase in the troop limits they'd agreed to three months earlier, because conditions had changed. Marshall's reply resulted in an embarrassing exposure of a willingness to sacrifice his integrity, as well as Chinese Government interests. His go-between at that point, a prominent local figure, told the press that Marshall assured the Reds he would guarantee an agreement within 24 hours if the Reds would clearly state their demands. If true, it seemed all Red demands were acceptable to Marshall. In addition to displaying Marshall's pronounced pro-Red

---

32   Marshall, *The Papers of George Catlett Marshall, Vol. V, p.518*

posture, it exposed an amateurish lack of discretion in selecting confidants.[33]

In early May, Government forces surrounded the Red 5th Division in Northern China. Although Marshall had ample evidence by that time that concessions to Chou brought no reciprocity, when Chou went to Marshall to save the division, Marshall arranged a truce.[34] There is no record of a Marshall request for concessions from the Reds for the salvation of the Red 5th Division.

In a communication to HST, on May 6, Marshall related his insight into the motives and thinking of the Chinese Communists. Mao's mass movement of troops into Manchuria in violation of his (Marshall's) mediation agreements was due to "The Communists became fearful of the good faith of the government party in carrying out the written agreements for the formation of a bona fide coalition interim government and the drafting of a constitution to be submitted to the Constitutional Convention scheduled for May 5." Marshall felt Red fears were justified by the anti-Communist demonstrations in Chungking and somehow aggravated by an earlier government proposal on truce team authority. Somehow, the Reds were justified in massive, deadly violations of his agreements if they convinced him they were fearful the opposition might violate his agreements. General Marshall's bottom line was the Reds were blameless and not to be held accountable. An amazing bias for the Presidential Representative, when the U.S. War Department had declared Manchuria critical to U.S.

---

33 Time Magazine, *5/6/46, Sliding Scale*

34 Sheng, *Battling Western Imperialism, p140*

interests. Mediator Marshall later clarified his unusual mediation posture in his farewell statement to Chou En-lai.[35]

The U.S. Navy failure to transport government troops, the State Department's restriction on transporting troops, the arms embargo and the truces that allowed the Reds to infiltrate and occupy Manchuria were not mentioned in Marshall's analysis. At one point, he admitted that the Russians gave Mao's Reds freedom of movement and Japanese military equipment stores including medium tanks, but he soon reverted to declaring the Soviets were "aloof" and blameless. It seemed reasonable to Marshall that because of his perception of doubt and fear in Communist minds, they were justified in any new demand. They now insisted on representation in the government of Manchuria, a direct conflict with U.S. War Department goals.

Similar to Marshall's acceptance of the Reds as equals at the mediation table, he moved towards accepting them as military equals in Manchuria. He then explained to Truman that he "permitted" movement of two Nationalist armies to Manchuria, but he declined to authorize movement of two additional armies because he "doubted U.S. Seventh Fleet ability to transport them." Thus, the desk soldier of WW2, who delegated decision making to subordinates, found reason to assume final authority on Chinese Army troop movements. It was less than six months after HST's decision to "not meddle in China's affairs". General Marshall "doubted seventh fleet ability" But he had not consulted the Navy, he had other reasons. According to CCP documents, Chou recommended they pressure Marshall

---

35   Foreign Relations of the U.S., *1947, vol.7, p.33*

to force Chiang to accept a ceasefire.[36] Chou En-lai easily put Marshall on the defensive with accusations that the U.S. Navy was transporting government troops to Manchuria. Although such a move would have been completely in keeping with U.S. rights and commitments, it put the ever compliant Marshall on the defensive. Marshall extended assurances to Chou that no Navy ships would be involved, but was unable to prevent the first two movements.

Despite Marshall's restriction on government troop movements, in late May, the Red Army in Manchuria was in trouble. Mao was on the verge of abandoning his last major city in Manchuria and dispersing his forces into guerrilla units. On June 3rd he issued the order to retreat. Two days later he learned of Chou En-lai's success with Marshall and dashed off a new order "Hang on... especially keep Harbin." The tide had turned. Marshall pressured Chiang to stop his advances in Manchuria. Chiang reluctantly agreed to a ten-day cease-fire. The Reds requested a month and Marshall went back and pressed Chiang to increase it up to fifteen days. On May 21, Chou En-lai formally requested that the coalition agreement be changed to allow an increase of Red divisions in Manchuria. Marshall supposed that an increase might be possible."[37] Marshall's initial agreement specified no Red divisions in Manchuria.

In less than five months, the mediation process had degenerated to the point where the Reds could abandon any agreement by citing a change in the situation and the government could be

---

36 Taylor, *The Generalissimo*. *P.348*

37 Marshall, *The Papers of George Catlett Marshall, Vol. V, p.562*

forced into nearly any concession demanded of it, in hopes of receiving promised aid. The negotiations were fast becoming a farce to all but General Marshall, who continued to sense fine liberal sentiments somewhere deep in the Red hierarchy and see dark motives in "reactionary" KMT circles. CCP forces continued to sabotage the infrastructure supporting the delicate balance of survival for the people of China. Ambassador Stuart, traveling at the end of April noted "the railways had all been cut by the Communists."

While Generalissimo Chiang Kai-shek contended with Mao's growing army, Red sabotage, U.S. reneging on promised aid, Soviet aid to the insurrectionists, post war recovery problems and General Marshall's "mediation," Mme. Chiang was busy in the United States contacting and then organizing influential Americans into a political support group for China. Marshall, under pressure, approved a six month supply of ammunition for the small, U.S. armed, segment of the Government army. But he soon added obstacles to obstruct the shipment of the ammunition. He then made a high level concession to the Reds.

When Ambassador Hurley resigned and Marshall was appointed Presidential Representative to China, General Wedemeyer was offered the position of Ambassador. Marshall advised him to turn it down. Months later, Marshall reversed himself and urged Wedemeyer to take the position of Ambassador. Wedemeyer's recent successful experience in China made him the ideal candidate. But after he accepted, purchased his diplomatic wardrobe and arranged travel to Chungking, Dean Acheson abruptly notified him the appointment was off. The reason: Chou En-lai was displeased with the choice of Wedemeyer as Ambassador. It seemed the Red insurrectionists held veto power over the selection of the U.S. ambassador to an ally. It's ironic that the Reds were able to cancel Wedemeyer's appointment with a simple objection where previously Chiang was plagued with Joseph Stilwell for several years and then had to confront FDR before getting relief.

The relationships and power positions of Chiang, Chou En-lai and General Marshall in the mediation process were again clearly defined in a seeming minor issue that Marshall fumbled into crises. He'd planned to place three man observation teams in the field to monitor his upcoming ceasefire. Chiang proposed the American member of the team should have final voice when disagreements arose. Marshall was elated and reported as much to Washington. However, after a six hour meeting with Chou En-lai, Marshall appeared completely reoriented on the issue.[38] On leaving Chou, Marshall attacked Chiang Kai-shek for causing the integrity of his position as mediator to be challenged. Chiang's proposal suddenly became a serious offense. Marshall presented it to President Truman as an excuse for large scale Red attacks that violated his ceasefire. Marshall's criticism of Chiang's proposal on the three man truce team displays the peculiar gaps in the famous Marshall intellect. Chiang's proposal was a proposal, nothing more. If Marshall accepted it and came to grief, unless he, Marshall, was a simple messenger, he, George Catlett Marshall was solely responsible. The acceptance of this issue to somehow justify Communists attacking and killing

---

38 Taylor, The Generalissimo, p.352

human beings tells much about the limitations of the data processing intellect.

On June 3, Chiang Kai-shek and Mao Tse-tung issued cease-fire announcements. Three hours later Government commanders reported attacks by PLA troops. 50,000 Red troops surrounded the port of Qingdao. Chiang asked for U.S. transport of his troops to reinforce the city. Marshall refused. Then, after talking to Chou En-lai, he reported to Truman the Red attack was provoked by two non-violent events. One was the Chiang proposal to give Americans the deciding vote on the truce monitoring teams the other was his (Marshall's) absence from Nanking.[39]

As the PLA flooded into Manchuria, it seems Marshall, after five months mediation, became aware of a common negotiating technique and briefly interrupted his harmonious relationship with Chou En-lai. Chou again requested an extension of time in order to travel to Yenan and gain Mao's approval on issues he, conveniently, was not authorized to resolve. On June 6 Marshall suggested "Chou become well-informed at Yenan as to just what lengths he could go in negotiations." In his irritation, Marshall, at long last, raised the issue of Communist sabotage, he termed it "disrupting communications." On June 12, he again raised the sabotage issue and asked Chou to stop destruction of railways and other infrastructure, curiously adding "unless they are absolutely forced to do so by circumstances...."[40] People in the cities could freeze and starve within six months if fuel and food shipments were blocked by Red demolition of railroads. Marshall did not define "circumstances"

39   Taylor, *The Generalissimo*, p.353

40   Marshall, *The Papers of George Catlett Marshall, Vol. V*, p 589

that would justify such avoidable tragedy. Along with the obvious Red disinterest in the people's welfare, Chiang Kai-shek in a meeting on June 27 pointed out another significant and easily verified fact. He knew of no instance where the inhabitants of a region occupied by the government had fled to a region controlled by the Communists, whereas over 5 million people had already fled from Communist-controlled regions. Marshall was not impressed.

On June 19, Dean Acheson, unaware the Reds had rejected Marshall's "Red West Point" scheme, moved ahead to secure funds for the project. He told the House Committee on Foreign Affairs "General Marshall had agreed to training and supplying Red forces as part of his program." During that period, Congress, along with the American public, believed the Chinese Government was receiving the promised flow of U.S. aid.

The month of July 1946 exposed State's policy of impartiality as a myth. After six months, red tape excuses for holding up arms shipments were wearing thin. Dean Acheson attempted a formal embargo. He proposed that munitions shipments be designated only for an integrated Chinese Army. The integrated Army was an army the Reds had no intention of joining. During that period, at the request of General Marshall, the State Department secretly refused licenses for the export of the ammunition that Marshall had previously agreed to. He admitted later that it amounted to an embargo. No reasons were offered.

On June 22, Mao Tse-tung had demanded that the U.S. end all aid to China. One month later, on July 22, Gen. Marshall advised Congress that he no longer supported a China aid bill then under consideration. By the end of the month, the Whitehouse issued an executive order denying the Chinese Government U.S. war surplus weapons which could be used in fighting a civil war. Thus, any aid that might do harm to the Communists was officially prohibited.

As summer wore on, the time came for the Communists to live up to their promises to General Marshall. The Reds had committed to reducing their Manchurian forces to a ratio of 1:14 vs. Government forces and reducing their total forces to 18 divisions. Promises they never intended to keep. They realized they'd gotten nearly all the concessions available from Marshall's "mediation." Chou reported to the CCP Central Committee "the chances of making use of the United States and Marshall are diminishing daily...."[41] Chou En-lai's charming presence, warm, friendly mannerisms and meaningless concessions were coming to an end. But General Marshall maintained his course.

Soon, PLA cease-fire violations increased to the point where even Marshall recognized the trend toward open war. On July 7, Marshall advised visiting Secretary of the Navy Forrestal that negotiations had taken a very sharp turn for the worse. He admitted his truces had worked "to some extant" in favor of the Communists. Marshall told Forrestal that, if negotiations to preserve the settlement broke down, he would recommend a period of withdrawal so that the United States could take two or three months for reappraisal and reevaluation of their policy toward China. "Withdrawal" meant continued denial of aid and further draw down of the Nationalist's depleted supplies. Forrestal also met with Admiral Cooke, Wedemeyer's replacement as commander of U.S. military

---

41   Taylor, *The Generalissimo,* p.351

in China and heard dire warnings. Contrary to Marshall's negative remarks and views on China, Cooke saw, in China, the potential for making a great nation. He believed the Chinese were like
Americans in that they prized personal liberty and freedom of the
individual, but they lacked knowledge of the principles of management needed to govern effectively.

Failure of Marshall's mediation left him adrift. This was the
situation Truman and Byrnes had specified would trigger U.S.
support of the Chinese Government. Despite conflicting public
statements, the President's formal orders to General Marshall had
not changed. But Marshall did not seek clarification of his original orders from President Truman or Secretary of State Byrnes.
On July 2, Marshall reached down and sought the advice of Dean
Acheson. True to form, Acheson recommended if war ensued, the
U.S. should end all material support and withdraw all military
personnel.

As the month of July advanced, Marshall's reaction to several
incidents confirmed his mindset. In Kunming, unknown assassins
killed two leaders of a minor political party and the freedom of
the press that Chiang recently granted came back to haunt him.
Partisans in the Chungking press accused the KMT party and
Chiang Kai-shek of complicity in the murders. The Reds exploited
it fully and Marshall accepted the killings as a plot by KMT reactionaries possibly involving Chiang Kai-shek. Why Chiang, nearly
submerged in economic disaster and civil war would kill two obscure politicians defies explanation. The only winners were the
Communists. Despite no evidence of KMT guilt, Marshall believed
in an evil, "reactionary" KMT. Meanwhile, three hundred Red

troops ambushed fifty-five U.S. Marines killing seven. Marshall declared it was "definitely the work of the Communists," but he didn't raise the issue with Chou En-lai. Chiang thought Marshall acted as if nothing had happened.[42] Marshall's papers indicate the issue of Americans slaughtered was dropped. It was a hint of the future. General Marshall did express concern that the "reactionary clique" in the Nationalist Government would use the killing of Americans to damage the Reds.

In mid-August, while Chou En-lai readied to abandon the new Constitution that Marshall considered his crowning achievement in China, mediator Marshall made a gushing admission that completely clarifies his performance in China. He openly assured Chou En-lai of his "unique position" in his (Marshall's) faith and high regard. "Much that we have done and have endeavored to do has been based almost exclusively on that faith".[43]

Meanwhile, Chiang Kai-shek, frustrated by increased concessions to the Communists and Red disregard for agreements and treaties, had no alternative but to work through Marshall and hope to gain the promised U.S. aid. He boldly proposed that Marshall be empowered to settle all Nationalist-Communist disputes.[44] It seemed the Government was ready to share power, but the Reds dedicated to the goal of total power, refused. As fighting increased, Marshall's answer was a letter to Chiang signed by Truman. The letter threatened the end of "America's generous attitude." Before any of

---

42 Forrestal, *The Forrestal Diaries*, p364

43 Foreign Relations of the U.S., *1946, vol.7, p.33*

44 Time Magazine, *6/17/46, Breathing Spell*

Marshall's well publicized, token shipments of arms left the dock, the State Department stopped licensing military equipment shipments to China.

Marshall's next concession to the Reds abandoned all pretense of adhering to the initial ground rules of his mission. He'd been sent to China to mediate a fusion of opposing parties that would combine all armed forces thereby preventing civil war. On June 13, he advised Chiang Kai-shek that he'd changed his thinking. He no longer believed it urgent to bring Red forces into the National Army. He now believed that for six months to a year, a purely Communist army would prove a more practical arrangement.[45] The sole justification stated by President Truman to push for a coalition government was the combining of autonomous armies. That goal suddenly evaporated. General Marshall's "faith and high regard" for Chou En-lai seemed unlimited. The timing of Marshall's new policy coincided with an internal declaration by Mao stating "we can defeat Chiang Kai-shek. The whole party should be confident of this."[46]

In August, Mao Tse-tung announced his army was ready to confront government forces in North China. The western media broadcast wild estimates. The New York Times reported millions of Reds mobilized for an all-out offensive. Other sources reported one million Red regulars and two million guerrillas.

Mao's offensive was a complete flop. Chiang Kai-shek's forces pushed Red opposition aside and moved through Communist areas with surprising ease. But Chiang's goal was; protect the Manchurian railroad artery from Peking to Mukden. In northern

---

45   Marshall, *The Papers of George Catlett Marshall, Vol. V, p.592*

46   Griffith, *The Chinese Peoples Liberation Army, p.85*

Manchuria, it was near impossible. Mao's demolition crews could strike anywhere, at any time, and government railroad outposts could be easily overwhelmed by mass attacks.

Below Manchuria, in North China, the Government's immediate offensive goals included the city of Kalgan, the gateway to Manchuria. Possession would not only impede Red movements into Manchuria, but also provide security for Peking and weaken the CCP's position throughout North China. By that time, Mao's recent confidence in his army had evaporated. He directed Chou En-lai to apply full pressure to gain a cease-fire and Marshall, responded. At that point, Chiang had military advantage in his grasp and refused the cease-fire proposal. Marshall threatened to quit China completely. When Chiang found that Marshall had sent a radiogram to Washington for his recall, he agreed to a ten-day truce. The CCP then upped their demands. They demanded a permanent truce for Kalgan equating to permanent Red control of the "Gateway to Manchuria". Chiang reacted, on October 10, 1947. Government troops assaulted Kalgan and captured 100,000 Reds. Marshall pressed Chiang for more concessions for the Reds and Chiang now holding the advantage, conceded. But the Reds saw no further gains in continuing to work Marshall. It was time for them to live up to the troop ratios and other agreements they made on paper. They walked away from Marshall's mediation process and constitution, marking his efforts in China as total failure.

The draft Constitution, previously agreed to by the CCP and all other parties, was to be adopted at a National Assembly. The Reds suddenly declared the Assembly illegal. Because the procedure for fixing its date was improper.[47] The charming, clever Chou En-lai had agreed to Marshall's proposed Constitution articles in order to cultivate the General's favor and gain military advantages. It worked for ten months. The arms embargo, truces, restriction of Government troop moves and other impediments succeeded in severely weakening the government's ability to protect the railroad system and provide food and fuel supplies, for the Chinese people. Meanwhile, it gave the Reds necessary time to organize an army.

Despite his recent military defeats, ever tenacious Mao Tse-tung sensed a weakening of his enemy's resources. The Reds lost nothing by walking away from Marshall's mediation. The door would always be open. But it was time to live up to previous commitments to incorporate Red units into the National Army. Something Chairman Mao never intended to follow through on. Why make real concessions, if the prize could be won outright? Information the Reds possessed led them to believe the U.S. would continue to deny aid to the Government. They saw in the future a crumbling ill-fed, ill-equipped Government army deprived of ammunition. An army fielded by a government presiding over economic chaos. Whether that future was one year or ten years away mattered little to ever-tenacious Mao Tse-tung.

Towards the end of 1946, the overall military situation changed. In Manchuria, the Russians initially supplied the PLA the full array of captured Japanese equipment and followed that with Russian war surplus weapons when supplies of Japanese caliber

---

47   Stuart, *Fifty years in China*, p.170,171

ammunition ran out. They'd organized and entrenched Red troops in strategic positions and blocked the U.S. Navy from delivering Government troops into the province. The State Department and General Marshall had curtailed the promised ground and air transport of Government troops. In fourteen months, Mao's forces, initially barred from Manchuria by General Marshall, brought much of the province under their control.

Other than Manchuria, Red errors during most of 1946 could have spelled their doom. They failed to effectively train enough troops to successfully confront Government forces in battle. Mao's declared strategy was "step by step" "to wipe out the enemy forces one by one." Instead, The Chinese Army over ran Communist areas, easily defeating Mao's raw troops. Mao's Eighth Route Army acclaimed for years by western admirers, was no match for Chiang Kai-shek's Nationalist forces. Fictional victories against the Japanese did not create veterans. Another Red myth was punctured, but went unnoticed.

Faced with major reverses on the battlefield, Mao decided to change his strategy.[48] The Reds would continue to pursue their military advantage in Manchuria aided by the Russians. In North China they would avoid major armed conflict with Government forces and concentrate on sabotage and terrorism.[49]

During 1946, a completely ruthless Chiang Kai-shek could have wiped out Mao's activities in North China just as the Japanese "Three all" campaign quelled Mao's aggressive behavior years earlier. In November 1946, Chiang still had the power to close off

---

48   Griffith, *The Chinese Peoples Liberation Army, p.89*

49   Time Magazine, *10/21/46, On the Great Wall*

Manchuria and sweep through Red controlled areas of North China with kill and destroy scorched earth tactics. He could have annihilated or forced Mao's faction out on another "Long march" to the wastelands. Instead, he took a moderate tack. In November 1946, Generalissimo Chiang Kai-shek convened the National Constitutional Assembly to approve a Constitution created by all of China's political parties under General Marshall's mediation. All parties, except the Communists attended.

The question for Chiang was could the government maintain a viable economy in the face of Communist guerrilla warfare and sabotage supported by the Russians, without U.S. help? The question for President Truman was would the United States walk away from the inclusive government Marshall had urged on China now that the Communists refused to join? During this period, a frustrated Marshall, seemed to abandon his customary courtesy with Chiang, but move even closer to the agent of his frustration. Similar to his past unshakeable support of Vinegar Joe Stilwell and Lloyd Fredendahl, Marshall's "Faith and regard" for Chou remained undiminished by the Red scuttling of his Constitution. In one of their friendly meetings, General Marshall revealed to Chou that the U.S. regularly intercepted weekly propaganda orders from Moscow to Shanghai. He revealed classified information to an active enemy of America's WW2 ally. He admitted to it later and attempted a lame excuse.[50]

Marshall's naïveté extended beyond his lack of negotiating experience. Evidence indicates his appointments secretary in China, was a Red agent. It appears, Ching Nu-chi, screened out and

---

50   Taylor, *The Generalissimo,* p.359

rejected visitors deemed undesirable by the Reds. Thus Marshall had no contact with any who might report on the ruthless methods the Reds used in their drive to absorb and mobilize the flood of people then coming under their control.

A Belgian missionary, Raymond de Jaegher, after six years in Communist controlled areas, was thoroughly familiar with Communist methods of controlling the people. A member of Marshall's staff advised de Jaegher to see the General and relate the realities of peasant life under the Chinese Reds. The American officer who was to make the appointment was suddenly sent off to another city. After a few days, de Jaegher went to Marshall's office and met the appointment secretary. Ching Nu-chi, responded, "The General is very busy. He won't be able to see you. . . . Besides, he knows whatever it is that you think you can tell him!" de Jaegher found out later he was a marked man with respect to the Communist Chinese. When he discussed his rejection with the American Charge de Affairs he was told, "Perhaps the staff around Gen. Marshall are deliberately keeping certain persons from seeing him."[51] Nothing was done. Marshall retained both his Red secretary and his unblemished view of the Red Chinese. In April 1949, Ching Nu-chi went public in Red China. He published *Secret report on the United States . . . Chiang Kai-shek conspiracy.*[52] In addition to his secretarial duties, Ching had access to all communications in Marshall's office. As Chou En-lai negotiated with the Government, he knew the concessions that were available and the restrictions Marshall imposed on the Government.

---

51   deJaegher, *The Enemy Within,* p.276,277
52   Ibid, *p. 277*

Before year's end, Marshall threw up his hands and left for the U.S. He'd spent nearly a year in a cycle similar to Patrick Hurley's fruitless negotiations. The processes differed in that Hurley's meetings had no negative impact on China's future while Marshall's mediation set the stage for the complete abandonment of Manchuria that began at Yalta. More importantly, his "mediation" gave the Reds time to organize their newly acquired population and resources in North China. For the Chinese government, Marshall's effective blocking of arms resulted in a year of draw down of China's depleted resources and a year of downward spiral in economic conditions. Overall, he'd set the stage for a national crises in China. On leaving China, he indicated the new Constitution met his approval. He said Chiang had gained a great moral victory.[53] Once again, Marshall's words were not reflected in his subsequent behavior. President Truman had promised full resumption of aid on adoption of Marshall's constitution. All parties other than the Communists convened and the Reds opted to not attend. The Constitution was adopted. Similar to Chiang's earlier compliance with Marshall's military demands, compliance with his political document brought no relief from the array of licensing and other restrictions holding up promised U.S. aid.

During the winter of 1946/1947, as arms and supplies were depleted, the momentum of government military operations declined. There was an increasing awareness that time favored the Communists. Government forces were free of Marshall's restrictions, but they were starting to see a new type of enemy. Russian-led training and mobilization in Manchuria was bearing fruit. At the same time, National

---

53   Marshall, *The Papers of George Catlett Marshall, Vol. V, p.765*

Government tactics on the battlefield were increasingly dictated by the quantity of ammunition and supplies available and quantities expected to be available in the future. Rather than surprise assaults, and counterattacks, lack of ammunition and supplies dictated a static defense or, as ammunition was exhausted, retreat. After nine years of warfare and little assistance from the United States, the Chinese economy was in a shambles. The government announced another austerity program and cut wages as inflation destroyed the real value of currency. Soldiers were hungry and paid next to nothing. Unable to purchase food they took from the peasant's they felt they were defending. Public support was crumbling.

The harsh reality on the ground at that point was: the government, with limited and diminishing resources, could not rebuild railroads, dams and bridges as quickly as the Reds could blow them up. While the Reds destroyed infrastructure, Marshall denied aid needed to rebuild. Morale plummeted as it became apparent there was no good end in sight. China's civilian population looked for an end, any end, to their long struggle...

When questioned, Marshall defended his embargo as showing proof to the Russians that America was not interfering in China. He frequently voiced concern for avoiding Russian criticism of the U.S. role in China. He failed to explain why the U.S. convinced the British, the French and the Belgians to also embargo ammunition shipments to Nationalist China.[54]

It seems Chou En-lai had gained entry into the blind spot in Marshall's judgment formerly occupied by Joseph Stilwell. Despite a complete lack of supporting evidence, Marshall continued to voice

---

54 Foreign Relations of the U.S., *1947, vol.7, 3/25/47 and 4/4/47*

belief in progressive elements within the Red hierarchy. He was blind to what General Wedemeyer saw, early on, "The great advantage of the Communists both before and after VJ day consisted in their utter irresponsibility for the fate of the Chinese people. The Nationalist Government was trying, however ineffectually, to defend what was left of free China. The Chinese Communists . . . played the role of jackal or hyena against the wounded and suffering Chinese elephant who would not submit to his enemy."

The progress of the "golden decade" when China made its greatest social and economic advances in history under Chiang Kai-shek[55] was halted by the Japanese attack in 1937. After eight years of total warfare followed by an insurrection supported by a neighboring super power, China abandoned by America, was disintegrating. Foreign Minister T.V. Soong declared "the house is burning down . . . and I am too busy putting out the fire to rebuild." Government forces continued to dominate in battle, but a critical year, 1946, had passed, a year when Chiang could have easily wiped out Mao's forces. Instead, Government efforts were frustrated by U.S. failure to transport troops, Marshall's truces and aid embargos. Another factor that Chiang admitted to later was his own overconfidence, a view point that led him to agree to Marshall's costly truces.

On Marshall's last day in China, he displayed his peculiar tendency to seek advice from subordinates rather than follow direction from above. He asked Ambassador Stuart, in view of the breakdown of peace negotiations, what form should American policy take toward China? Stuart outlined three alternate policies: to give active assistance, to drift along with no strong program or: withdraw entirely.

---

55   Marks, *Wind Over Sand, p.355*

He recommended active assistance or, if not, withdraw. Marshall said he agreed in principle. However, he quickly reverted to form.

When he arrived in Washington, he said Chiang had to get along with the Communists or without help from the U.S.[56] The general who installed and supported the abusive Stilwell in China, had pursued the first portion of his assignment in China with uncharacteristic vigor. He spared no effort in forcing Chiang Kai-shek's cooperation. Past that point, he ignored the President's directive to support China if his negotiations failed. Viewed from the standpoint supporting the Chinese Government, his strategic thinking seemed to contradict his U.S. Army background. He'd advanced in an Army dedicated to the concept of focusing total, devastating efforts on the enemy and forcing a breakthrough. From Bedford Forest's "getting there fustest with the mostest" and Sherman's march to the sea, to Patton's race across France, the U.S. Army believed in concentration of all resources on the enemy, force a breakthrough, pour in and prevent the enemy from regrouping and developing a new defense or counterattack. In China, when Nationalist forces broke through Red defenses and forged ahead, Marshall pressed for a truce. Admiral Cooke, U.S. Military Chief in China testified in Senate hearings "several times in 1946 . . . when they had the Communists licked, a truce took place . . . because the Communists would say-well we are going to play ball now."[57] The Marshall denial of promised ammunition and weapons left China's army with

56   Wells, *Seven Decisions tha Shaped History,* p.219

57   Senate Committee on the Judiciary, *10/51* , *p.1502, Disarming China*

worn out American and Chinese weapons and a shrinking inventory of ammunition. When Marshall returned from China, he continued an embargo of .30 caliber ammunition, for the divisions bearing U.S. rifles, and a cutoff of explosives for the Chinese armories attempting to supply the remaining 300 divisions with 7.92 mm cartridges. It was a shameful betrayal. It meant defeat on the battlefield was simply a matter of time.

In the late 1940s, Americans on the street and in Congress were increasingly focused on Soviet Cold War aggression in Europe. Any public awareness that the Soviet Union was actively aiding Mao's rebels would have forced the release of a flood of aid to China. The enablers adjusted their misinformation accordingly. In 1946, Soviet treaty violations in Manchuria, closing Dairen (Dalian), training and entrenchment of PLA troops, and attacks by Russian troops and Japanese POW tanks were vaguely admitted but dismissed by General Marshall as rash, independent acts of individual Russian commanders. Then, as Cold War hostility to Soviet aggression heated up, Marshall adjusted accordingly. He'd previously admitted the Russians were aiding Mao's Reds. He suddenly switched to complete denial of Soviet aid to Mao's forces. He declared the Russians were completely "aloof" in Manchuria. He made risky statements that could easily be challenged and refuted, but his cloak of prestige and America's preoccupation with Europe carried the day for his purposes.

At the end of World War II, American war production in high gear resulted in huge quantities of ships and aircraft mothballed in remote areas and great supply dumps of small arms, artillery and ammunition throughout the world. Although, several small nations purchased or were given small quantities, without a major war, these war materials would soon rust and decay into worthlessness. Whenever aid to China was debated, Marshall and the State Department stressed its cost to the taxpayer. The arms and ammunition promised and desperately needed by, the Chinese Government were left-over from WWII and of rapidly declining value to the United States. Despite this, Marshall frequently cited exorbitant cost to the taxpayer as justification for not supporting the Nationalist Chinese.

Before long, the U.S. "hoarding' of war surplus ammunition and weapons would have a deadly impact on young Americans. The first half of the "Forgotten War" was fought with old, deteriorated WW2 ammunition and weapons and Americans died as a result. Thus, WWII ammunition that could have saved China later caused American deaths in Korea.[58]

---

58   Drury and Clavin,   *The Last Stand of Fox Company,*   *p.351*

17

WE MUST DO MORE

O N RETURN TO Washington, General Marshall fumed against reactionaries in the Chinese National Government who opposed "genuine" coalition government. But the new Chinese Constitution, the form of government China had adopted, was his creation. He also spoke out against the Communists. Strong words, but not borne out by his upcoming performance. Marshall, who believed in managing situations and avoiding direct confrontation[1] used words to fit the occasion and then acted independently of those words in order achieve his covert goals. Later, before testifying at a Congressional Committee Meeting, he requested his testimony be secure from outside distribution and then proceeded to contradict every military opinion voiced at wars end.[2]

---

1 May, *The Truman Administration and China, p.21*

2 House Committee on Foreign Affairs, *2/20/48*

When his proposals and agreements were honored by Chiang Kai-shek and rejected and broken by the CCP, Marshall completely shifted focus from the specific agreements at hand and voiced unsubstantiated concepts of evil reactionary factions within the KMT Government and virtuous progressives inside the Red power structure. If results did not develop as planned, he simply looked further for anything that would serve to avoid making a change in direction. He admitted, "The National Assembly has adopted a democratic constitution," and commented, "Unfortunate that the Communists did not see fit to participate in the assembly, since the Constitution that has been adopted seems to include every major point they wanted." Included in General Marshall's China orders from HST was a new promise of vast aid if China adopted the Marshall Constitution. When China adopted the Constitution, General Marshall flouted a third Presidential promise.

Shortly after his return to Washington, Marshall issued a peculiar statement; "I believe our government must shortly do more for China in this matter than give advice . . ." Then, he proceeded to define "doing more for China." "We must clear our hands. Get out as quickly as possible in order to avoid the inevitable Russian recriminations . . . we must move all the Marines out of China."[3] Meanwhile, the Russians did nothing to avoid American recriminations. They blocked another American naval vessel from entering the "open" Port of Dairen. Former Davies colleague John Carter Vincent, then on the rise in the State Department, authorized a public statement saying the Russians were acting within their rights in the Dairen situation.

---

3   Truman, *Memoirs, Vol.2, p.77*

In reference to the deteriorating China situation, Marshall declared later: "I specifically was endeavoring to see what support could be given to the Generalissimo . . . the situation was such that we would literally have to take over control of the country in order to ensure that the armies functioned with efficiency." All experts at ground level contradicted that statement. Major General John P. Lucas, head of the skeleton Army Advisory Group in China was clear and specific. Lucas was a West Point graduate and World War II Corps commander in Italy. He stated his MAG group could build a first-rate Chinese Army and defeat the Communists in two years, if the U.S. provided arms and supplies equivalent to those needed for 10 American divisions and if he could more or less control strategic and operational planning.[4] He pointed out that military units deteriorated very rapidly in battle and needed frequent relief and retraining to operate effectively. Government forces at war for a decade were in dire need of retraining. Despite General Marshall's repeated criticism of Chinese Army efficiency, his papers show no hint of anything remotely similar to his "Red West Point" plan for training Red Army officers. He totally ignored the official Military Advisory Group's proposals for the Chinese Army. The MAG advisor for China's Air Force, Brigadier General John P McConnell advised China's air force could be rapidly made efficient and effective if it were only suitably equipped and trained.[5]

When asked later if substantial military aid could have changed the results, Marshall told Congress the Chinese Army lacked the support of the people. But his Communist appointments secretary

---

4   May, *The Truman Administration and China*, *p14*

5   Ibid, *p.14*

in China had precluded contact between the icy, aloof, general and the people of China. General Marshall, by virtue of the informal titles bestowed on him early in WW II and President Truman later positioning him as a "the greatest living American," was able to make weighty statements on subjects where his specialized military background and anti-social characteristics prevented inflow of information. Yet, in a Washington totally focused on the Soviet threat in Europe, General Marshall's version of the China situation went unchallenged. Similarly, when hemmed in by contrary information on aid to China, Marshall would resort to opinions such as," I don't believe the American people are ready to . . . (aid China). This while Gallup polls indicated a heavy majority of the public favored "giving Chiang Kai-shek more military supplies, goods and money."[6] Marshall's statements coupled with his tactic of vastly overestimating the dollar cost of aid were effective. Typically, Marshall would furnish no detail to back up his cost estimates while others did furnish complete proposals with cost estimates that were modest compared Marshall's estimates and a small fraction of the aid dollars approved for Europe. Marshall's costs were essentially an accounting masquerade. As outlined previously, the surplus munitions denied the Chinese were valueless and were decaying as the charade continued.

Former ambassador William C. Bullitt wrote in *how we won the war and lost the peace*: "In the field of aviation, General Marshall's actions were even more damaging to China and the U.S. In September 1946, he deliberately broke the contract of the American government to deliver to the Chinese government planes to maintain 8

---

6   Public Opinion Quarterly, *Fall, 1948, p.548*

1/3 air groups for three years, and spare parts to cover replacements, and ammunition, and materials needed for ground services during the same period. From September 1946 to March 1948 not a single combat or supply plane was delivered to China under this agreement. The conduct of the American government in this matter was strictly dishonorable. General Marshall was responsible for this conduct." These aircraft were obsolete for the U.S. Air Force but would have given China complete control of the air vs. Red ground forces. It was not to be.

On February 1, 1947, Mao Tse-tung noted: "Our army has improved in both equipment and tactics. From now on the central task in building our armed forces is to make every effort to step up the building of our artillery and engineer corps."[7] The Reds had no capability for manufacturing Russian caliber artillery. It could only be supplied by the Soviets. Soon, Americans would be killed and maimed by Russian caliber weapons fired by Mao's Red Army. Weapons that General Marshall declared did not exist. Marshall's denials did not flow from a lack of awareness. The previous May 13, Chou En-lai radioed Moscow Central committee that Marshall told him he was aware of "Soviet support to us" in the Northeast."[8]

In early February 1947, Marshall again stated "I believe our government must shortly do more for China . . ." and he completed arrangements for withdrawal of the Marine force protecting the Peking rail line from Communist sabotage. He claimed the withdrawal would blunt Communist charges of U.S. imperialism.

---

7   Mao Tse-tung, *Selected Works of Mao Tse-tung, Vol. IV, p.123*

8   Taylor, *The Generalissimo, p.349*

During the withdrawal, Marine brass decided, rather than add to the already excessive surplus stocks of ammunition throughout the Pacific, the China Marines would leave their surplus ammunition in China. The question arose destroy it or leave it for China's use? Destroying explosives is inherently dangerous. Destruction of explosives, in India, bound for China at wars end had resulted in serious casualties. The existence of this issue as a subject for discussion indicates that the concept of disarming China had gained legitimacy. All military, from Theater Commander on down, were firmly in favor of leaving the ammunition accessible to Government troops. Only John Vincent Carter, Assistant Secretary for Far Eastern Affairs, objected. He wanted the ammunition destroyed. In this instance, the military prevailed.[9] Later Marshall and Carter claimed credit for this modest aid to China.

As news of China's dire situation leaked out, the press raised questions, but nothing was pursued in depth. Later, Congressional inquiries indicated Congress and President Truman had little knowledge of Marshall's activities during China's crises. In February 1947, a concerned HST asked Marshall if the time had come to supply ammunition to China. Marshall replied that giving ammunition would open the United States to Soviet charges of aiding the civil war in China.

During the month of February 1947, President Truman had to decide what role the U.S. should play in Greece as Great Britain, in economic decline, pulled their support of anti-Communist elements in both Greece and Turkey. Both countries were under extreme pressure from the Soviets. Secretary of the Navy James Forrestal, equating the

---

9   Senate Committee on the Judiciary, *10/51, p.1499, Admiral Cooke*

Greece and Turkey situations to China's, voiced suggestions for support of China to General Marshall. On February 27, he wrote Marshall detailing his proposal for a mission to China. It would include an infusion of practical experts to revitalize the Chinese economy. There's no record of a Marshall reply. Nothing came of the proposal.

When the House Foreign Affairs Committee addressed China aid, on March 20, 1947 Marshall Aide, Dean Acheson, testified to a Congress then considering China aid "the Chinese government . . . is not approaching collapse. It is not threatened by defeat by the Communists. The war with the Communists is going on much as it has for the past 20 years." Less than four weeks later, Mao Tse-tung announced conditions were favorable for the final annihilation of Government forces. Acheson's testimony was a blatant but effective lie. No aid was voted.

In China, the Government effort to defeat the Red army, while defending thousands of miles of rail lines, was on the verge of a transition. Nationalist forces continued to advance. They took control of 120,000 square miles and 18 million people. But, without ammunition and rations, the Army would soon collapse. The economy was sliding into ruin and feeding the Army became a critical problem. The wily Mao Tse-tung resorted to hit and run tactics to draw the National forces deeper into Red territories thereby stretching their supply lines. On April 15, 1947, 26 days after Acheson lied to Congress, Mao declared ". . . in the last 20 days we have achieved the objective of tiring him and considerably reducing his food supplies, thus creating favorable conditions for tiring him out completely, cutting off all his food supplies and finally wiping him out."[10]

_____

10 Mao Tse-tung, *Selected Works of Mao Tse-tung, Vol. IV, p133*

The following month, China's credit was exhausted. Manufacturers, unable to buy raw material for their factories, closed down. Inflation rates were meteoric. Communist Commissioner Yeh Chien-ying boarding a plane in Chungking for return to Yenan taunted "Long live Chinese-American cooperation!"

In May 1947, Dean Acheson substituting for President Truman announced a massive aid program to rebuild war damaged nations. He said "Europe and Asia were totally exhausted after a terrible war and after two horrible winters. It was necessary for the United States to help them recover, and to do that, huge sums of money would have to be appropriated. And it must all be done soon." Acheson went on to say. "That was the way the President saw it, and that was the way it was. As Mr. Truman has very often said of very many things that was all there was to it."

But that was not all there was to it. China was soon deleted from the plan. Billions would flow into countries in Europe and Japan while surplus weapons and ammunition promised repeatedly to China rusted and decayed. HST rewarded his much favored Secretary of State by, christening the enormous aid package "The Marshall Plan" citing the General's input on the scope of the plan[11]. Elimination of China from the plan was the only substantial change in scope. In regard to Asian nations other than China, Marshall had no reservations on a separate $270 million grant to Japan. Thus the defeated WW2 enemy, with relatively minor problems, was receiving American aid while the ally devastated by that enemy was denied aid. In addition to the $270 million, Japan also enjoyed an annual influx of $600 million introduced into the Japanese econ-

11   Truman- *Memoirs, Vol. 2, P. 114*

omy by American occupation forces. Japan was obviously not in Moscow's crosshairs at that time.

On May 18, Ambassador Stuart conveyed the latest Chiang Kai-shek request that the promised ammunition and the promised 8 Air Group agreement be promptly and fully executed.[12] He reported "They (the Reds) were counting on preventing American aid to the Government..... and are intensifying their vituperation to this end" he went on "the cruelly authoritarian nature of communist domination and the revulsion of the population... against their leadership."[13]

By June, 1947, a half-year had passed since Chiang Kai-shek complied with the most recent requirements for gaining U.S. aid, by adopting Marshall's constitution, a half year since Marshall declared "we must do more for China ..." and then did less by taking out the Marines and continuing his arms embargo. After six months of ignoring proposals from fellow cabinet members and military advisors, Marshall declared, "I have tortured my brain and I can't now see the answer."[14]

On June 9 the Joint Chiefs of Staff submitted their study of the military aspects of U.S. policy towards China. It challenged the great dichotomy in existing U.S. policy. The Joint Chief's goal was define the best policy to further United States interests in the world. They were not concerned with visions of reactionaries in the Kuomintang political party, liberals in the Communist party or maintaining image with the Soviets.

---

12   Foreign Relations of the U.S. 1947, *vol.7, p.706*

13   Ibid, *p. 707*

14   May, *The Truman Administration and China, p20*

The study concluded: (1) the United States must prevent the growth of any power or coalition to the point that it threatened the Western Hemisphere. (2) U.S. security demanded that China be free from Soviet domination. (3) It was truly in the interest of United States security that Eurasian nations oppose Soviet expansion. (4) Soviet expansion is furthered by the Chinese Communists. (5) Soviet expansionism is incompatible with U.S. security. (6) With Japan disarmed, the only nation in Asia capable of resisting Soviet expansion is Nationalist China. (7) Unless the National government is given sufficient military help to resist Communist expansionism the government will collapse. (8) U.S. commitments to the United Nations, in which China is listed, at U.S. insistence, as one of the great powers, requires that we support Nationalist China in getting control of Manchuria. (9) Chaos in China works to the advantage of Soviet Russia, unless immediate military aid is given in accordance with an overall plan. The plan should take in account aid for the Nationalists to meet and ultimately eliminate all Communist armed opposition.

These findings by the best military minds in America had no effect on Secretary of State Marshall's China policy.

As summer approached, Marshall's lack of action on China became conspicuous to his fellow cabinet members. On June 23, Marshall announced he was searching for positive suggestions. His skills in manipulating colleagues were apparent. It seems Marshall had kept his subtle aid embargoes hidden from his fellow cabinet members. The discussion concerned the continuance of aid to China rather than the resumption of curtailed aid. Three days later, at a cabinet meeting, he again asked for suggestions and commented "it was very difficult to help them." When Navy Secretary Forrestal proposed shipping the military aid we'd promised, Marshall did not reply. He repeated he needed suggestions and abruptly left the meeting. In a meeting the following day Marshall reinforced the misconception that the U.S. was then aiding China. "The Secretary of State outlined the situation in China . . . : and whether to continue to supply armament and arms to the Chinese National Army . . ?" He again voiced concern over Russian sensibilities, and grasping at straws, he suggested the Russians might be upset because they hadn't received a World Bank loan. In addition to the prestige and accolades collected early in WW2, the "Greatest living American," had become the administration's "China Expert." Fellow cabinet members, absorbed in critical issues in Europe and domestic problems, did not question Marshall's statements on China.

During his China "agonies" Marshall found time to convey advice to Chiang on how to run the country. On July 6, he belittled the impact of military aid. What China needed was greatly increased civil liberties. A high sounding call to a nation fighting for its life, but one that flies in the face of history and common sense. In America's two deadliest wars, President Lincoln suspended civil liberties and FDR imprisoned an entire ethnic population. There's no record of a Marshall call for increased civil liberties in Communist territories during his close association with number two Communist Chou En-lai or his meetings with Mao Tse-tung.

While General Marshall belittled military aid to China, on September 18, the Office of Intelligence Research warned of the potential danger to the security of the U.S. in the existing China situation and estimated 30 Government divisions, adequately trained, armed and supplied would restore China proper to Government control.[15]

More than two years earlier the U.S. Ambassador to Moscow had detailed Russian motives and practices and advised "the Soviet Program is the establishment of totalitarianism ending personal liberty and democracy." Since that time, most Americans who dealt with the Russians confirmed and added to the Ambassador's negative conclusions. Yet, as China disintegrated, Marshall convinced his fellow cabinet members he was striving for cooperation with the Russians. Therefore, in deference to Marshall's grand plan for cooperation, the U.S. should not offend the Soviets by aiding China. Meanwhile, Washington was unconcerned with offending the Russians in Europe. The enormous "Marshall Plan" aid to Western Europe was a direct blow to any Soviet expansion plans for Europe. Full-fledged support of the Marshall Plan by those, who worked so diligently to block China aid, suggests Moscow Cold War strategy may have been "Threaten Europe and Gain China." Marshall's concern that China aid would offend the Russians was flimsy logic since the Russians had signed a treaty to support the Nationalist Chinese Government. But Marshall did not have to explain. Unfortunately for China, and later, for America, Marshall was able to misrepresent facts, ignore or divert inquiries and proposals from fellow Cabinet members, from the Joint Chiefs, from

---

15   Foreign Relations of the U.S. 1947, *vol.7 p.286,287*

Congress and from the military advisors he'd sent to China. He would soon compromise his ethics further in order to divert the attention of the President of the United States.

While General Marshall "tortured his brain" on how to help China, the U.S. acted decisively in Greece. The Greek government faced a situation similar to China, but on a miniscule scale. In 1947, the U.S. poured in arms and assigned frontline military advisors and a top combat commander to fight Greek Communists. There was no agonizing indecision, and no concern of Soviet recriminations. This and a few lesser efforts would soon be publicized as "The Truman Doctrine" and the "Containment Strategy", proof of the Administration's and Marshall's fight against Communist expansion. General Marshall was positioned to save 9 million Greeks and betray 450 million Chinese. For Stalin and international Communism it was an excellent trade. For Red enablers in Washington, it worked as long as the Truman Doctrine and the Containment Strategy could distract attention from their efforts against China.

In China, in 1947, Mao's Reds rejected food and non-military aid from the United Nations Relief Agency, UNRRA, in order to gain secrecy and keep the lid on a massive increase in Russian weapons shipments. Unlike the U.S., where war surplus arms and ammunition were left rusting into obsolescence, the Russians committed their war surplus to the cause. The UN Aid Director was abruptly refused entry to Red territory. But news continued to leak out. The Chinese Central news agency reported

30,000 Japanese Prisoners of war and 90 tanks were leading a Communist offensive in Manchuria. Its correspondent in Mukden reported a special bureau of a "certain" nation was supplying the Communists with equipment for 20 divisions. "Certain nation" was the usual designation for Russia in the Chinese press. Also reported, the Japanese were manning the tanks then spearheading the Communist offensive. In another issue, the news agency told of more than 100,000 Russian trained Koreans and a cavalry division from Outer Mongolia in the attacks against Chinese Government forces.[16] If Mao's rabble militia needed more training to face Chiang Kai-shek's National Army, the Communists had other resources. The new Red cloak of secrecy along with General Marshall's concept of "aloof" Russians effectively masked the acceleration of Stalin's rearmament of Mao's forces. A myth was floated describing the Reds gaining great quantities of U.S. Arms from surrendering Government troops. No evidence existed to support this myth. The only American weapons shipped to China during this period were boltless inoperable rifles. A few years later, when Mao attacked Americans in Korea, all the Japanese arms gained in Manchuria had been replaced by Russian versions. Americans in Korea faced Russian Burp guns and Russian 76 mm artillery.

As the situation in China deteriorated further, word of the massive impending loss and the lack of effort to prevent it was leaking. The June 9, 1947 Joint Chiefs of Staff Report had pointed out the Chinese Communists "should be regarded as tools of

16   Utley, *The China Story,* p.51

Soviet policy." It cited the great advantages Mao received in the form of Soviet aid and support. It summarized "had the Soviets not thus assisted the Communists in Manchuria it is quite possible that the National Government would long ago have been able to eliminate the Communist forces in the Northern and Eastern China."[17]

Gestures were needed. Marshall announced America would "sell" arms and ammunition to China. However, there was no mention of previous Presidential pledges to directly aid our now bankrupt ally. Marshall required that each purchase receive advance approval, which could take months and then incur licensing and other delays. The only transfer of ammunition that took place consisted of 130 million Gimo Chinese caliber cartridges (approximately 40 cartridges per man for Chinese troops). Using Marshall's U.S. Army guidelines for ammunition needed in combat, he provided the Chinese Army with cartridges for less than eight hours of rifle combat or possibly a minute of machine gun fire. Marshall advised Ambassador Stuart by telegram on June 11, 1947, and explained the ammunition produced during World War II had not been shipped (for two years) "because of transportation difficulties." He also advised Stuart "prohibition continues on... explosives."[18]

General Marshall, after a year in China and back in Washington only six months, next stated he needed a new survey of the situation. He selected his former subordinate General Wedemeyer as the ideal candidate for the mission. He believed Wedemeyer's

---

17 Foreign Relations of the U.S. 1947, *vol.7, p.840.841*

18 Ibid, *p.848*

image as former China commander and Chief of Staff to Chiang Kai-shek would provide credibility and felt Wedemeyer, as a former subordinate, could be managed. HST appointed Wedemeyer Special Representative of the President and assigned him to make an "open-minded" assessment and report on the China situation and on neighboring Korea.

Later comments from China indicated Wedemeyer's appointment schedule in China might have been rigged. Many Chinese complained the American spent too much of his month's inspection tour talking with the government critics. China's Premier Chiang Chun said he had not been granted a thorough interview with Wedemeyer. The Chairman of Shanghai business and industrial organizations protested to President Truman they had no opportunities for presenting their views.

As China's clock ticked down, General Wedemeyer collected "new" information on China and Korea. After several weeks in China, he returned and presented a comprehensive report that recommended immediate aid to China. He cited the obvious, but much ignored, WW2 surplus arms that would cost American taxpayer nothing. He also reported our South Korean ward was neither trained nor armed to resist an invasion from Communist North Korea, and he made recommendations for correcting that situation.

Soon after submittal, he was told that Secretary of State Marshall wanted certain portions of the "open minded" report deleted. Marshall would be angry if he didn't comply and the report would not be distributed unless those revisions were made. Wedemeyer, compliant until that point, had enough. He refused.

Wedemeyer had been encouraged to comment frankly on Nationalist China's shortcomings. He did so, both to Chiang Kai-shek and in his final report to Marshall. The State Department gleaned all negative comments on China and Chiang Kai-shek from the blacked out report and leaked them to the press. Marshall, then officially suppressed the "Open minded" report. All Congressional inquiries on the contents of the report were rejected.[19]

The assignment, the weeks in China, the report, the review and the delay before the suppression of the report covered an additional several months of inaction by Secretary of State Marshall while China's decline accelerated. Wedemeyer had gone to considerable effort and did a thorough job, but, in retrospect, his mission was simply window dressing. When Wedemeyer left for China, Marshall Radiogrammed Ambassador Stuart that the mission of the Special Representative of the President was "a temporary expedient."[20]

Pressure to open the Wedemeyer report increased, and Marshall resisted declaring it would "fan the fires of U.S.-Soviet conflict." But, under increasing pressure from Congress, he announced he would release shipments to China. The rifle and machine gun ammunition Chiang needed so badly amounted to only 3% of the supplies Marshall released. The remaining 97% included useless items from the scrap heap such as obsolete gas masks and artillery shells, (China had no artillery.) The Chinese salvaged rubber from gas masks and dismantled war surplus artillery shells to provide powder to manufacture rifle cartridges. The independent

19   Time Magazine, *12/29/47, Gesture*
20   Taylor, *The Generalissimo, p.376*

newspaper, Ta Rung Pao stated: "The diplomatic attitude of the U.S. during the past two years has been permeated with arrogance and prejudice (and) contempt...."

October 1947, marked the beginning of the end for Nationalist China. Communist sabotage of rail lines and bridges meant adequate food and coal would not reach the major cities that winter. Ruinous inflation would accelerate even more dramatically. Government armies, stretched thin, were unable to protect railroads and infrastructure. Outposts were easy prey for massed Red attacks. The Reds wasted no resources on P.O.W. camps. Captured defenders had the choice of joining the Red Army or death. The loss of isolated outpost units, some up to regimental size, not only reduced the troop strength of the Government army, it severely eroded morale. As conditions in the cities worsened, China's long enduring will to fight was reaching the breaking point.

On October 29, 1947 Ambassador Stuart, belatedly, assessed the Nationalist Government. He wrote ". . . the men at the very top are of high integrity and continue to struggle bravely against terrific difficulties. There are many more like them within and outside the government."

The following month, Secretary of State Marshall reported to President Truman and the cabinet on the existing world situation. He stated the "advance of Communism has been stemmed and the Russians have been compelled to make a re-evaluation of their position." When he uttered these words, he presided over the fall of nearly 20% of the world's population to Communism.

Later that month, Marshall announced the end of his China agonies. Pretending there had been a great difference of opinion, he said "Everyone now agrees that we wish to prevent Soviet domination of China." Exactly two years earlier, President Truman and Secretary of State Byrnes had instructed him that if all else failed; he should support the Nationalist government. Two years of "tortured" study brought him to the action that he was originally ordered to carry out. Two years that doomed nearly one fifth of the world.

His announcement was another time consuming ploy. After two years of ignoring proposals from fellow cabinet members, the War Department and the Military Advisory Group in China, He boldly stated: ". . . the immediate problem is to determine what we can do effectively." Of course, by that time, it was too late for effective action. China was beyond salvation. Marshall went through the motions of considering various measures that he had ignored for the past two years, measures that no longer fit the deteriorated situation on the ground. He could agree on military advisers with respect to reorganization of the Chinese army services of supply (For an army then starving and nearly out of ammunition.) He qualified even his belated concessions. He was not willing to accept responsibility for Chinese strategic plans and operations. Only eighteen months earlier, Marshall, in China, blocked reinforcements to Manchuria and other military operations. He forced major changes in Nationalist strategic plans and operations with his disruptive truces, limitations on troop movements and munitions embargoes. Considering the disastrous condition of China's army in late 1947, Marshall was simply redecorating his stalling and stonewalling tactics. The much touted top military mind of World War II had been unable to execute the President's order to aid China if all else failed. For two years, he could not respond to proposals advanced by others, and couldn't explain the reasons for restrictions he imposed on the Chinese Government contrary to the Presidents original directions.

As the year ended, Congress smelling a cover-up, summoned General Wedemeyer. He told them the President had bound him to secrecy but, as an ordinary observer, he felt he could give them his personal opinions. He urged an immediate, full-fledged effort in dollars and munitions, (his official report had called for aid within 60 days. That deadline had expired while the report was locked away). Wedemeyer again emphasized the munitions China needed were lying in supply dumps throughout the Pacific. On Chiang, he pointed out "the man has fought Communism all his life. He stood by us as an ally in the war when he might have accepted favorable peace terms from Japan in 1944." He added: "I personally think he is a fine character. He is a logical leader of China today. . . . He needs our help and he should get it."

By February, 1948, more than a year and a half had elapsed since Marshall told Navy Secretary James Forrestal he would take "two or three months" to decide what do about China.[21] When General Marshall's immense prestige finally succumbed to pressure to help China, other obstacles and delays were still available. Marshall's ability to quickly ship arms to China had been demonstrated by his recent token shipment of rifle ammunition to China and his prior hurried arrangements to supply weapons and ammunition to the Reds under his Red West Point plan. As China succumbed, he shuffled the China aid issue off to Congress.

---

21   Forrestal, *The Forrestal Diaries, p.174*

While Congress deliberated, Marshall muddied the waters by introducing an option never considered, an option impossible to execute, yet one that would arouse universal, emotional rejection. He alluded to putting boots on the ground in China. He opined the "Communists could not be wholly overcome by the Nationalists . . . for the United States to underwrite the Nationalists war would involve obligations and responsibilities . . . the American people would never knowingly accept."

Marshall, who had previously stated the army had insufficient personnel to send a few thousand advisers to China, suddenly raised the scenario of the U.S. Army combat divisions fighting in China. It was a clever ploy to defuse the upcoming outcry when China fell. The concept of the American Army fighting in China was impossible from a military standpoint. Marshall knew one simple fact; there was no Army to send to China. The Army that conquered Hitler's Panzer Corps and the fanatical Japanese Army, only a few years earlier, was a skeleton by 1948. It was totally and completely incapable of operations on the Chinese mainland, a situation that would soon become apparent in Korea.

As Congress deliberated, Dean Acheson proclaimed "our military observers on the spot reported the Nationalists lost no battles due to lack of weapons and ammunition." But, on March 3, 1948, Ambassador Stuart had reported "General Wei Li-huang seems to be a really good man but his desperate need of ammunition has been fully reported by us."[22] In regard to "military observers on the spot" in China, the Marshall/Acheson State Department had recommended to an unwitting Congress that U.S. military advi-

---

22 Foreign Relations of the U.S. 1947, *vol.7, Stuart to Sec. of State*

sors in China be forbidden from entering combat zones.[23] Clearly, flagrant deceptions continued.

As 1948 progressed, Marshall and Acheson buried increasingly alarming reports from China. On February 5, 1948, Ambassador Stuart belatedly reported "the situation is very definitely one to cause pessimism . . ." On March 17, 1948 Stuart reported "in their despair all groups blame America for urging structural changes . . . or reforms which they feel they themselves (the government) would carry out if their immediate internal problems were not so acute, while America still delays the long promised aid upon which the survival of the democratic institutions depends."[24] On March 31, he reported "the Chinese people do not want to become Communists, yet they see the tide of Communism running irresistibly onward. In the midst of this chaos and inaction the Generalissimo stands out as the only moral force capable of action."[25] Stuart was appointed Ambassador when the Reds, seeking a more amenable American, objected to Wedemeyer's appointment. Stuart's alarm was much too late. His early reticence may have been due to a misconception of the China situation given him by the State Department. He'd been told, in 1946, China had received well over two billion dollars of aid since the Japanese surrender. Stuart was biased going in. He believed the government had every advantage when their power was actually beginning a steady decline. He awakened too late.

---

23 Wedemeyer, *Wedemeyer Reports*, p.401

24 Foreign Relations of the U.S. 1947, *vol.7, p.155, Stuart to Sec. of State*

25 Ibid, *vol.7, 3/31/1947 , Stuart to Sec. of State*

The issue had been would the U.S. abandon China? And the answer, created through clever and devious methods, although yet unspoken, appeared to be yes. Not by a sudden, direct proclamation, by slow, persistent, inside maneuvering. The U.S. aid cut off, the strategic, tactical and financial restrictions Marshall imposed on Nationalist forces created such uncertainties that the Nationalist Government was unable to make any meaningful plans for the future. The initiative was solely in the hands of the Communists.

18

THE FINAL ACT

1948 OPENED WITH China on the brink. Secretary Marshall was called to testify before the House Committee on Foreign affairs on Feb. 20. There was much to explain but Marshall, the conference room warrior, was in his element. He opened by boldly requesting that his remarks not be "distributed in any way" in order to prevent "great harm to the Government of China." The only "great harm", at that point, would fall on Secretary Marshall if his remarks were not confined to the domestic politicians in the room. Any, who knew the realities of the China situation, would refute most of his story. His opening sentence was blatantly false "on VJ Day, in 1945 ". . . in the opinion of virtually every American authority, (it was) impossible to conquer the Communist armies by force...."[1] Every informed American military authority outside that hearing room would have contradicted Marshall. On VJ Day, the Communists

---

1   U.S. House Foreign Affairs Committee, *2/20/48, p.160*

had no army. They needed truces to gain time to build an army from a rural population. The General went on to paint a picture of a Chiang Kai-shek devoted to war on the Reds. He described a pitifully weak National Army, but didn't explain why his training efforts ignored the Chinese Army but focused on training and arming the Reds under his Red West Point plan. He didn't explain why his "mediation" efforts restricted Government troop movements but did nothing to impede the Reds. He mentioned "private investigations" that, he said, corroborated Red victory claims, but, no records were cited. He didn't explain the successive defeats suffered by the Red army until his arms embargo silenced Government guns. The austere Secretary of State even gave Congressmen, in close touch with their constituents, his insights on what "the American people would never knowingly accept."

Marshall admitted the Communists brought about "terrible destruction." However, even there, somehow the Government was to blame. He'd predicted it "frankly and forcibly" to the Government many times. He boldly pushed "The Big Lie" claiming vast aid and support was given China, despite routine State Department internal memos confirming a complete ban on shipment of combat materials.[2] Inside the Committee room, it seemed his years of "agony", his clever ploys, the web of licensing delays and other red tape obstructions had never happened. He claimed he "tried to expedite the surplus property affair." and used his influence to "force down the price for China, prices that would soon be inflated tenfold. Since acceleration of Cold War hostilities negated his justification of "Avoiding Russian recriminations," for removal of the Marines,

---

2   Foreign Relations of the U.S. *1947, vol. 7 , 3/25/47   Acheson to Kirk*

he cited a "tremendous pressure" by businessmen from Shanghai and elsewhere to remove the Marines. Marshall testified it was he who directed that Marine ammunition be left for the Government Army. (Marshall was in Moscow at that time and, as noted, his State department subordinate in China demanded the ammunition be destroyed.)

Marshall, isolated from contact with ordinary Chinese by his Communist appointments secretary and influenced thoroughly by his close contact with Chou En-lai, went on to relate unlikely stories of hands on experiences dealing with ordinary people in China, stories that invariably reflected badly on the Chinese Government. In closing, he even resorted to using the old Davies-Stilwell slander of the Chinese stepping aside to let others fight.

He referred to, but did not identify, "representatives in Manchuria and other places," who reported diverse political thinking in the CCP and declared the "Russian have played with clean hands, if you forget Dairen" On Feb. 24, 1948, Marshall's Consul General in Mukden. Manchuria, reported Soviet Union delivered 1960 rail carloads of equipment and ammunition to the Chinese Communists the previous calendar year. Also reported: Soviet instructors now training 60 regiments for Chinese Communist Army in North Manchuria.[3] Russian 76 mm. artillery, Russian carbines and Russian Burp guns in the hands of the PLA would soon kill Americans in Korea.

Marshall's prestige seemed to carry the day until one Congressman who had knowledge and experience in China

---

3   Foreign Relations of the U.S. *1947, vol. 7 , p.111*

spoke. Walter Judd, a former missionary in China who later, as a Congressman, met with Chiang Kai-shek and others, took issue with Marshall's testimony. Judd quoted his Nationalist contact "I yielded to General Marshall and signed that truce agreement." —"I will curse myself until my death. At that time the Communists had only 60 counties, at the end of the year, they had 300 counties." Marshall had no defense. He shifted to generalities. By meeting's end, General Marshall had taken full advantage of the confidentiality he'd requested going into the hearing. Most of his testimony wouldn't stand the light of day outside Committee chambers.

In February 1948, at a National Security Council meeting, Marshall said he feared China would be an unending drain upon our resources. But he would recommend aid to China to be administered by the European Recovery Program, an agency with no capability for handling war surplus rifles, ammunition, etc. An ill-advised Congress realized some semblance of aid to China was needed. In April 1948, $128,000,000 was provided.[4] To preclude any chance this modest aid would revive China, the last act of the "We must do more" charade ensued.

The Whitehouse handled the appropriation with a peculiar lack of urgency and State Department deception and obstruction exceeded their prior performance. When the Chinese Ambassador in Washington requested implementation of the program, he received no reply for two months until Senator Bridges sent a strongly worded letter to President Truman. After that, Secretary Marshall waited over three weeks until the end of June before replying to the Ambassador. Even then, the Chinese could not acquire arms and ammunition because

---

4 Wedemeyer, *Wedemeyer Reports,* p.400

the President authorized only commercial transactions and the munitions could be obtained only from government stocks. Another month passed before the President issued the required directive. On July 28, procedures were finally in place. Contrast that with FDR's response to an aid request from Great Britain before the U.S. entered World War II. FDR had shipments en route to England within a week.[5]

On March 31, 1948, Ambassador Stuart reported to Secretary Marshall "Demoralization and deterioration….have continued at an accelerated pace….Chinese people do not want to become Communist, yet they see the tide of Communism running irresistibly forward…"[6]

By August 1948, munitions were still not shipped to China. Much accounting, listing and pricing was done along with setting of priorities, obtaining export licenses. When shipments were finally made, it was found the $128 million appropriation bought only a fraction of the quantities intended. Investigation revealed prices charged for surplus rifles, ammunition, etc. had been inflated five and 10 fold thus negating the intent of Congress. A World War II surplus rifle that had been sold to other nations for $5.10, cost China $51, exactly 10 times the standard price. The greatest distortion was in ammunition pricing. The ammunition most critically needed by Chinese soldiers. The Chinese were being charged more than 18 times the price charged of other nations. Pricing of other armaments showed the same disparity or worse. China's price for a bazooka was 44 times the established surplus price.[7]

---

5   Utley, *The China Story*, *p.44,45*

6   Foreign Relations of the U.S. *1948, vol. 7 , p173*

7   Utley, *The China Story*, *p.47*

The audacity of this move to obstruct the will of Congress indicated an urgency to remove the last possible obstacle to Communist domination of China. But there was more. When the rifles finally arrived in China, Chinese soldiers found the bolts and firing pins had been removed[8], rendering the rifles useful only as clubs. The last hard fighting remnants of the Government Army, waiting expectantly for rifles and ammunition, had to choose surrender or futile death.[9] Secretary Marshall defended the delayed delivery of weapons, declaring the Chinese were questioning the pricing. He offered no explanation for the disarming of the rifles. It was the final treachery in the four year betrayal of China. Later it was claimed weapons given to Chiang's forces were readily captured by the Communists. But no useable weapons had been delivered up to that point. General Marshall had a flimsy defense for the exorbitant price levels; they reflected the cost of newly manufactured weapons. No one questioned why surplus materials would be replaced or why other aid recipients and buyers had enjoyed prices that were fractions of the cost charged to the Chinese.

In his 1948 testimony to the Foreign Relations Committee, Marshall, attempted to soften the way for the upcoming fall of China. He contradicted the Truman Doctrine and the "Containment Policy" commitments to resist Communist expansion throughout the world. He argued against "the tendency to feel that wherever

---

8 All surplus WW2 rifles were stored intact. Korean War U.S. Army and Marine infantry were issued these rifles from the same WW2 surplus inventory. The Korean War rifles came out of storage intact (no missing bolts and firing pins) covered with cosmoline protectant that was applied when the rifles were mothballed.

9 Senate Committee on the Judiciary, *10/51, p.1499, Admiral Cooke, p.1504*

Communist influences is brought to bear, we should immediately meet it . . ." He apparently felt 20% of the world's population was not worthy of the President's policy.

In September 1948, before the final curtain fell on China, Marshall and the State Department announced a change in policy. Nearly two years after the Reds walked out of his mediation, Marshall declared the United States would no longer push for Communist inclusion in the Nationalist government. The United States would now recognize China's struggle was part of the struggle against world Communism. At that late date, no flood of dollars and munitions could be released in time to help China and the Communists had dropped any pretense of interest in a coalition government. The only positive impact, on the dispirited Nationalist Chinese, might be a morale lift if they realized they were not in the fight alone. Marshall and Acheson prevented even that slim possibility. They classified the policy change as secret. America would ostensibly work in common cause with China but China must not become aware of this. The Chinese were denied any whiff of encouragement. By virtue of its "secrecy", this major policy change had absolutely no effect on the situation it addressed. Its purpose was a soothing of Congressional alarm and a securing of safe positioning for the major players before the upcoming fall.

As the enablers became fully aware of the magnitude of their accomplishment, they prepared for backlash. On March 15th 1949 Dean Acheson in a letter to Senator Connally, head of the Senate Foreign Relations Committee, misrepresented U.S. total aid to China claiming over 2 billion since the end of World War II. This was the same figure Acheson quoted to Ambassador Stuart in 1946. Thus even Acheson's fraudulent accounting inadvertently acknowledged China received no U.S. aid during their struggle. Major portions of Acheson's two billion aid claim were expenditures that disadvantaged China. These were dollars spent hurriedly transporting Japanese troops and civilians back to Japan leaving China without port and city administrators. Rather than abruptly pulling the Japanese out, China would have benefited if the former invaders were put to work repairing the devastation they'd created and continuing in bureaucratic positions until China could more smoothly phase them out. Acheson also ignored his President's designation of Japanese repatriation costs as World War II expenditures, rather than postwar expenditures. Acheson's two billion also included nearly one billion non-itemized "economic aid", a half billion "unidentified" aid and, by peculiar accounting, funds received from China for miscellaneous surplus material "sold" to China. Sold items included the half-million obsolete gas masks from which China salvaged the rubber for use in the civilian economy and various other quartermaster supplies.

U.S. official accounting of China aid substantially agreed with China's figure. The United States estimated the total of all aid "appropriations" for China after the end of WW II at $360 million. (This included the belated $128 million Congressional appropriation, the inflated prices and boltless rifles). Shipments covered by that appropriation, were soon canceled. Deducting the cancelled $128 million from the total appropriated $360 million produces a figure of $232 million of China aid shipped. This substantially agrees with China records listing $225 million received after WW2.

Whether China aid amounted to $225 million or $232 million, either is miniscule in size and quality compared to U.S. aid to other nations in need at that time. Billions flowed to Europe and Japan, ironic that aid to the enemy, who'd ravaged China for eight years, was not blocked by General Marshall. Aid to Japan and other countries did not include obsolete gasmasks, boltless rifles, etc. and aid dollars weren't subverted by fraudulent, inflated item costs.

Records prove George Catlett Marshall and Dean Acheson perverted every truth necessary to prevent China from gaining promised weapons, ammunition. Their performance conformed to the Red anti-ethic "The end justifies the means."

Marshall, Acheson, the Davies group and others, primarily in the State Department, through subtle or overt means exerted all efforts to undermine China. They subverted the will of Congress and the American people. The President intent on battling Communist aggression in Europe, labor unrest at home and other post war domestic problems relied on a State Department that he'd inherited and a reputed military genius he'd appointed. He was persuaded to compromise his own views and accept the deceitful advice of the "experts". When inconsistencies and contradictions appeared, his dependence on the State Department and General Marshall was too far advanced to allow correction. He issued statements to fit the moment. In a March 11, 1948 press conference Truman said his earlier statement requiring "fair and effective representation" for the Communists "still stood" but then contradicted that saying "we did not want any Communists in the government of China." By 1948, he'd completely delegated the China situation to Marshall. In November 1948, some six months after Congress had passed the belated China Aid bill, while red tape was still holding up deliveries, the Chinese United Nations delegate appealed to Marshall. Marshall replied he would refer requests to Washington. He offered no encouragement and advised against a Chinese appeal to the UN. The damage had been done. Nationalist troops lacking food, clothing and ammunition were capitulating to the Communist Chinese who were, by that time, well supplied by neighboring USSR. At that point, the State Department floated versions of China's armies readily capitulating and surrendering weapons they'd not yet received. This was contradicted by Major General Barr, head of the U.S. Military Advisory Group in China who criticized the inability of Government troops to recognize that discretion was the better part of valor, they too often believed stubborn defense could defeat overwhelming odds.[10] General Marshall, referring to the promised 8 Air groups he'd denied China for three years, cited the danger of committing all U.S. resources to China.[11] The promised 8 Air groups were long into obsolescence and had no value to the U.S. Their significance lay in the fact that they would have given Government forces domination of the air over all battlefields. The Reds had no air power.

During 1948, Russian equipped Chinese Communist forces completed the take over of Manchuria, and rolled south into China. Government forces fought stubbornly on occasion, but the Army was plagued by shortages of food and ammunition and demoralized by knowledge that the future could only be worse. Chiang Kai-shek selected the island of Formosa as his ultimate fall back position. When all possibility of victory on the mainland vanished, Chiang evacuated hundreds of thousands of troops and his remaining navy and air forces to the island. He declared Formosa would be the base

10   Utley, *The China Story, p.42*

11   Foreign Relations of the U.S. *1947, vol. 7 , p.512-517*

for counterattack and recovery of mainland China, brave words to restore shattered morale.

In August, 1949, the Nationalist Government divisions remaining on the mainland surrendered and two months later Mao Tsetung proclaimed the founding of the People's Republic of China.

The State Dept. hurriedly issued a "White Paper" stating the U.S. had stayed out of the Chinese "Civil War" because it should not and could not influence the outcome. But rather than "stay out", interference was the name of their game. They did their best to maintain the allusion that aid was flowing to China while they interfered. In regard to "could not influence the outcome" U.S. military opinion agreed that China could easily defeat the Reds with modest U.S. assistance. The only exception was George Catlett Marshall, who only voiced the "could not win" opinion after he'd blocked aid for two years. The paper ignored the FDR and HST promises of vast postwar aid. In regard to the pledge of full aid if China adopted the Marshall Constitution, a new requirement appeared in the White Paper; the adoption of the Constitution was only a beginning, development of a "truly liberal group in China" was required.

America awakened abruptly. The obscure picture of distant China came into focus as a shock. The Containment Strategy, the Truman Doctrine and Secretary Marshall's assurances had conditioned Americans to believe their government had the China situation under control. Suddenly, the public awoke to the cataclysmic loss of nearly one fifth of the world's population to Communism. The Administration faced a political storm. Less than a year after Harry Truman's great election victory over New York Governor Tom Dewey, his administration was close to panic.

Subsequent Congressional investigations found Marshall again ignoring the truth, claiming no part in the policy that abandoned

China. He testified falsely that when the policy was issued ". . . I was on the ocean going over there." He was contradicted by Admiral Leahy, Secretary of State Byrnes and HST's letter of assignment. All stated "these documents . . . have received your approval." President Truman had no criticism for the Communists or General Marshall. He declared "Chiang Kai-shek would not heed the advice of one of the greatest military strategists in history and lost to the Communists." Harry Truman's support of Marshall was an extreme example of his reluctance, almost an inability, to turn away from errant subordinates.

General Marshall's efforts sealed China's fate. That is a matter of record. His motivation is a mystery, was he a dedicated under cover Communist or a willing dupe? Marshall voiced no evidence of Communist leanings, and his position on "Containment" in Europe seemed in line with HST's views. Of course, Marshall would have been discredited if he attempted to apply his China tactics in Europe and it's possible the entire Soviet aggression program in Europe may have been a dramatic feint to distract America and takeover 20% of the world in Asia. It cost Stalin nothing to blockade Berlin, but the dramatic airlift response sucked in U.S. resources from all over the globe. There were many other similar crises large and small in Cold War Europe that distracted America from China and allowed the enablers full latitude.

In June, 1950 good fortune smiled once again on George Catlett Marshall. All media and Congressional inquiries on the loss of China were cut short by a crisis on a small peninsula in Asia. George Catlett Marshall would again preside over supply of armaments for opponents of Mao Tse-tung.

19

A WAR THAT MUST BE FORGOTTEN

K OREA, "THE LAND of the morning calm" is a small peninsula projecting from the land mass of Asia. Tribes that crossed the land bridge to present day Alaska and moved south to spread across North America, some 25,000 years ago began their migration in the Korean corner of Asia. The peninsula, being well off the path of the great Asian movements of armies and the nature of the fiercely independent people, made Korea unattractive to expansion minded neighbors. Despite common borders with powerful warring neighbors, Korea remained relatively unscarred by major wars for thousands of years.

America's first contact with Korea was violent. When a Yankee trading ship ran aground on that remote peninsula, Koreans massacred the crew and burned the ship. Following that, in 1870, U.S.

Marines landed and stormed the forts protecting the imperial palace, but the king refused to treaty with the foreigners. Five years later, the Japanese induced the Koreans to sign an agreement. In 1882, the U.S. concluded a treaty and American missionaries entered the country. In 1906, at the conclusion of the Russo-Japanese war, a peace treaty, mediated by future American President Theodore Roosevelt placed Korea under Japanese influence. A few years later, Japan formally annexed the peninsula and from that point Koreans were subjected to oppressive authoritarian rule until Japan surrendered ending WW2.

Throughout WW2, the Soviet Union carefully avoided war with Japan. Then, when the U.S. devastated Hiroshima and Nagasaki with nuclear bombs, the Russian army attacked and rolled through Japanese occupied Manchuria and the Korean Peninsula.

In the early harmonious days after Japan surrendered, the U.S. and the USSR agreed to halving occupation of the peninsula along the 38th parallel of latitude. The Soviets occupied the mountainous northern half containing 1/3 of the population and high capacity hydroelectric plants that supplied the entire peninsula. The more populous, U.S. occupied, south was less mountainous, primarily agricultural and dependent on the north for electric power. The border initially had no meaning for Koreans, who considered themselves one people. They were hardy, eager for independence and expected to regain their national identity soon after Japanese were evicted. However, Cold War confrontations interrupted any possibility of a normal process of development. Soon, each side promoted its own political system. In the north the Soviets installed a militant communist, Kim IL Sung as dictator and proceeded to regiment the country along Soviet lines.

In the south the U.S. installed Syngman Rhee, a Korean National who'd lived in exile in the United States for 36 years. The arbitrary 38th parallel divided geography but not people's political beliefs. Those who held democratic principles in the north soon submitted to communism, prison or death. In the south, rightists led the country. Communists infiltrating from the north initially attempted to take over the labor movement and influence nationalist political factions in the south. Violent clashes were a common occurrence. Gradually, North Korean adherence to the Moscow line became obvious and aroused the distrust of South Korean Nationalists. In 1946 the Reds were able to call a general strike in the South, but by 1948 their influence in the labor movement had diminished well below that point. North Korea then shifted focus to infiltrating and inciting rural South Koreans to form an anti-government guerrilla force.

The Rhee government's moves to suppress the guerrillas were clumsy and harsh. It's estimated 100,000 Koreans died during that period. As South Korean Government forces gradually pushed the guerrillas into remote areas, the guerrillas resorted to aggressive forays into villages and towns in search of food. The countryside that formerly sympathized with the Reds turned on them. The government then offered an amnesty program that won over 40,000 guerrillas and following that, instituted a land reform program making tenant farmers into landholders of small plots. The rural guerilla threat was eliminated.

As the South evolved unevenly towards democratic rule, South Koreans, many with relatives in the communist north, became increasingly aware of the extreme oppression and suffering Kim

IL Sung inflicted on his northern subjects. Gradually, most South Koreans evolved to hold firm anticommunist views. By 1948 the overwhelming majority could be ranked as anticommunist.

The agreement on the 38th parallel demarcation line included a schedule for a general election to unite North and South Korea. However, since southerners far outnumbered northerners, the Soviets avoided free elections and focused on developing a small well-disciplined North Korean army complete with tanks, artillery and air force.

When the Americans landed in South Korea after WW2, the United States committed to organize and arm South Koreans sufficiently to balance the military power of the north. However, similar to U.S. performance in China, excuses were soon created. Aid opponents claimed that President Rhee, if armed would invade the north. At first glance, it seemed a logical. Both Rhee in the south and Kim Il sung in the north had voiced intent to unite Korea under their flags and border incidents along the 38th parallel were frequent and violent. On closer examination, it was a flimsy, easily refuted excuse for disarming South Korea. The U.S. was fully capable of arming South Korea with selected defensive weaponry without enabling Rhee to invade North Korea. U.S. war surplus antitank guns rather than tanks, fighter planes rather than bombers, land mines and fixed artillery and fixed antiaircraft weapons could be massed to defend effectively without providing offensive capability. As with China, arms were available, but were denied the South Koreans in their time of need. A second option that would provide defense and yet restrain South Korean offensive action was proposed in General Wedemeyer's 1948 report to President Truman, the report that was suppressed by General Marshall.

By 1948, some two years after the Japanese were evicted from the peninsula, South Korea had evolved to be the Republic of Korea (ROK). Despite domestic upheavals and overt threats from their northern neighbor, the small nation was unevenly moving toward true democracy, a concept, at that time, foreign to that part of the world. Three tumultuous years after the United States installed Syngman Rhee to head the fledging nation, elections were sufficiently free and competitive for Rhee's party to lose its majority in the legislature. Economic progress paralleled political development. Amazingly, the small country cut off from the hydroelectric power of the north and lacking in raw material, was starting to prosper. Rhee's land reform program energized agriculture and with the reduction of Red incited labor strife and civil unrest in the cities, the domestic situation brightened. Unfortunately, another problem loomed.

The U.S. State department cited a UN recommendation that occupation troops leave the peninsula. The United Nations, in existence for all of three years was markedly responsive to requests from the U.S., its primary source of funding. At that time, the U.S. could get UN approval for anything that didn't arouse Russian veto. Its' obvious, the UN recommendation for troop withdrawal from Korea, if not instigated by the U.S. Representative at the UN, was not resisted. As time wound down U.S. troop evacuation was deferred for six months. The Russians had fully armed and trained their satellite North Korea but the South Koreans were suddenly faced with the loss of their only protection. U.S. troops would soon disappear. Then, while U.S. aid flowed out to Western Europe and recent enemy Japan, American aid to South Korea was cut back from 137 million to 92.7 million. Rhee's urgent pleas for promised aid were ignored or rejected and Rhee was positioned as a Fascist dictator. U.S. State Department posture on South Korea closely resembled its China policy of slander and disarmament.

United States formally recognized South Korea as the Republic of Korea (ROK) on January 1, 1949 and eight days later advised Rhee that U.S. troops would be pulling out as a "normalization of relations....." As the pullout date approached, in February 1949, the CIA submitted their analysis of the Korean situation to President Truman. It concluded that U.S. troop withdrawal would probably result in a collapse of the Republic of Korea, an event which "would seriously diminish U.S. prestige and adversely affect U.S. interests in the Far East....and would be felt most acutely in Japan." JCS Chief Omar Bradley, who'd presided over the recent disarming of the U.S. Army, demurred and pushed for the pullout. Wedemeyer's report, warning that removal of troops would incite a Red invasion, remained locked away.

January 1949 was a fateful month for The Republic of Korea. Secretary of State Dean Acheson warned Rhee his "aggressive reminders of promised aid could have serious consequences." JCS chief General Omar Bradley submitted a National Security Council study and recommendation to the President. A peculiar study that rejected substantial military aid to protect the Republic of Korea and recommended the entire Korean situation be passed on to the United Nations. It then went on to expose that proposal as meaningless by recognizing that the fledging U.N. was powerless to help the Republic of Korea. The following month, the CIA reported on the political/economic status of ROK. "Communist capabilities in South Korea....at a low level....further reduced if the Republic continues its present trend toward increased stability[1]. In a separate report the CIA stated that withdrawal of U.S. forces from Korea would probably be followed by invasion which would "seriously diminish U.S. prestige and adversely affect U.S. security interests in the Far East." It went on to recommend a moderate force be retained in order to discourage Red invasion plans, etc.[2]

In June 1949, 45,000 U.S. troops were pulled out of South Korea leaving a token military advisory group. The State Department justified the pullout as complying with the UN Resolution of Dec. 12, 1948 and declared the U.S. "has given unstintingly."[3] Meanwhile, ROK pleas for promised aid were ignored. A consensus was developing in the State Department, the Army high command, Congress and the White House, a concept that saw South Korea as relatively inconsequential to United States. The Joint Chiefs of Staff, led by General Omar Bradley, declared " Korea is of little strategic value to the United States ....a commitment to the United States use of force in Korea would be unwise and impractical----". South Korea was about to be written off.

Six months later, in January, 1950, for reasons never explained, Secretary of State Dean Acheson went public and exposed South Korea's complete vulnerability to the long threatened attack from the Communist North Korea. For Communist leadership, this

---

1   CIA Doc. ORE 32-48

2   Ibid, 3-49

3   Dept. of State 1/9/49 p. 59,60.

removed any lingering doubts on Washington's lack of commitment to South Korea. The Administration's abandonment strategy
was firmly in place. Following that, in March 1950, Congressional
thinking was publicly stated by the Chairman of the Senate Foreign
Relations Committee "I'm afraid it's going to happen, that is, the
abandonment of South Korea, whether we want it or not." Other
than Japan, Asian nations were largely ignored by the Truman doctrine, the Containment policy and the Marshall plan. It seemed the
continent of Asia was being silently conceded to Communism.

The abandonment strategy was adopted by all branches of government and became the bedrock of U.S. policy on Korea. The Reds
knew South Korea was ripe for the taking and events accelerated. U.S.
Army intelligence, predicted the North Koreans would attack south
in March/April 1950 and then revised that with a prediction of a June
invasion. Ominous reports of North Korean troop movements and
evacuations of civilians along the border surfaced as June approached.
All available information seemed to confirm a June invasion, but the
warnings aroused little interest in Washington.

By June 1950, the U.S. political scene was in disarray. The
Administration seemed ineffective and the President was taking a
severe beating in the polls. Americans had been rudely shocked
10 months earlier, in August 1949, when the Soviets successfully
detonated an atomic device and the United States lost its position
as the sole nuclear power in the world. Only weeks after that,
Mao Tse-tung's Reds completed their conquest of mainland China.
Shock waves reverberated through Congress. The administration
found itself in critical condition. Republican opposition charged
Red influence in the State Department and rampant espionage by

Red agents. Influential democrats grudgingly concurred. Despite a powerful PR campaign, public and Congressional confidence in the administration reached a new low. The consequences of further retreat and failure by the administration were unthinkable. The stage was set for a dramatic move that would reassert American authority and regain public confidence.

June 25, 1950, President Harry Truman, enjoying a quiet Sunday at his home in Missouri, received a phone call from Secretary of State Dean Acheson. Acheson advised the President of a new, but not unexpected, development on the Korean peninsula in Asia. Carefully developed strategy was in place. Official Washington had seen no strategic value at risk and conceded that South Korea, ROK, would likely be overcome by the Communist North.

However, that view and policy was adopted before America lost its monopoly on nuclear weapons, before it lost nearly 20% of the world to Communism. That Sunday afternoon in Missouri, consensus strategy met political reality.

When U.S. Secretary of State Acheson advised the President of United States that North Korea invaded South Korea, Truman responded "Dean, we've got to stop the sons of bitches no matter what." That evening daughter Margaret recorded in her diary "we are going to fight." The following day she added "last night dad said we would resist the aggression of North Korea.....he is going to send planes and troops"[4]. The guiding strategy of the United States for the past three years suddenly evaporated. The President and the country were not ready to lose again in Asia. HST's war

---

4   Truman, M, *Souvenier, p.275*

decision was formalized at hurried meetings in Washington, where warnings, from Army brass, of a weakened U.S. Army, were ignored. An unexpected Soviet absence from United Nations allowed the U.S. to avoid Russian veto and gain U.N. sanctions on North Korea and token commitments of troops from individual U.N. members. With HST's hometown decision properly dressed with congressional and U.N. approval, America entered its first undeclared war and declared it a Police Action. On June 25, 1950, Korea "the land of the morning calm" plunged into modern total warfare that would kill and maim millions.

The North Koreans attacked south with 137 WW2 Soviet medium tanks, a tiny force by recent WW2 standards, but ROK forces had no weapons capable of stopping them. Red tanks roamed at will, disrupting ROK communications and morale. Most of the Republic of Korea, forces displayed their lack of combat training and inadequacy of weapons with disorganized retreat. Seoul, the ROK capital, fell in days and the government fled south.

In Washington, the President Truman moved quickly, but ineffectively. He ordered a blockade in the Straits of Formosa, ostensibly to protect Chiang Kai-shek's Formosa, but the Reds had no naval forces capable of attacking the island. The blockade had a reverse effect. It halted Chiang Kai-shek's attacks on the Red mainland and resulted in freeing Red Defense troops for other deployments, including Korea.

In regard to the major issue, stopping the North Korean invasion of South Korea, HST soon discovered he had no army to deploy. Post WW2 demobilization had been followed by extreme budget cuts and Army effectiveness had been further reduced by a peculiar government committee that relaxed army discipline standards. Five years after WW2 ended, nearly all combat experienced captains, lieutenants and sergeants, the people who provide leadership in combat, were pursuing civilian careers. Infantry divisions based in nearby Japan and Okinawa were seriously understaffed. Combat units in Japan had succumbed to soft occupation duties and it was found later that lower ranks from Okinawa lacked the most basic infantry training.

The first deployment of troops from Japan to Korea was limited due to only six C-54 transport planes available. The budgeted air fleet had been sent to assist the Berlin airlift and remained there. Although none of the listed combat units were ready for actual combat, they were inserted piecemeal to stop the North Koreans. Then, more shocking news emerged. The United States Army that knocked out thousands of Hitler's Panzer tanks a few years earlier had only 18 armor piercing artillery shells in the entire Asian theatre and its anti-tank mines were duds. One unit carefully mined an approach road and watched as Red T-34 tanks came at them. Not one mine detonated[5]. The richest, most powerful country on earth had nothing to stop North Korea's small tank corps. Troops exposing themselves to direct tank fire in order fire bazooka anti-tank rockets, found their missiles bouncing harmlessly off Red tank turrets. WW2 hand grenades hurled at enemy infantry had a failure rate as high as 50%[6] and unexploded grenades could become lethal at any time. In the heat of battle, orders were not communicated. There was a shortage of communications wire and

---

5   Sandler, *The Korean War*, p 66, 70

6   Drury & Clavin, *The Last Stand of Fox Company*, p 351

outdated radio batteries lasted only a few hours. The combination of untrained troops, inexperienced squad, platoon and company leaders along with useless, dangerous weapons and ammunition and a general relaxation of discipline fostered a new term in the U.S. Army. "Bugout" became the word of the day. The Air Force discovered their own shocking situation when they faced the Russian Air Force. The Russians, noted for inferior aircraft recently in WW2, flew MIG jets that outperformed American Jets.

Washington waffled between urgency and panic. The nation that supplied its allies so generously during the recent world war, 'The arsenal of democracy", resorted to collecting armaments from Post Office lawns to equip troops in combat. The Marine Corps, threatened with extinction only one year earlier, called up veterans of Guadalcanal and Iwo Jima. Many said farewell to young wives and babies and bled out storming Seoul or breaking out of the Frozen Chosin. When U.S. KIA (killed in action) figures exceeded 1000 per month, the President's misnomer "Police action" was quietly dropped from Washington bulletins. As word of defective weapons and ammo leaked back to the U.S, the public was baffled. The President had only recently acclaimed U.S. Army superiority[7].

On the ground, in Korea, the small but well-disciplined North Korean Army rolled south almost unimpeded. ROK forces dissolved and U.S. forces retreated, surrendered or died. A last ditch defensive line, the Pusan Perimeter, was set up in the southeast corner of the Korean peninsula and reinforcements were rushed in. Included was a British contingent that represented the UN's first

---

7 NY Times, 4/22/50, *p. 8, HST at Fort Benning; ..The immense strength of theU.S....*

troop contribution. From that point on military forces in Korea were officially identified as UN rather than U.S. forces. In total, UN members would contribute approximately 10% of the U.S. led ground forces in Korea. The much touted UN participation came at price that would soon come due.

As U.S.-UN reinforcements, including combat trained troops, poured into Pusan, time began running out for the North Korean invaders. Their small army would soon be out-numbered and their extended supply lines were open to air attack. However, they fought stubbornly and kept UN forces penned up at Pusan until General MacArthur masterminded a surprise amphibious landing near the 38th parallel, in the north. The 1st Marine Division landed at Inchon and advanced on Seoul. Threatened with complete cutoff, the North Koreans put up a stubborn resistance at Seoul to allow their forces to escape from positions further south. Their retreat continued and UN forces kept the pressure on, crossed the 38th parallel and pursued into North Korea. By the end of October, 1950 Americans were ap-proaching the Yalu River, the North Korea-China border. Troops were told they'd be home for Christmas.

Some six weeks earlier, before U.S.-UN troops crossed the 38 parallel into North Korea, the CIA reported nearly half a million Chinese Communist troops near or moving toward the Yalu River, the China/North Korea border, and Red Chinese aircraft arriv-ing in the same area. The CIA warned it "may be stage-setting for an imminent overt move." Red China then issued two warnings threatening to interfere if U.N. troops crossed into North Korea. Both warnings were ignored in Washington.

While Macarthur urged his troops further north to the Yalu, masses of organized Chinese "Volunteers" infiltrated and launched surprise attacks on over-extended US/UN units. An overconfident General Macarthur, instructed by Washington to invade North Korea, ignored the immediate threat and attempted to push northward against what turned out to be overwhelming forces. MacArthur's forces were surrounded. Many fought their way out. Many more had to abandon their equipment to make their escape. Some didn't get out. The U.S Army 31st Regimental Combat Team surrounded in the mountainous north east, was massacred despite rescue forces close by. The army's rebuilt WW2 radios were incompatible with Ist Marine Division radios only 15 miles away.

UN forces retreated southward and re-crossed the 38th parallel into South Korea. Seoul fell to Communist invaders once again. General Ridgeway took over command of U.S.-UN forces in Korea, organized retreating troops, dug in on a line across the peninsula south of Seoul and counterattacked.

The Chinese invasion forced a decision on Washington. Mao's Red Army was killing Americans. How resolutely would America react? The much heralded UN troop contributions to HST's "Police Action" now exacted a price. MacArthur reported Red Chinese troops "pouring" over the Yalu River into North Korea and ordered his B-29s to bomb the bridges. However, Washington had promised to consult with the British before any action that might affect Manchuria and other UN allies were also included in strategic and tactical decisions. The decision, conditioned by UN influence was new in the annals of warfare. Enemy reinforcements were allowed to flow across the Yalu bridges and MIG jets (piloted by Russians masquerading as North Koreans) were allowed safe passage back to bases in Manchuria after attacking Americans. Manchuria was established as a safe sanctuary and supply depot for enemy troops intent on killing Americans, unprecedented in the history of warfare. It was justified as preventing world holocaust, but at that time, although the Russians had tested an atomic device, they were not armed with atomic weapons; they had no meaningful naval forces and only limited strategic bombing capability.

While Mao Tse-tung's decision to go to war with the U.S seemed more than reckless, he may have had reason to believe the U.S. would break with traditional methods of warfare and allow him safe sanctuary while he killed American's nearby.

Along with UN participation in war decisions, another price for UN participation was soon exacted. Foreigners, UN people, gained access to U.S. classified information and the State Department carried this concession to an extreme. British Foreign Office official Donald Maclean and others enjoyed complete access to nearly all U.S. military and atomic secrets. Maclean had access to security information denied U.S. Congressmen and he, for some unexplained reason, carried an escort-free pass to all U.S. Atomic energy facilities. At that time, U.S. world strategy was based on America's position as sole possessor of operational atomic weapons. The recent extreme military staff and budget cuts had been justified by the belief that Stalin would curb his aggressions in the face of U.S. nuclear capability. All defense issues hinged on Soviet belief in U.S. nuclear superiority. But, in reality, the U.S. nuclear arsenal was disarmed. Maclean knew America had no atomic bombs ready for war. When Maclean defected to Moscow in 1951, it was apparent Stalin and Mao knew that America's immediate nuclear threat was a bluff. Secretary of State Dean Acheson's reaction to the defection was reported as "My God, that sonofabitch knew everything." In addition to top secret info, "Everything" included the knowledge that Mao's troops and Stalin's pilots would enjoy safe sanctuary in Manchuria while they killed Americans in adjacent Korea.[8]

In April, 1951, General MacArthur wrote a politically embarrassing letter to Republican Congressional leadership. HST reacted by relieving the General. Since that time MacArthur has been blamed for disregarding Red Chinese warnings and invading North Korea. However, Dean Acheson, not MacArthur's office in Tokyo, received and ignored the Red warnings and only the President is authorized to make the decision on invading a foreign country. General Ridgeway was elevated to replace MacArthur in Tokyo. General Van Fleet, recent savior of Greece, once again called upon in a crises, took command in Korea.

As summer approached, Van Fleet launched a full offensive. Seoul was retaken and Communist forces retreated northward. (Van fleet later reported to Senators in a secret session, "We had the Communist Armies on the run."[9]) When the Reds called for truce talks, Van Fleet was ordered to halt his offensive. Once the advance was halted, the Reds dug in. Truce talks droned on and the Communists built a near impregnable defense line from which they

---

8   Sandler, *The Korean War, p. 110,111*

9   NY Times, 3/23/53, *Truce Talks Halted His Victory March,*

launched deadly attacks on UN troops. The bedrock Red defense line, along with the safe sanctuary in Manchuria already granted to the enemy, removed any pressure on the Reds to come to terms. Ground combat turned into World War One type trench warfare. Each night saw deadly firefights and ambushes in the "no man's land" between the opposing trench lines. The Reds continued to build up their forces. They launched intense artillery bombardments and attacked selected "high ground" locations in force. UN forces resisted and counterattacked, but they fought without the enemy's increasing resources. Inexplicably, despite the vast WW2 surplus ammunition supplies, ammunition was, at times, in limited supply on the front lines and after more than a year of warfare, a year to produce new ammunition, none was available.

Truce talks dragged on for nearly two years while casualties mounted and the Reds became more aggressive. The war continued as HST's term in office ended. He became the first American President to not seek reelection during wartime. Public dissatisfaction with the war and other administration embarrassments gave General Dwight Eisenhower an easy road to the Presidency. Ike visited Korea before taking office, gained firsthand information and acted. He pledged to end the enemy's safe sanctuary, bomb Manchuria and turn to all out conventional warfare. He also removed the seventh fleet blockade from Formosan waters. The Reds soon came to terms and the killing ended. Eisenhower detractors claim Stalin's death precipitated the peaceful change in Red posture and the truce. But Russian influence in North Korea had shifted to China two years earlier, when Mao rescued North Korea from MacArthur's October, 1950 offensive.

During the last year of the war increasing reports of ammunition shortages on the front lines raised congressional inquiries. When President Elect Dwight Eisenhower visited the front in Korea, he'd found "Certain problems of supply ---require early correction."[10]

The first two years of the three year war had been fought with huge left over supplies of WW2 ammunition. The use of old ammo allowed two full years to bring production of new ammunition up to a fraction of the quantities recently produced during WW2. Reported shortages seemed incomprehensible. However, on December 29, 1952, after 2 ½ years to bring new ammo production up to a fraction of WW2 levels, General William Reeder of G-4 logistics admitted that troops in combat in Korea were being rationed on artillery ammunition. The 1st Marine Division, blocking the invasion route to Seoul, reported critical shortages of hand grenades, 81 mm mortar rounds and artillery ammo rationing that "allowed the enemy to show himself almost at will without receiving fire."[11] This meant Americans could only watch while the enemy massed his forces to attack.

Congressional investigators heard flimsy excuses, the steel strike was blamed, (the steel strike lasted six weeks). "We thought it would be a short war". (When China entered the war, nearly three years earlier, no sane mind expected a short war.)

---

10   Time Magazine, 12/29/52, *Heavy Caliber Cover-up*

11   USMC Operations in West Korea, Vol. V *p. 193*

How could it be that the greatest country on earth, the "Arsenal of Democracy" of WW2, after a two year startup, failed to produce a fraction of the recent WW2 ammunition output? Was this a two year plague of national incompetence? No credible explanation was offered. In January 1952, after 18 months of war and 18,000 Americans dead, the administration declared "tremendous advances" in production.[12] But the shortages increased. Time magazine called that a "Heavy Caliber Cover-up." In 1953, the Senate Armed services subcommittee found "needless loss of American lives" because of ammo shortages. Democratic Senator Byrd blamed the President for ordering a slowdown of ammo procurement but further investigation pointed to then Secretary of Defense George C. Marshall. Marshall claimed he was acting on an estimate made before China entered the war.[13] But China entered the war only four months after the first shot was fired. Marshall didn't explain why he left the ammo production slowdown in force for years while the enemy reached and exceeded UN firepower on the front lines. Sending young Americans into combat and deliberately depriving them of ammunition is a concept nearly beyond belief, but the unexplained ammo shortage fit the Marshall pattern. Troops opposing Communist Mao Tse-tung, whether Chinese or American, were denied ammunition and died.

Similar to the China betrayal, information on the Korean War ammunition shortage and other legacy-sensitive aspects of the Forgotten War have been successfully covered up for over a half century.

---

12   NY Times, 1/7/52 , *Wilson Forecasts--*

13   Ibid, 5/9/53, *Byrd Ties Truman to Shell Shortage*

20

CONCLUDING IRONIES

WE NOW KNOW the Great Teacher was beyond ruthless, but he was also surprisingly ignorant. In addition to his terror campaigns, his blunders killed millions. He seemed totally unaware of China's historic agricultural limitation. For centuries despots and warlords alike limited their military conscriptions in order to maintain a critical level of farm labor. A population level required to stave off cataclysmic famine. Mao Tse-tung carelessly drew down the rural population for his great Leap Forward and other grand schemes and millions starved. While his deadly programs proceeded in mainland China, Mao failed to overcome Chiang Kai-shek's modest forces on Taiwan and gradually faded into isolation as less extreme factions evolved in Communist China.

Chiang Kai-shek proved to be a prime example of the power of the smear. His life story, rising from abject poverty to unite the largest nation on earth, his long tenacious fight against the cruel

Japanese, add to that his rise from defeat to form a thriving democratic nation and it's truly a phenomenal life story, one that would suggest a Chinese George Washington. It's a story that his worst detractors don't deny. But the "corruption" charge has clung despite the intensive FBI investigation that came up empty and more recently, Chiang's wealthy relatives, purported receivers of vast corrupt funds, have died off leaving settled estates that show relatively modest wealth.

Chiang Kai-shek, in Formosa, moved quickly to govern by Sun Yat-sen's three principals. On February 4, 1949, he launched a "land rent reduction program". It aimed to implement Sun Yat-sen's slogan "land to the tillers". Within four years of peaceful transition, 80% of arable land was owned by those who tilled it. The reckless "dare to die" revolutionary who rose to unite China and fight Japan to a standstill, only to be abandoned by his ally, was not finished.[1] After weathering a succession of invasion threats from Mao's Mainland China, the much maligned Chiang and his son guided Taiwan's growth to thriving, democratic nationhood: a beacon of freedom lying adjacent to a monolith of terror and suppression.

The Red takeover of China fulfilled a Communist world strategy outlined by Lenin in 1922, attempted unsuccessfully by Stalin in 1928, and executed successfully after WW2. It resulted largely but not entirely from America's abandonment of China. Other factors contributed. In 1943, FDR signed a treaty renouncing all preexisting exploitive claims on China port sovereignty but one year later, he turned and awarded Russia "preeminent" authority over Manchurian ports and railroads. In 1945 HST granted the Soviets authority over Manchuria's

---

1   Crozier, *The Man Who Lost China,* P 352

principal port, Dairen and then allowed them to close it to U.S. and Chinese vessels. In 1945, the U.S. promoted a China-Russia Friendship Treaty and then completely ignored multiple flagrant Soviet violations.

Chiang Kai-shek was not blameless. He failed to update his views of Mao's Red forces as they progressed from a rural militia to the well trained, well-armed army developed by the Russians during Marshall's truces. Chiang failed to recognize the deterioration of his army after a decade of war. He failed to penetrate Marshall's skillful "managing" techniques and failed to recognize that the continuing red tape delays of arms shipments constituted a concerted effort to disarm his forces. A clearer view of this situation would have allowed him the quick response that characterized his career before he cast his lot with America and George Marshall.

However, all of the above would have amounted to nothing but for George Catlett Marshall's maneuvering and deception. Marshall's misfit protégé Stilwell installed the slander program that set China up for betrayal. Patron Marshall, after WW2, exhibited new levels of initiative and commitment. He sacrificed his ethics and his country's welfare in his drive to subvert the faithful ally who'd so recently saved countless thousands of American lives. The kindest view of George Catlett Marshall would picture him as a well-intentioned dupe. His early WW2 dedication to a suicidal invasion of France and his allowing the Russian Army more U.S. trucks than Eisenhower's forces in Europe could be viewed either as errors or efforts to aid the Communist cause. His easy violation of Judeo- Christian and West Point ethics could indicate adoption of the Red anti-ethic *the end justifies the means.* His responsibility in the Korean War ammunition shortages that killed Americans may define the character of George Catlett Marshall.

Dean Acheson's misinformation campaign contributed much to the betrayal of China. His false claims of two billion post war aid to China provided cover for General Marshall's arms embargos. His false report to a Congress then considering China aid; "The Chinese government is not threatened by defeat by the Communists," effectively stifled aid from a budget conscious Congress. His declaration to Congress that "our observers report no instances of battles lost due to ammo shortages---" was deliberately false. Acheson supported and promoted the "bright young men" of the State Department who could find no fault with any Communist action. His public exposure of South Korea's vulnerability invited North Korea's attack and the war that followed. It has been lamely passed off as a simple gaffe, but the United States Secretary of State does not ad-lib major policy announcements. Every word is carefully evaluated, reviewed and voiced for a specific purpose. His failure to act on Red China's threat to enter the war cost thousands of American lives. Acheson's career bio carefully avoids any mention of his many misstatements that invariably aided the Communist cause. In his private life, he was a staunch friend of convicted spy, Alger Hiss. When the flow of torn bodies from Korea increased, Dean Acheson found it advantageous to transform himself into a Cold War warrior.

President Truman's concepts of Chiang Kai-shek and China underwent a 180 degree change during the years he was counseled by George Catlett Marshall and Dean Acheson. On taking office, he believed "That Chiang's government fought side by side with us against our common enemy, that we have reason to believe that the so-called commies in China not only didn't help but on occasion helped the Japs." Two months later on January 5, 1946, he wrote "We should rehabilitate China and create a strong central government there; we should do the same for Korea."[2] Later, after years of Marshall/Acheson advice, he described a "crooked old Chiang Kai-shek" whose "downfall was his own doing." General Marshall's influence on his President is indicated in an HST letter to wife Bess. "....I'd very much like to explode on the Bolshies – but Marshall hopes I won't. So, of course, I won't..."[3] HST's total reliance on Marshall and Acheson insulated him from any objective view of the China situation. General Wedemeyer's special report and the regular reports from the U.S. Ambassador in China pictured Chiang Kai-shek in only positive terms. Wedemeyer described Chiang as "A fine character. ---The logical leader of China today...". Ambassador Stuart reported on Oct. 29, 1947 "...the men at the top are of high integrity and continue struggle bravely against terrific difficulties. There are many more like them within and outside the government. On March 31, 1948, Stuart reported "the Chinese people do not want to become communists,...the Generalissimo stands out as the only moral force capable of action." Such reports did not reach HST.

President Truman was diverted from following through on his original intentions by trusted advisors who subverted his goals for China while he addressed critical issues at home and in Europe. The Administration in office during the growth of the "corrupt" Chiang Kai-shek slander retreated from office under charges of corruption. Harry S Truman, the first American President to take office of a United States that had reached world supremacy, was the

---

2   Truman, *Memoirs Vol. 2, P.80*

3   Truman, *Dear Bess, P. 545*

first American President to not seek reelection during wartime. Truman left office with the lowest Gallup Poll approval numbers on record. HST had many fine qualities, but as he readily admitted, he was thrust onto the grand stage, ill-prepared and the challenges were enormous.

Harry S Truman, inserted into an incredibly complex world of high stakes situations, placed complete trust in a reputed Great American who, with a small segment of government bureaucracy, conveyed 20% of the world's population to communist terrorism in Asia while he, HST, led the fight to stop Communism in Europe.

When records are examined, two overriding facts are clear and fully documented. While fighting the bulk of the Japanese Army throughout WW II, China's government was subverted by emissaries from the United States. After WW II, China was subverted by the U.S. Secretary of State and abandoned to a terrorist insurrection, resulting in a regime that killed tens of millions of Chinese and tens of thousands of Americans. The sheer magnitude of the numbers killed in China made this the deadliest manmade horror in world history and the American enablers made this a stain on the greatest country in world history.

Dwight Eisenhower's pre-election trip to Korea has been criticized as a publicity stunt. But only at the front lines could he get the real facts on the peculiar ongoing ammunition shortage. Facts that were blocked from his predecessor by trusted subordinates. Eisenhower brought stature to the Whitehouse. Communist Cold War challenges subsided for eight years and then emerged with the election of a young, inexperienced Chief Executive. Eisenhower while faulted for a "Missile gap" vs. the USSR, installed missiles ranging on Moscow and initiated recon flights over our Cold War enemy. Red China's challenges toward Chiang Kai-shek's emerging democracy on Taiwan were effectively blocked. With eight years of peace, the first modern highway system was developed and, after two wars in the past decade, Americans focused on home and family. It was an eight year hiatus from strife and major national problems.

* Ike's warning that we must not forget the "harrowing decades" that "poisoned our national life," referred to an era when U.S. Army decoding of espionage messages revealed, and Soviet records confirmed, the identity of 329 Americans imbedded in the U.S. Government and working as Soviet agents. An era when the American Communist Party, advocating the violent overthrow of the U.S. government, listed 70,000 registered members. Ike's warning is long forgotten, today, our school systems teach our children "....it may be that none of these people was ever a Communist..."[4]

THE END

---

4   Boorstin & Kelly, *A HISTORY of the UNITED STATES, P. 722*

BIBLIOGRAPHY

Acheson, Dean G. Present at the Creation.

NY: Norton, 1969

Ambrose, Stephan, E. Citizen Soldiers. NY: Simon & Schuster, 1997

Belden, Jack. China Shakes The World. NY, Monthly Review Press, 1970

Berry, Henry. Hey, Mac, Where Ya Been? Living Memories Of The U.S. Marines In The Korean War. NY: St. Martin's Press, 1985

Bjorge, Gary J. Merrill's Marauders: Combined US Army Command and Operations in North Burma. Kansas: General Staff College, 1944

Bjorge, Gary J. Leavenworth Paper Number 22: Combat Studies Institute Press, Fort Leavenworth, KS

Braim, Paul. The Will To Win: The Life Of General James A Van Fleet. Annapolis, Naval Institute Press, 2001

Buhite, Russel, D. Patrick J Hurley and American Foreign Policy. Ithaca, NY: Cornell Univ. Press, 1973

Bullitt, William C. How We Won the War and Lost the Peace. Life Mag. 8/30/48

Burkitt, Laurie, Scobell, Andrew, Wurtzel. The Lessons of History: The Chinese Peoples Army, Strategic Studies Institute, 2003

Byrnes, James F. Speaking Frankly. NY: Harper Bros., 1947

Carlson, Evans Fordyce. Twin Stars of China. NY: Dodd, Mead & Company, 1940

Carlson, Evans Fordyce. The Chinese Army. NY: Institute of Pacific Relations, 1940

Carter, Caroll J. Mission to Yenan. KY: Lexington Univ. Press, 1997

Chang, Jung and Holliday, Jon. Mao: The Unknown Story. NY: Anchor Books, 2006

Chennault, Claire, Lee. Way of a Fighter. NY. Putnam & Sons, 1949

Chiang, Iris. The Rape Of Nanking. NY: Basic Books, 1997

Chiang Kai-shek China's Destiny And Chinese Economic Theory. NY: Roy Publishers, 1947 Editor: Jaffe, Phillip

Clark, Mark. Calculated Risk. NY: Panther Books, 1956

Cloud, Stanley and Olson, Lynne. The Murrow Boys. NY: Houghton Mifflin Co. 1996

Cray, Ed. General of the Army: George C Marshall Soldier and Statesman. NY. Norton and Co. 1990

Crozier, Brian. The Man Who Lost China. NY: Charles Scribner's & Sons, 1976

Davies, John Paton. Dragon by the Tail. NY. Norton & Co., 1972

De Jaegher, Raymond J. and Kuhn, Irene C. The Enemy Within. Garden City, NY: Doubleday & Co,1952

Detzer, David. Thunder of the Captains. NY. Crowell & Co. 1972

Donovan, Robert J. Tumultuous Years. NY: Norton, 1982

Drury, B and Clavin, T. The Last Stand of Fox Company. NY: Thorndike Press, 2009

Eastman, Lloyd. The Nationalist Era in China. NY: Cambridge Univ. Press, 1991

Fairbank, John K. and Fuerwerker, Albert. The Cambridge History of China, Volume 13, part 2. London. Cambridge University Press, 1986

Feis, Herbert. The China Tangle. NJ: Princeton Univ. Press, 1972

Fenby, Jonathan. Chang Kai-shek: China's Generalissimo and the Nation he Lost. NY; Avalon Publishing Group, 2005

Fitzgerald, Charles P. Revolution In China. New York: Frederick A Praeger, 1952

Forrestal, James. The Forrestal Diaries. New York: Viking Press, 1951

Gorcharov, Sergei N. Uncertain Partners. Stamford, CA: Stamford Univ. Press, 1993

Griffith, Samuel B. The Chinese Peoples Liberation Army. NY. McGraw-Hill, 1967

Heiferman, Ronald I. The Cairo Conference of 1943. NC: McFarland & Co. 2011

Hanson, Haldore. "Humane Endeavor" NY: Farrar & Rinehart, 1939

Hanson, Victor Davis. Soul of Battle. NY: Random House Inc., 2001

Hart, Liddell. The Red Army. NY: Harcourt, 1956

Hastings, Max. Retribution. NY: Random House, 2007

Haynes, John E. Venona: Decoding Soviet Espionage in America. CT: Yale University Press, 1999

Hilger, G The Incompatible Allies: A History Of German-Soviet Relations. NY. Macmillan, 1953

Hunter, Charles N. Galahad: San Antonio, TX: The Naylor Co. , 1963

Larrabee, Eric. Commander in Chief: NY: Harper & Rowe; 1987

Lautenschlager, Stanton. Far West In China. NY: Friendship Press, 1941

Leahy, William D. I Was There. NY: McGraw- Hill, 1950

Liang, Chin-tung Gen. Stilwell in China. NY: St. John's Univ. Press, 1972

Li, Laura Tyson. Mme. Chang Kai-shek: China's eternal First Lady. NY: Atlantic Monthly Press, 2006

Liu, F F. A Military History of Modern China; 1924-1949. CT: Greenwood Press,1981

Lohbeck, Don. Patrick J Hurley. Chicago: Henry Regenery Co., 1956

Mao Tse-tung. Quotations from the Chairman: CA: China Books, 1990

Mao Tse-tung. Selected Works of Mao Tse-tung Vol. 1-5 NY: Pergamon Press, 1977,

Marks, Frederick. Wind Over Sand; GA. Univ of GA Press 1988

Marshall, George C. The Papers of George Catlett Marshall. Vol. 1, 2, 3, 4, 5. Baltimore, MD Johns Hopkins Univ. Press, 1981

May, Ernest R. The Truman Administration And China; 1945-1949. Philadelphia: J B Lippincourt Co., 1975 Editor: Hyman

Mosher, Stephen W. Broken Earth. NY: Free Press, 1983

Pakula, Hannah. The Last Empress. NY: Simon & Schuster, 2009

Pogue, Forrest C. George C Marshall: Statesman 1955-1959 NY Viking Penguin 1987

Prefer, Nathan. Vinegar Joe's War. NY: Presidio Press, 2000

Romanus, Charles F. and Sunderland, Riley. Stilwell's Mission To China. Washington, D.C.: Dept. of the Army, 1953

Romanus, Charles F. and Sunderland, Riley. Stilwell's Command Problems. Washington, D.C.: Dept. of the Army, 1956

Rose, Lisle A. Dubious Victory; US and the End of World War II. Kent State Univ. Press, 1973

Rose, Lisle A. The Roots of Tragedy. Westport, CT: Greenwood Press, 1976

Sandler, Stanley. The Korean War. KY: Univ. Press of Kentucky, 1999

Schaller, Michael. The U.S. crusade in China, NY: Columbia Univ. Press, 1979

Schmidt, Donald E. The Folly of War: American Foreign Policy, 1898-2005. NY: Algora Publishing, 2005

Sheng, Michael M. Battling Western Imperialism. Princeton, NJ. Princeton Univ. Press, 1950

Sherwood, R. E. Roosevelt And Hopkins; NY. Harper & Row, 1948

Shewmaker, Kenneth E. Americans and Chinese Communists, 1927-1945 NY: Cornell University Press, 1971

Short, Phillip. Mao ; A Life. NY: Henry Holt & Co. , 1999

Sinclair, William Boyd. Confusion Beyond Imagination. Idaho: Joe F Whitley, Publisher, 1986`

Stilwell, Joseph W. The Stilwell Papers. NY: Da Capo Press,1948

Stuart, John Leighton. Fifty Years in China NY: Random House, 1954

Sutter, Robert G. U.S. – China Relations, NY: Roman & Littlefield, 2010

Suverov, Victor. The Liberators. NY: Norton & Schuster, 1983

Taylor, Jay. The Generalissimo. Cambridge, MA. Harvard Univ. Press, 2009

Tong, Hollington K. Chiang Kai-sheik Volume One Shanghai: The China Publishing Co. , 1937

Truman, Harry S. Memoirs, Volume 2. Garden City, NY: Doubleday & Co., 1956

Truman, Harry S. Dear Bess. NY: Norton & Company, 1983

Truman, Harry S. Off The Record. NY: Harper & Rowe, 1980

Truman, Margaret. Harry S Truman. NY: Murrow, 1973

Truman, Margaret. Souvenir. NY: McGraw-Hill, 1956

Tsou, Tang. America's Failure In China; 1941-1950.Chicago: Univ. of Chicago Press1963

Tuchman, Barbara W. Stilwell and the American Experience in China 1942-1945. NY: Macmillan Publishing, 1970

Tuchman, Barbara W. Sand Against the Wind. London: MacMillan

Tzouliadis, Tim. The Forsaken; An American Tragedy In Stalin's Russia. NY: Penguin, 2008

Utley, Freda. Last Chance in China. NY: Bobbs-Merrill Co. 1947

Utley, Freda. The China Story. Chicago: Henry Regenery Co. 1951

Vladimirov, Petr. China's Special Area; 1942-1945 Bombay: Allied Publishers, 1974

Wedemeyer, Albert C. Wedemeyer Reports! NY: Henry Holt Co, 1958

Weinstein, A and Vassiliev, A. The Haunted Wood. NY: Random House,1999

Wells, Sumner. Seven Decisions That Shaped History. NY: Harper Bros. 1950

White, Theo. H and Jacoby, Annalee. Thunder Out of China. NY: W. Sloane Assoc., 1974

Wou, Oderic Y K. Mobilizing the Masses. Stanford, CA: Stanford Univ. Press, 1994

OFFICIAL DOCUMENTS

U.S. Department of State: Foreign Relations of the United States- Diplomatic Papers 1942 *China*

Foreign Relations of the United States- 1945 *The Far East and China,* Vol. VII

Foreign Relations of the United States- 1946 *The Far East and China,* Vol. VII

Foreign Relations of the United States- 1947 *The Far East and China,* Vol. VII

Foreign Relations of the United States- 1948 *The Far East and China,* Vol. VII

U.S. Senate:

-Committee on Foreign Relations- Hearings on China, December, 92nd Congress- July 21, 1971

-Committee on the Judiciary, Subcommittee testimony of Admiral Cooke re; George Marshall Disarming China, October, 1951

U. S. House of Representatives:-Committee on Foreign Affairs, February 20, 1948

U.S. War Department, July 1945 – Report on -The Chinese Communist Movement, Edited by Lyman P Van Slyke, Stamford Univ. Press,

U. S. CIA Documents ORE 32-48, ORE 3-49

PERIODICALS

New York Times
Time Magazine